The
Secret
Life
of
Word

*A Professional Writer's Guide
to Microsoft Word Automation*

Robert Delwood

The Secret Life of Word

Disclaimer

Trademarks

XML Press
Laguna Hills, California
http://xmlpress.net

First Edition
ISBN: 978-0-9822191-6-4

Table of Contents

Preface

Describing Microsoft Office Word as just a word processor understates the capabilities of this versatile application, which is used by nearly a billion people worldwide. The designers anticipated a broad range of possible uses and planned wide latitude for customization. Word is now part word processor, spreadsheet, database, and Web editor. It's also a programming platform.

After the introduction of the Visual Basic editor in Word 97, Word gained popularity for its ability to automate the most mundane and repetitive tasks. Complex calculations can be performed in automatically updating containers (called "fields"), and strings of tasks can be chained together into a single operation (called a "macro").

This book introduces two forms of Word automation:

- **User interface:** This form of automation uses items that can be selected from the user ribbon or placed in the document. Examples include user forms, fields, Quick Parts (new in Office 2007), and user controls such as text input areas, and checkboxes.

- **Macros:** The other form of automation, macros, is perhaps less familiar. Macros let you record and recall tasks so you don't have to repeat them step-by-step. Your use of macros can include: running ones others provide to you, recording your own, modifying recorded macros, and programming macros.

Each chapter focuses on one aspect of automation, providing examples, techniques, and where applicable, macros.

Who Should Read This Book

This book is for Word users who want more control and insight into Word's automation capabilities. Automation was never intended to only be for programmers. Instead, automation is equally useful for writers. To be clear, this book is not about programming or making you a programmer. I understand not everyone is interested in becoming a programmer just to accomplish everyday tasks. Instead, I intend to jump start the automation process and enable you to write automation solutions yourself.

I assume you have some experience with Word. Although many of the examples include detailed step-by-step procedures, this is not a Word tutorial. Automation is partly about stringing Word functions together, but knowing what those functions are – their options, the right combination, and the right sequence – is up to you. Seasoned Word users, or "power users," can benefit from this book, but so can less experienced users.

Word Versions

Most of the examples and topics are applicable to all versions of Word, including Word 97, Word 2000, Word XP, Word 2003, Word 2007, and Word 2010. Where this is not the case, I will state which versions apply. For example, Building Blocks and Quick Parts were introduced in Word 2007 and will not be applicable to earlier versions.

How to Use This Book

This book takes a pragmatic and realistic approach to learning automation. It is part cookbook and part tutorial. I encourage you to work through the examples line by line. For code examples, you can type the code into the integrated development environment (IDE) or copy and paste from the electronic samples provided on this book's website[1]. Feel free to experiment and try variations.

The coding style and examples are different throughout the book, allowing you to see differences and make your own choices. For example, unless otherwise noted, samples use `For...Next` loops and `For...Each` loops interchangeably. Since the automation challenges differ for each writer, no book of examples can address them all. Instead, study several examples and use whichever examples and code work best to construct the solution you need.

Book Structure

This book uses a tutorial and cookbook approach to introduce Word's automation concepts. Each chapter introduces a new aspect of automation. I first explore basic procedures, followed by automation techniques, and finally VBA (Visual Basic for Applications) with code examples. VBA can almost always be used to supplement automation techniques available through the user interface. That means you can choose not to use macros at all, too.

Although I assume you have some experience with Word and the user interface, I do not assume any programming experience. If you want to get the most from using VBA, you should read and understand the first two chapters before reading other chapters. They explain basic automation principles and creating and modifying macros. The remaining chapters may be read in any order.

- ▶ **Chapter 2:** Introduces the basics of automation – when to use it and when not to – and discusses automation project management.

- ▶ **Chapter 3:** Covers recording and modifying macros from the Word code generator. Word can record and playback a series of user actions in procedures called macros. Recorded macros can be modified, or new macros can be created by hand. The chapter discusses each of these techniques, which will be used throughout the rest of the book.

- ▶ **Chapter 4:** Covers Find and Replace. This is a versatile utility that goes well beyond simply finding and replacing text. You can set up powerful replacements that can convert the messiest

---

[1] http://xmlpress.net/wordsecrets.html

of Word HTML into clean XHTML code. It also provides a powerful search language that uses wildcards, to find patterns of text, such as telephone numbers or part numbers.

- **Chapter 5:** Covers fields and form fields. Fields are automatically updating containers of text. Most readers know that page numbers, like "Page 1 of 10", are fields, but you may not know that you can craft your own fields to perform a wide range of calculations. Word tables can be used as small Excel-like spreadsheets, incorporating many of the same functions. Combined with other features, including bookmarks and macros, an impressive amount of information can be created, collected, or shared with minimal effort.

- **Chapter 6:** Covers the automatic placement or insertion of information. These features include AutoCorrect, which automatically fixes spelling errors – for example, switching *teh* for *the* – and an expanded feature in Office 2007, Building Blocks, which allows you to insert any amount of material – from a client's name to an entire document template complete with formatting and styling – into a Word document.

- **Chapter 7:** Covers Smart Tags, a capability that automatically highlights predefined terms or patterns in the text, such as names, acronyms, or addresses, with a purple underline like the underline used to flag misspelled words. Clicking on a highlighted term presents additional actions for that term, such as a link to a company website or a search page. Smart Tags terms and actions can also be linked with macros to help in collecting or identifying those terms. The chapter covers using default Smart Tags, creating your own, and creating and maintaining the terms list.

- **Chapter 8:** Covers the different ways that information can be imported to, exported from, or changed by Word. Word includes many features that go beyond common copy and paste. Dynamic links can be established to other documents; Word can query and collect data from MySQL, Oracle, and Microsoft Access databases; and Word can poll spreadsheets and documents, including plain text files.

- **Appendix A:** Contains a set of code examples. The examples cover a wide range of Word operations including: selecting a document to copy/paste, manipulating files, using special characters, and much more. The appendix is structured as a cookbook, with short examples you can insert into existing macros and complete examples that can be used as a starting place for your own code.

- **Appendix B:** Contains additional topics related to automation programming.

- **Appendix C:** Contains an ASCII table, which is useful if you want to access specific keys programmatically.

- **Glossary:** Contains definitions of important terms related to automation programming.

- **Resources:** Contains references to additional sources, books, and websites of interest to automation programmers.

- **Index:** There is a full index.

Typographical Conventions

The following text styles are used in this book:

Bold	Ribbon commands, user interface items (such as buttons or check boxes), and other direct commands are marked in bold. Example: In the **Paragraph** dialog box, set **Line spacing** to **Single** and then click **OK**.
The single bar (|)	The single bar separates ribbon command sequences or sequences in a dialog box. Example: Press **Home** tab|**Font**|**Bold** to make the selection bold.
`Monospace font`	A Monospace font is used for function and macro names (for example, the `AutoNew` function). It is also used for code examples and file names. For example:

```
Public Sub Macro1()
    Selection.Style = "StyleNameNotFound"
End Sub
```

Italics	An italic typeface is used to note a specific value or to show emphasis. Example: Use AutoText to change *hte* to *the*.

 This symbol identifies the associated text as an explanatory note.

 This symbol identifies the associated text as a caution. A caution is used to highlight situations where the wrong action might lead to lost data or other undesirable consequences.

Code Examples

The publisher and I want to make this book as useful to you as possible, so we have made most of the examples available for download at the book's website (http://xmlpress.net/wordsecrets.html). We encourage you to use the code examples in this book in your own applications. In most cases, you can do this freely without asking permission. The only exceptions would be if you wish to sell or distribute the examples, or you wish to sell an application that uses significant portions of the code. For more information, send email to permissions@xmlpress.net.

While we have made every effort to ensure that the examples are correct and work as described, we assume no responsibility for errors or omissions, or for any damages that result from using any of the information or examples here.

If you use some of our examples, it would be nice, but not required, to acknowledge the source with an attribution that includes the title, author, and publisher.

Help and More Information

We have tried hard to present this information in a meaningful, useful, and accurate manner. This includes explaining concepts, presenting examples, and providing a context for the solutions. If you have comments, find errors, or have questions, please let us know:

▶ **Book web page:** http://xmlpress.net/wordsecrets.html: contains code examples, errata, book extras, and information about the Facebook page for *The Secret Life of Word*.

▶ **Email:** mailto:wordsecrets@xmlpress.networdsecrets@xmlpress.net: for comments and questions.

It is not possible to cover all the topics in depth, so you may want additional information. There are many books and websites dedicated to programming in general and VBA in particular. In addition, the following websites may be useful:

▶ **Microsoft:** http://office.microsoft.com

The official site of Microsoft and Microsoft Office.

▶ **Microsoft Developer's Network (MSDN):** http://MSDN.microsoft.com

This is a Microsoft site and forum specializing in developer issues. It includes free online developer documentation for many Microsoft products. Of special note is the API (Application Programming Interface) documentation, which provides detailed explanations for each API.

▶ **Microsoft Help and Support:** http://support.microsoft.com

This is a technical site with a Knowledge Base, how-to articles, and other technical articles.

▶ **Microsoft newsgroups:** http://groups.google.com

Newsgroups are user communities and forums specializing in specific topics. Google Groups supports the following relevant newsgroups:

- Microsoft.public.office.developer.vba
- Microsoft.public .word.vba.addins
- Microsoft.public .word. vba.beginners
- Microsoft.public .word. vba.customization
- Microsoft.public .word. vba.general
- Microsoft.public .word.vba.userforms
- Microsoft.public .word.word97vba

▶ **Windows Secrets Lounge:** http://lounge.windowssecrets.com

Formerly known as Woody's lounge, this is an excellent starting point for Word and Word VBA questions.

▸ **Stack Overflow:** http://www.Stackoverflow.com

This is a more technical site that specializes in programming specific questions and issues. If your question is too general or is Word user interface related, you may be tersely referred to another site.

▸ **Word's MVP (Most Valued Professionals):** http://word.mvps.org

This site includes articles and code examples provided by MVPs. These are not Microsoft employees, but they are recognized by Microsoft as technical community leaders with an outstanding record for helping and assisting others.

Resources (p. 259) contains references to several useful books about Microsoft Word. And, you can often get specific answers by a well-crafted Internet search. Chances are someone has already asked that same question and had it answered on the web.

Acknowledgments

Writing a book became a great adventure. It started as an idea for a trade journal article and turned into so much more. Word automation is not the sole realm of the programmer, but too often that's how it's perceived. I believe the Word designers intended these capabilities to be available for all users, but that the message got garbled somewhere along the way. I hope this book helps you short cut the automation process through examples and little theory.

Special thanks needs to go to Richard Hamilton at XML Press for guiding this through completion and being a patient editor. Others provided technical help from websites like StackOverflow.com and Windows Secrets Lounge. Often they didn't know why I was asking questions, but they provided outstanding answers. They include Paul Edstein (who ended up becoming a technical reviewer) for his overall help, but specifically his work with field codes, and Graham Mayor (http://gmayor.com) and Greg K. Maxey (http://gregmaxey.mvps.org), who each write superb websites for Word automation. Special thanks to Paul Edstein for his guidance and suggestions with fields (Chapter 5 and Chapter 8), and for permission to use the code in Example 5.14 (p. 87). More of his fields calculations can be found at Microsoft Word Date Calculation Tutorial[2].

The technical reviewers lent considerable time and expertise to the development of this book. They provided invaluable comments, direction, and technical insight. Our thanks go out to Paul Edstein, David Kowalsky, and Alexandra Sihastra.

Thanks to my friends who were supportive and who endured barrages of questions. Finally, I want to thank my family, who put up with me during the long process. My children got used to me being gone on weekend nights, since they could stay up even later. My wife, Marianne, was the most patient, taking up the slack on most evenings; near the end she wanted the book done even more than I did.

---

[2] http://www.gmayor.com/downloads.htm#Third_party

2

Introduction To Word Automation

Automation Overview

From its 1983 beginnings on the Xenix operating system, Word has evolved to become one of the premier tool kits in business today. This is due in part to its versatility and customization, which is the foundation for Word's automation abilities. This versatility has several aspects:

- ► **Preferences:** Word has to conform to users' preferences and work habits. For that reason, the user interface (UI) is configurable. You can move Window panes, change defaults, and alter the user interface. No matter which version of Word you use, you can configure it to meet your needs.

- ► **Data transparency:** The Word designers understood that information will never again be isolated. Data transparency – recognizing that information comes from somewhere and goes somewhere – allows you to control that flow and in turn be more productive. You import, export, convert, or transform information easily. Data can be linked, copied, pasted, or queried to and from many sources, including the Web, another Word document, a spreadsheet, a database like Microsoft Access, Oracle, or MySql, or even a plain text file.

- ► **Functions:** Word contains many features and functions that are available through the user interface. Examples include table manipulation, sorting, formatting, referencing, and marking revisions. For reviewing and revision tracking alone, there are no fewer than 25 functions. Working with tables, you get two additional on-demand **Ribbon** tabs. Altogether, there are about 950 features and functions in Word.

- ► **Data-driven features:** Data-driven features are tools that you can create directly through the user interface to automate things like placement and formatting of data. These include fields, mail merge, Quick Parts (AutoText in Office 2003), and building blocks. They do not require programming; you control their options though the user interface. For example, you can insert a building block for text, assign it data automatically (perhaps from an XML file or database query), and format it. Then, when you open the document, the content updates automatically, requiring no additional attention from you.

► **Scripting and programming:** Since no single tool set addresses all user challenges, there are scripting and programming capabilities. Virtually the entire document object model (DOM) – the internal structure of Word and documents – is open to developers. Users at all levels of expertise can tap into these resources. The most convenient way is through recording a macro. This allows you to step through your sequence with the user interface, after which Word generates a macro automatically. You can re-run that macro as many times as you need, each time with the exact same sequence of events.

If you need additional capabilities, you can hand-modify a macro, changing it to more precisely meet your needs. And, you can write your own macros directly. Coding allows the most precise degree of automation because you can write code, add-ins, and applications to specifically address your customization needs. There are functions and features available only through programming. Although programming allows the most degree of customization, it can also be the most complex. Most of the time, you won't need to write code, but it is there as a last resort.

This book concentrates on data-driven features, scripting, and programming, but where appropriate will discuss other features, such as assigning macros to the Quick Access Toolbar or a keyboard shortcut.

Advantages of Automation

Given this large set of tools, you can assume that most tasks can be accomplished. However, just accomplishing a task isn't the point anymore. You need to accomplish your task efficiently, make modifications along the way, and be able to repeat the task. Moving from simply accomplishing a task to making it repeatable is the primary objective of automation. It aims to reduce manual effort, replace repetitive tasks with predictable and repeatable applications or scripts, and make processes better, faster, or cheaper.

Automation can take many forms, from simply using Word's F4 key to repeat the last command, to using copy and paste to avoid retyping text, to using built-in functions, to writing macros. You can pick the level of involvement that is right for you and your team.

The advantages of automation include:

► **Convenience:** You can replay almost any number of commands by invoking a single command or macro. Automation is based on the fact that if you do something once, it's likely you'll do it again. This is pure conservation of keystrokes. Furthermore, after creating a macro, you can assign it to a key or an icon in the QAT (Quick Access Toolbar, a customizable toolbar that appears by default next to the Microsoft Office button in the top left corner of a document).

► **Quality:** Reliably repeating a set of commands in the same order reduces the potential for errors. And, by saving the sequence, you don't need to remember every step. This becomes important three or six months later, when you will probably have forgotten all the steps and the reasons for them.

► **Leverage:** You may share macros among team members. Chances are if it's useful to one person, it will be useful to many.

► **Customization:** Macros can be created, run, and modified without involving a programmer. That means writing teams or individual writers can customize their own procedures. You can write macros as a one-time script, or as part of an ongoing process. You can even create a macro that itself runs other macros.

Types of Automation

In Word, there are three types of automation features: Atomic, Container, and Programmatic.

Atomic Features

Atomic features are the features and functions available through the user interface. They are single action functions that have no other components to them. Take as an example the Sort feature (**Home** tab|**Paragraph**|**Sort**). Although sort has options associated with it (ascending/descending, sort by paragraph, and so on), it's essentially a single action that once clicked performs one function. Atomic features are the first features users encounter with Word. Atomic features can be part of sequences that include other actions. Power users are often recognized for their expertise in creating atomic features that trigger long and complex sequences.

Container Features

Containers are components that perform actions or functions automatically. Fields and content containers (as of Office 2007) are examples of containers. Once defined, a container requires no action from the user to perform its function. For instance, a date field is a container that displays the current date. The contents update automatically whenever certain events occur, but once you have created the field, you do not need to do anything else. In the same way, a content container may include text from another part of the document, another document, or an external data source. Like fields, once you define the content container, it generally does not require any attention.

Programmatic Features

Programmatic features use code or macros to perform actions. Office lets you create macros by recording your actions and storing them for later use. Expanding on that feature, you can manually change the recorded code, or even write code without having to record a macro first.

Macros are recorded in the VBA (Visual Basic for Automation) programming language. However, you are not limited to VBA. You can use any language that supports automation calls, including Microsoft .NET languages and tools. Programming languages give you additional features that are not available in the user interface. These range from simple to complex. For instance, Word's SaveAs function actually has 16 options. You can also use features typically restricted to Windows programming, some 32,000 calls.

These three categories are not mutually exclusive; there is a lot of overlap among them, and no single approach is comprehensive. For example, in Chapter 4, *Find and Replace*, we will see an example that converts Word's HTML into clean XHTML using the Find and Replace atomic features, in this case nothing more than actions from the Find and Replace dialog.

Traditionally, documentation teams do not write software or develop customized software tools. Some companies consider those skills too specialized or costly to relegate to writing groups, or they do not see the advantages of automation. Many teams have never seriously considered programming, thinking that such an effort is out of scope or that the team does not have the proper skills. However, in this age of automation and convenient data access, you can make significant gains by using automation in support of documentation. As an experience Word user, you know the features, functions, and the sequence to do your tasks. Automation is just putting them together and letting Word do the rest for you.

An Example of Automation

As an example of the different levels of automation, imagine you have a series of tables and you want all the rows for each table to be kept together on the same page if possible. The manual way is to select the table, click the **Home** tab, click the **Paragraph** dialog button, select the **Lines and Page Breaks** tab, select **Keep with next**, and **Keep lines together**, and click **OK**. This is seven actions.

To automate this task, perform the sequence once, and since those actions all occur within one dialog, the **Lines and Page Breaks** of the **Paragraph** dialog, use the **F4** key to repeat them all. This is an excellent improvement, but it doesn't save the sequence. Once you perform almost any action other than typing **F4** (such as typing a single character or using another **Ribbon** command), you lose the entire sequence, and you would have to repeat all seven actions again to perform this action. A better way of automating it is to record the actions as a macro, which would then always be available.

Now, imagine the same set of tables, but this time you have to make sure the formatting is correct and consistent. Perhaps the first row of each table needs formatting with bold, white text, and black highlighting, and the other rows need to use the Arial font with a size of 14.5 pt. This automation is more complex since it's just not repeating the last few actions. Although they're related actions, the F4 key can't reproduce them using a single keystroke. Instead, it needs a macro, and a hand modified macro at that.

If your goal is to make an action or sequence repeatable in Word, the preferred way to do this is through macros. Macros are stored code, usually in the document or a template. They can be run using the **Macros** button of the **Developer** tab (also by **ALT-F8**), assigned to a button for the QAT, or assigned to a keystroke. Macros stored in documents are local to that document only. Those in templates can be run by any document with that template attached. Since that makes it more available, many users prefer storing them in templates. You can transfer macros to other documents or templates through the **Organizer** dialog, which is the same dialog for transferring styles (**ALT-F8|Organizer** button).

How Do You Create Macros?

There are two ways to create a macro. You can record it or manually write it.

Recording a macro

To record a macro, you set the macro generator to record and then perform the actions you want to record. Word then translates your actions into a macro. Click the **Developer** tab, click the **Record Macro** button on the **Code** panel, complete the **Record Macro dialog** information, and then perform your actions normally. When done, click the **Stop Recording** button in the recorder dialog. To use your macro, Click the **Developer** tab, **Macros** button, select the macro by name, and click **Run**.

As an example, you may need to insert tables that have the following characteristics: Arial font, 10 point type, five rows, two columns with widths of one inch and three inches respectively, top row shaded, table caption, and paragraphs before and after the table. This is about a 25-step process. If you perform the procedure once and record it as a macro, you can generate the table as many times as you need with one command.

Writing a macro

The other way to create a macro is to modify an existing macro or create a new one manually. As powerful as recording a macro is, writing a new macro or modifying an existing one extends the capabilities even further. Using the VBA (Visual Basic for Applications) editor, a built in feature to all Office suite applications, you can add custom code. Chapter 3, *Creating Macros*, shows how to take a recorded macro and add error checking code.

Direct coding allows you to do things that are not possible through the user interface. For example, you can add a message box, get user input, or display an open file dialog, to name a few. In addition, since VBA is a true programming language, you also have access to loops, decision statements, and error handling. While this is technically programming, you can easily add simple features to macros without being a programmer.

Summary

Word supports several types of automation using both programming and non-programming approaches. For non-programming approaches, you can use built-in features ranging from Undo (**CTRL-Z**) and Redo (**F4**), to inserting fields, to Building Blocks (predefined text). Programming approaches use VBA and Word's macro recorder to add an almost unlimited amount of versatility, ranging from the simple to the complex. The recorder lets you create macros from your actions. In addition, you can modify a recorded macro or write your own. You choose your level of involvement. That way, automation, or the ability to do more work in less time, is in your reach.

3

Creating Macros

The true power of automation comes into its own with Visual Basic for Automation (VBA). VBA is a programming language built into most Microsoft Office suite tools, most extensively into Word and Excel. It's a versatile tool that can be used in a wide range of contexts. At one end, you can use VBA as a programming language to create complex routines or even complete applications that can tap into the Windows operating systems, access other applications and databases, and use tools such as third-party dynamic link libraries (DLLs) and ActiveX controls. At the opposite end, you can record and playback almost any action performed through the user interface without knowing programming. Or, you can start with a recorded macro and hand-modify it until it meets your needs. Although I encourage everyone to learn more about the programming aspect of VBA, this section focuses on recording and modifying macros.

Macros help minimize the sometimes stultifying amount of repetition needed to create and modify documents. Whether this is making charts, formatting text, or finding the right phrase in a long document, the key is that a similar, if not identical, action repeats over and over. Office provides an easy way to speed this up. An action or sequence of actions can be stored and replayed later. This collected set of actions is called a *macro*.

Creating macros provides two benefits. The first benefit is that an action can be reliably and accurately repeated later, either immediately or months later, after you have forgotten the exact sequence. The second benefit is that you can share knowledge with others. They don't have to re-create work you have already done. Since the process is simple, it can and should be used frequently. The goal is, "If you do something more than once, automate it."

This chapter shows you how to record a macro, play it back, and share it with others. It also discusses security features and considerations. The chapter ends by showing you how to create and edit a macro using the built-in editor. These procedures will be used throughout the book.

Often the first step in solving an automation problem is to record a macro and see how far that can take you. Then, if you need additional steps, you can modify the code. Finally, if recording a macro won't do the job, you can write some code right from the start.

This section provides an overview of the macro making and playback process. VBA was introduced with Word 6 and is akin to, but not always compatible with, other versions of the BASIC language. If you have any BASIC language experience, you may see similarities with VBA. Recorded macros translate user actions into VBA code that can be read and edited.

Recording a Macro

Recording a macro allows you to perform a series of actions from the user interface and save that sequence. That sequence, called a macro, can be played back later. All Office suite applications have VBA support, although not all have it to the same extent. Word and Excel have the most extensive VBA tools and let you record and modify macros. PowerPoint and Outlook do not allow you to record macros, but you can playback imported ones and write your own from scratch.

The Developer Tab

Before recording a macro, you need to display the **Developer** tab of the **Ribbon** (see Figure 3.1). This tab includes many of the features you will need to record and play back macros.

Figure 3.1. Developer tab

Procedure 3.1 shows how to display the Developer tab, which doesn't display by default after the initial installation.

Procedure 3.1. Display the Developer tab

1. Click the **Microsoft Office** button.

2. Click **Word Options**.

3. Click the **Popular** category, if not already selected by default.

4. Under the **Top options for working with Word** section, check the **Show Developer tab in the Ribbon**. Click **OK**.

5. Click the **Developer** tab. The **Code** panel, which is to the left-hand side in Figure 3.1, is the one we're interested in.

Since Word usually gives you two or three ways to do the same thing, you don't have to display the **Developer** tab to record and play macros. The recording capabilities are available on the Word status bar (see Figure 3.2), and you also have options to play them back. However, the **Developer** tab is convenient and you'll eventually need it for more advanced features.

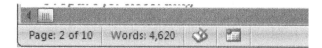

Figure 3.2. Word status bar: the macro record button is the last icon on the right

Using the Macro Recorder

You're now ready to record a macro. During a recording session, almost every action you make in a document will be saved. One oddity is that while the actions a mouse click performs are recorded, the actual mouse click is not. That means you can't click or select text with the mouse when you're recording. If text or an object needs to be selected, select it before you start the recording session or use the keyboard during recording to select it.

It's good practice to know the exact sequence ahead of time. You might have to rehearse the steps several times or make several recording attempts. Don't worry about making mistakes. If the action is minor enough, it may not matter. There is no way to remove an action once it's recorded this way, but if you don't like the way the macro turns out, you can always delete it and start over.

Procedure 3.2 shows how to record a macro that creates and formats a table.

Procedure 3.2. Record a macro to create and format a table

1. Open a new document.

2. In the **Developer** tab, click **Record Macro**. The **Record Macro** dialog displays (See Figure 3.3).

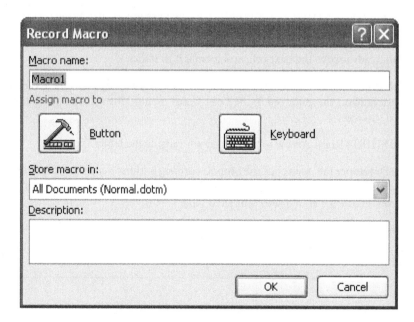

Figure 3.3. Record Macro dialog

3. In the **Macro name** field, give your macro a name. By default it will be given a name like Macro1, but you can change it to a more meaningful name such as CreateTable.

4. In the **Store macro in** field, specify the document to store the macro in. This is where the macro gets stored, and the choices include any currently open document or attached template (by default Normal.dotm). I suggest you select the current document, instead of the default, by selecting Document1 (document) from the drop-down list. Changing the location protects the Normal.dotm template since we're only practicing and bound to make mistakes. There are other options on this dialog that I will discuss later. See the section titled "Sharing A Macro" (p. 23) for additional information.

5. Click **OK**. This starts the recording session. When the dialog box closes, the cursor will change to the tape cassette icon, and the **Record Macro** button name will change to **Stop Recording**.

    You are now ready to start recording your actions.

    The following steps create a table and enter data into it.

6. Click the **Insert** tab, and in the **Table** drop-down select a 2x2 table. After creating the table, the insertion point will be in the first cell.

7. Type **R1c1**, press **Tab**, type **R1c2**, press **Tab**, then for the second row, type **R2c1**, press **Tab**, and type **R2c2**.

8. Press **SHIFT+TAB** three times to get back to the first cell. You can use any keyboard sequence to do this, but you can't use the mouse.

9. Click the **Bold** button (**Home|Font|Bold**). This changes the format of the text in this cell to bold.

10. Press **Tab** to advance to the next cell, and format it in *italics*.

11. Press **Tab** to advance to the next row, and select the entire row by pressing **SHIFT+Right Arrow** twice. Select the color red in the **Font Color** menu. This will change all text in the second row to red.

12. Click the **SHIFT+Right Arrow** to put the cursor outside the table.

13. Click the **Developer** tab, then click the **Stop Recording** button to end the recording session. Alternately, you can click the **Stop Recording** icon in the status bar; it appears as a blue square icon. Figure 3.4 shows the completed table.

Figure 3.4. Table generated by Procedure 3.2

Playing Back a Macro

With the macro recorded, you can now play it back (Procedure 3.3). The macro creates a new table wherever the insertion point is, so you should first either erase the contents of the file by pressing **CTRL-A** and then **Delete**, or position the cursor elsewhere in the document.

Procedure 3.3. Play back the table macro

1. Position the cursor where you want to insert the table.

2. Click the **Developer** tab.

3. Click the **Macros** button. This displays the Macros dialog box(see Figure 3.6).

4. Select the macro name, `CreateTable`. Click **Run**. The table is created.

Editing a Macro

The previous parts of this chapter gave a brief introduction for recording macros. But there's much more. While there is a lot that recorded macros can do, there is even more they can't do. To tap into these missing capabilities, you'll have to change the code directly.

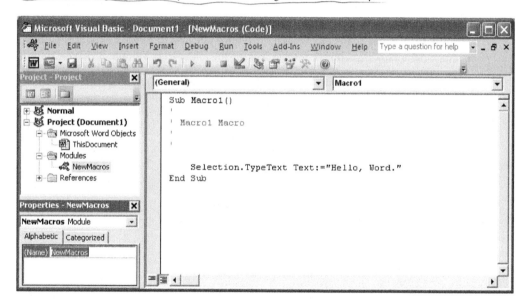

Figure 3.5. IDE screen

In the **Developer** tab, click the **Visual Basic** button. This opens a new screen, the IDE or "Integrated Developer Environment" screen (See Figure 3.5). It's appropriately named. First, it's integrated into each Office suite tool, meaning you don't need to load or install a separate application; you can create or modify macros from any computer loaded with almost any edition of Office. Second, it's a tool for developers and development. Third, it's a complete programming environment. It comes with a built-in code editor, debugger, and programming tools. There are a lot of tools in the IDE, but don't worry, I will only discuss the most important ones. Close the IDE for the moment using the **Close** button in the top right side of the window.

The IDE is your main workshop. You will write, edit, debug, and run the macros from here, at least while you're creating them.

Using the IDE

To get started, record the following macro:

1. In the **Developer** tab, click **Record Macro**. Use all the defaults, except store the macro in the same document, as you did in Procedure 3.2. Click **OK**.

2. Enter the text `Hello, Word`.

3. Click **Stop Recording**.

Once you have recorded your macro, you can use the IDE to modify, run, and test it. Procedure 3.4 shows how to do this.

Procedure 3.4. Modify and run a simple macro

1. In the **Developer** tab, click the **Visual Basic** button. The result will be similar to Figure 3.5 (the IDE Screen) except that the main portion of the screen will be empty.

2. In the **Project** window on the left, top side (labeled **Project - Project**), expand **Project (Document1)**, if not already expanded, by double clicking it. Expand **Modules** by either clicking on the expansion box or double clicking the folder icon. Double click **NewMacros**.

3. The macro code displays in the main window (see Example 3.1):

```
Sub Macro1()
'
' Macro1 Macro
'
'
    Selection.TypeText Text:="Hello, Word."
End Sub
```

Example 3.1. "Hello, Word" macro

4. In the IDE, modify "`Hello, Word.`" to "`Hello, there.`"

5. In the **Run** menu of the IDE, select **Run Sub/Userform**. If the **Macros** dialog appears, the cursor was not in the `Macro1` code; select `Macro1` and click **Run**.

   The phrase "Hello, there." is added to the document. It should be right after the existing "Hello, Word." This is correct because the macro simply adds the text at the insertion point, which was never moved after creating the macro.

6. Delete all the text in the document and run the macro again. The macro can either be run from the IDE, as in the previous step, or from the **Macro** button of the **Developer** tab. Now, "Hello, there." appears by itself.

Deleting a Macro

Procedure 3.5 shows how to delete a macro.

Procedure 3.5. Delete a macro

1. Click the **Developer** tab.

2. Click the **Macros** button. This displays the **Macros** dialog (See Figure 3.6).

3. Select the `CreateTable` macro. Click **Delete**.

4. Click **Yes**.

 The **Macros** dialog also lets you edit and run a macro.

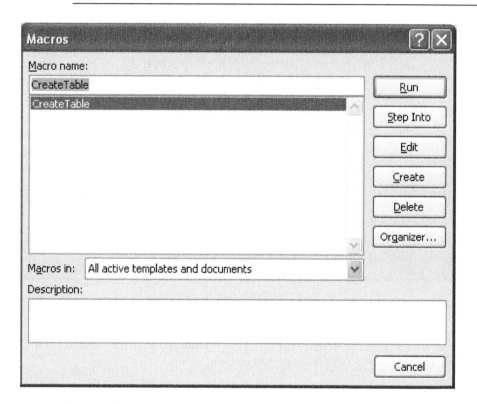

Figure 3.6. Macros dialog box

Accessing a Macro

Another set of options to consider is how you access macros. In Procedure 3.3, you used the **Macro** dialog to select one from a list. This is the most comprehensive way, but it's neither the only way nor the most convenient. What if you wanted to run the macro many times in quick succession? It would be annoying to go through four clicks each time. There are two other ways to do this: the "button method" and the "keyboard method."

Button Method

The button option (see Procedure 3.6) allows you to assign the macro to a button, but only through the Quick Access Toolbar (QAT).

Procedure 3.6. Assign a button to a macro

1. Start recording another macro (see the first four steps in Procedure 3.2 (p. 15)).

2. In the **Record Macro** dialog, fill in the **Macro name**, **Store macro In**, and **Description** fields (**Description** is an optional field for passing notes or instructions on to other users). The button will be named whatever is in the **Macro name**. For now, you can leave the default.

3. Click **Button** to assign the macro to run from a button. This displays the **Customize** screen (the same one as the Office button **Customize**). The macro name will be something generic like `Normal.NewMacros.Macro2` (see Figure 3.7).

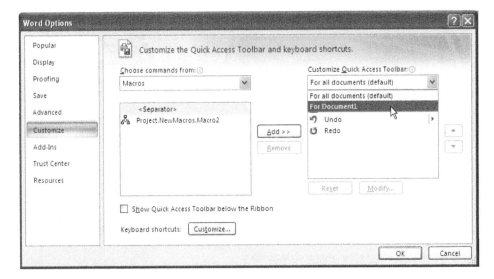

Figure 3.7. The Customize screen during a button assignment

4. Since we want to keep the macros local, select **For Document1** from the **Customize Quick Access Toolbar** drop-down list in the right column.

5. Select the macro (in this case, `Normal.NewMacros.Macro2`) and click **Add**. This will move it the right column, which lists the current set of Quick Access tools (See Figure 3.8).

6. Click **OK**.

7. Finish recording the macro.

When you're done, you will see an icon for your new macro in the QAT (see Figure 3.8). To test the macro, click the icon.

Figure 3.8. Macro added to Quick Access Toolbar

Procedure 3.7 shows you how to customize the icon and name of your macro.

Procedure 3.7. Customize a macro name and icon

1. Right click the macro's icon in the QAT. This displays a pop-up menu. Choose **Customize Quick Access Toolbar** to see the **Customize** dialog.

2. Since the macro was assigned to the local document, use the right column drop-down list and choose **For Document1**. The list of macros in the right column changes; in this case it's just `Macro2`.

3. Click the macro name in the right hand list, if not already selected.

4. Click **Modify**. This displays the **Modify button** dialog.

5. Select an icon from the **Symbol** icon list.

6. (Optional) Rename the macro in the **Display name** text box.

7. Click **OK**.

8. Click **OK** to leave the **Customize** screen.

The QAT will now have the new icon, and if you changed the **Display name**, the tool tip will show the new name. You can also set the icon and **Display name** before recording. To test the macro, click the icon and the macro will run.

Keyboard Method

The keyboard method (see Procedure 3.8) allows you to assign a macro to a keyboard key.

Procedure 3.8. Assign a macro to a keystroke

1. Start recording another macro (see the first four steps in Procedure 3.2 (p. 15)).

2. In the **Record Macro** dialog, fill in the **Macro name**, **Store macro In**, and **Description** fields (**Description** is an optional field for passing notes or instructions on to other users). The button will be named whatever is in the **Macro name**. For now, you can leave the default.

3. Click **Keyboard** to assign the macro to run from a button. This displays the **Customize Keyboard** dialog (see Figure 3.9). The macro name will be in the **Commands** list and will have a generic name like `Project.NewMacros.Macro2`.

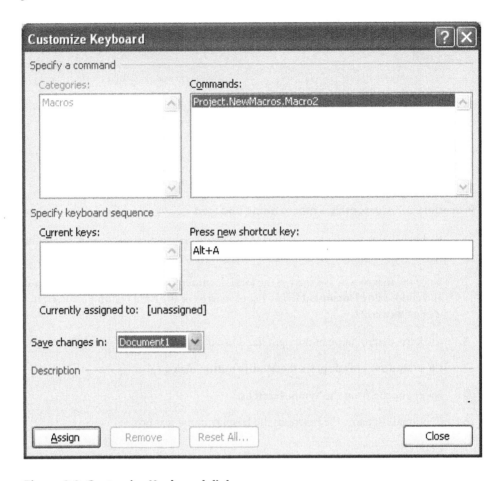

Figure 3.9. Customize Keyboard dialog

4. The cursor should be in the **Press new shortcut key** text box but if not, click there.

5. Using the keyboard, press the key or combination of keys you want the macro to be assigned to. For example, press **ALT-A**. That combination appears in the text box. If that combination is already assigned to another command, you will see additional information, for example, "Currently assigned to: Normal.NewMacros.Macro1." Clicking the **Assignment** button will overwrite the existing the key assignment with the new one.

6. When you decide on the correct keyboard combination, use the **Save changes in** drop-down menu to save your changes. To keep the macro local, select Document1 to keep the macro local.

7. Click **Assign**.

8. Click **Close**.

9. Finish recording the macro.

To test the key assignment, open the document and press the keys you assigned. The macro should run.

This is a simple example to be sure, but it should be clear how powerful macros can be. There is practically no limit to how many steps can be recorded. And, as helpful as macros are to you, they can be equally helpful to others. Once a macro is created it can be shared. The next section describes how to do this.

Sharing A Macro

In the examples above, the macros were kept in the local document. However, it is likely you will want to share your macros. The developers of Office think so, too, and they set most options to default to the most public option available, usually listing the templates first.

You can share macros in two ways: through a document or through a template. You can share macros from both places at the same time, but no two macros can have the same name. Where you place a macro determines its scope, which in turn determines how easily available it will be to others.

 Be sure to note where you store your macros. It's easy to lose macros, especially with all the options Office presents.

Sharing Through Documents

The first option is to save the macro in the document itself. The document has to be saved in an Office 2007 macro-enabled document (`.docm`) or in Office 2003 format (`.doc`). By saving it in the document, the user can access the macro only if that document is the active one. This has two important implications. First, the macro is available only when the document is open. Second, if the document is copied, the macro will be copied, too, and you will have two copies of the macro, one in each document. If you want to change the macro (such as adding to it or fixing a bug in it), you will have to change it in each document, separately. Obviously this can be a maintenance problem if you need to keep changing the macros.

Nevertheless, saving macros in the document has advantages. The macro may be specific to the document and not generally useful. Or, it might be a one-time tool, and after you use it, there may be no need to keep the macro around. In either case, saving it in a document is a good option.

Sharing Through Templates

The second option is to save the macro in a template. Templates allow you to share Word information such as formats or Building Block text, and sharing macros is no different. The template has to be saved as a macro-enabled template (`.dotm`) or in Office 2003 format (`.dot`).

Storing macros in a template gives them wider usability. First, since all documents must have a template attached to them anyway (by default Word uses `Normal.dotm` even if that means creating a new template if `Normal.dotm` does not already exist), you automatically have a logical place to store them. This required template is called a "document template."

Second, in addition to the one required document template, you can have up to 150 additional templates. These are called "global templates." This gives users better granularity, allowing them to add (or not add) templates selectively. For example, if a macro is so specialized that only a few users would be interested in it, it makes little sense to add it to the required template. Instead, a new template can be created just for the users who need it.

Third, You can place the templates in centralized network locations. This ensures that all users within a team, group, or company access the same macros.

You decide where to store a macro during the recording set-up (see Procedure 3.2 (p. 15), step 3). The **Store macro in** drop-down of the **Record Macro** dialog lists all the available documents you can store the macro in.

Security

Macros are excellent mechanisms to carry viruses or malevolent code. Given that macros have virtually unlimited access to the computer, the operating system, and your data, Microsoft Office incorporates several features to help improve security.

 ### Viruses, Malevolence, and Mistakes

The word *virus* is now a generalized term for any harmful or malevolent software. Technically a virus is any program capable of copying itself to another computer with no, or very little, action on your part. In contrast, users more commonly get malevolent software, also called *malware,* by running a program that infects the computer. They obviously don't know the program is malicious, or else they wouldn't run it.

A *Trojan horse* is an application that looks safe, but installs unwanted software. This can be either a program that is run explicitly (for example, unwanted code that runs when you think you're installing a useful and safe application) or run when you visit a website. VBA relies on ActiveX controls to provide Internet capabilities, but those controls are vulnerable and can be used to spread malware. As a result, many companies attempt to reduce their usage.

That's not to say all bad code is intentionally malicious. Mistakes happen. Legitimate software can have bugs. Your own code can, too. You could also have logic errors, where the code performs as you intended, but with unexpected or unforeseen results.

Document Type

Your first line of defense is the file type. Microsoft created two new types of documents in Office 2007: the -x and the -m file types, which are identified by the file suffixes .docx and .docm. Other Office tool suite applications have similar naming, such as Excel's .xlsx, and PowerPoint's .pptx suffixes. The -x versions cannot contain macros at all. If you're concerned about harmful macros, use a .docx or the corresponding template .dotx filename. Recipients of these document types should be assured they're free of any macros.

Others can't fake the type by simply changing a -m filename to -x (to make you think it's a safe file), or conversely from an -x to an -m. Files having their extensions changed, either with or without macros, display an error upon opening the name changed file, and the file is never actually opened. To change the file type you have to use the **Save As** option once the file has been properly opened. The other formats – .docm and .dotm – do allow macros. Care must be taken for documents from Word 2003 and earlier since they do not have this naming safety net. A Word 2003 or earlier .doc or .dot file can contain macros.

In addition, there are three other security features: digital signatures, digital certificates, and trusted publishers.

Digital Signatures, Digital Certificates, and Trusted Publishers

These three techniques attempt to vouch for the authenticity of the code. They do not ensure the code isn't malicious or capable of causing harm, just that the code comes from a known source and that it hasn't been changed since the authentication took place. These options have a digital or electronic means of verifying the source.

A "digital signature" is a timestamp and encryption method for verifying that the contents of the macro have not been changed since it was signed. If you trust the signer, then a valid digital signature indicates that the macro is exactly as the signer intended and that it has not been modified since it was signed.

A "digital certificate" is like an electronic ID card, such as a passport or driver's license. In either instance, you provide proof of identify to a third party – in the case of a driver's license it would be the state – and the third party issues a certificate that identifies you. A driver's license is trusted since the issuer, the state, is trusted. In the same way, if the recipients of a file trust the issuer of the certificate, then they can be assured that the macro came from the source the issuer says it came from. There is a strict certification process and usually a cost for a third party issuer (called a certificate authority or certification authority (CA)). You can create a certificate yourself, called "self-certification," but the certificate is valid only on the computer that created it.

A "trusted publisher" (not to be confused with a trusted location, see the section titled "Trusted locations" (p. 26)) is a Microsoft Office digital signature and digital certificate management system. Office can be set up to run all macros (and ActiveX controls, add-ins, and applications extensions) from developers you have defined as trusted publishers. This designation allows you to accept new macros and changes without re-validating developer's credentials.

Security Level

The next line of defense is the security level. Office prevents macros from being run without some sort of explicit permission. Procedure 3.9 shows how to set the security level.

Procedure 3.9. Set macro security level

1. Click the **Office** button, and then click **Word** Options. This displays the **Word Options** screen.

2. Click **Trust Center** on the left, then the **Trust Center Settings** button. By default, the **Macro Settings** screen displays (See Figure 3.10).

3. Select the level in the **Macro Settings** area. The safest setting is **Disable all macros with notification**. With this option, Office prompts the user each time a macro is run. For now, consider selecting that option.

 In a corporate or government environment, there may be security policies that dictate the security level you must use. Consult your IT department for their policies.

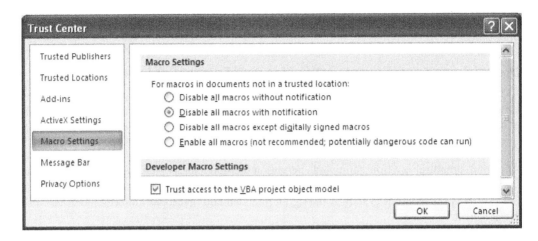

Figure 3.10. Trust Center screen

When the **Disable all macros with notification** setting is in effect, you will see a prominent warning under the tool area when Office encounters a macro (See Figure 3.11). Procedure 3.10 shows how to enable a macro in this situation.

Procedure 3.10. Enable macro execution

1. Click **Options** from the **Security Warning** bar. The **Security Alert - Macro** dialog displays.

2. Click **Enable this content** to run the macro.

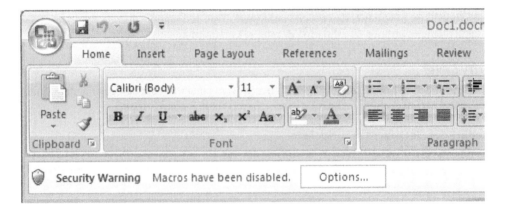

Figure 3.11. Macros disabled security warning

Trusted locations

Having to click two buttons to run any macro may get annoying, so there is another option: The "trusted location." This is a folder that you explicitly designate to contain only safe macros. That means any macro found in that location will always run, even without notification from the security level. In a corporate setting, for example, a network share can be designated as a trusted location so that team members can put their macro-laden templates for users to connect to. Procedure 3.11 shows how to set up a trusted location.

Procedure 3.11. Set up a trusted location

1. Click the **Office** button, and then click **Word Options**. This displays the **Word Options** screen.

2. Click **Trust Center** on the left, then the **Trust Center Settings** button.

3. Click **Trusted Locations**. The **Trust Center**'s **Trusted Locations** screen displays (See Figure 3.12). This lists all the folders declared as trusted locations. If the location you want is there, note that location. Any files placed there will be trusted. If the location is not listed there, you can add one.

4. Click **Add new location**. The **Trusted Location** screen displays. You can type in the full path name or navigate to it using the **Browse** button. In either case, click **OK**. The newly added location appears in the list. Click **OK** and then click **OK** again to leave the **Word Options** dialog.

5. Test the location by placing a document with a macro there and running the macro. Even with a high security level, the macro will run.

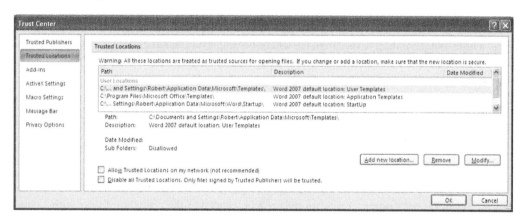

Figure 3.12. Trust Center Trusted Locations screen

Documenting Macros for Others

Just handing another team member a template with a macro in it really isn't that useful. Additional help is needed. The user needs to know three things at a minimum:

► **The name of the macro:** Users need to know what name to use to invoke your macro. Consider the name carefully, there are good and bad ones. `MyMacro` or `TableThing` are hardly useful to other team members. You can be verbose. `CreateAndFormatPersonnelRequirementsTable` is good. This name borders on self-documenting since it gives users an idea of what the call does and is not likely to be used by others.

► **How to invoke the macro:** Users need to know how to start the macro. Here are three options:

  1. Include it only through the **Macros** dialog. This is the least interesting, but safest, method.

  2. Use a keyboard combination. This is risky because you may use a combination that is already taken or that a future macro writer will use.

3. Assign it to a button. This is less risky than a keyboard combination, but requires more work from the originator.

▶ **Prerequisites:** These are the conditions that need to be set before using the macro. Some important factors to consider include: Does the insertion point need to be at a certain location? Does the macro start inserting text at the insert point or some other location within the document? Does the macro insert or delete any data?

Advanced Features

VBA is a deceptively simple language with powerful underlying features. The following sections present a selection of the most important advanced features. Not all of these features are required to use the samples in the book, but understanding these features may make the process more convenient and versatile.

Creating Code

At this point you have recorded several macros and done some basic modifications. Now let's create a macro from scratch. This topic will only be a very brief overview of VBA programming. The examples in the following chapters are complete programs; you do not need to write any code yourself to use them. However, you may want to modify the examples to fit your own needs. For that, a little understanding of the language will be helpful. You can either type the examples in the editor or cut and paste them from the code examples associated with the book.[8] Procedure 3.12 shows how to write a VBA program.

Procedure 3.12. Create a new code module

1. Open the IDE if it's not already opened (see the section titled "Editing a Macro" (p. 17)).

2. Right click on **Project (*Document1*)** (*Document1* will be replaced by the name of your currently open document).

3. Select **Insert|Module**. A new module will be created in the `Modules` folder with a name like `Module1`. The module will open automatically, and a blank document will appear.

4. Type "Option Explicit" in the first line (The IDE may have already done this).

5. Press **Return** twice. Note: this is different from Word. In the IDE, programmers use returns to create white space.

6. Enter or paste the contents of Example 3.2 into the IDE.

```
Sub ThisisText()
    Selection.TypeText "This is my first program."
End Sub
```

Example 3.2. Simple code example

 When you type in an example from the book, if the example has line numbers, do not include them. The examples on the companion website for this book do not have line numbers and can be used as is.

7. Run the program. In addition to the ways I have already discussed, another way of running the program is to place the cursor somewhere in the program and press **F5**. The text "This is my first program." will appear in the active document.

Analyzing Example 3.2, you can see that each program has a beginning statement, an ending statement, and a name; these are the only required parts. Sub (short for subroutine) opens the program, End Sub closes it, and the name is ThisIsText.

Example 3.3 replaces Sub/End Sub with Function/End Function. A function is like a subroutine except that it returns a value.

```
1 Function ThisIsAFunction() as long
2        ThisIsAFunction = 5
3 End Function
```

Example 3.3. Simple function code example

Functions have two additional requirements. First, you must declare the type of value the function will return. In Example 3.3, the return type is declared to be of type long[1] by the statement: as long. Almost any value can be returned, it just has to be declared. The second requirement is that the actual value returned is assigned to the name of the function, as though it were a variable. In Example 3.3, the value 5 is assigned as the return value in line 2: ThisIsAFunction = 5.

Return values are useful. You can write your own procedures, customizing the value and what kind of information is returned. For example, Example 3.4 returns the value π (Pi to two decimal places).

```
Function GetPi() As Double
    GetPi = 3.14
End Function
```

Example 3.4. Function that returns the value of Pi to two places

You can combine your function with a calling subroutine. Example 3.5 displays the value of pi.

```
Sub DisplayPi()
    MsgBox GetPi()
End Sub

Function GetPi() As Double
    GetPi = 3.14
End Function
```

Example 3.5. Calling the GetPi function

You can pass a parameter, or a starting value, to the function. Example 3.6 calculates the circumference of a circle, passing in the diameter as a parameter. The CalculateCircumference function returns the circumference.

---

[1]The data type long declares an integer that is stored in enough space to contain a large value.

```
Sub GetCircumference()
    MsgBox CalculateCircumference(5)
End Sub

Function CalculateCircumference(diameter As Long) As Double
    CalculateCircumference = diameter * 3.14
End Function
```

Example 3.6. Function to return the circumference of a circle

The last of the basic statements is the `Public`/`Private` declaration. Each subroutine or function (collectively referred to as a routine or procedure) has to be declared as either `Public` or `Private`. A `Public` routine can be called from macros in other modules or even other templates. It also allows that macro to be displayed in the **Macros** dialog (**Developer|Code|Macros**). A routine without any explicit declaration defaults to `Public`. A `Private` routine can neither be called outside of its module nor listed in the **Macros** dialog. You may wish to use a `Private` routine if you don't want users to call the macro directly.

IntelliSense

The IDE helps you, too, with *IntelliSense*, a form of autocomplete (See Figure 3.13). If you manually entered the code above, you may have noticed that after typing the period following `Selection`, a series of choices popped up. This is IntelliSense, and it displays a set of options you can select from. You could have then entered `TypeT` and the choice would have become `TypeText`. To complete the statement you press the space bar or type a period (.).

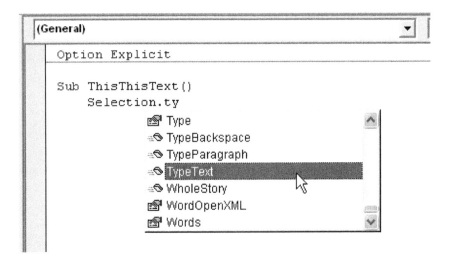

Figure 3.13. Using IntelliSense

Learn to rely on this to complete statements. The drop-down list shows the available and valid commands, either for the properties (items that hold a value) or methods (items that take an action) for the selected item. In addition to showing the valid options, it also displays the parameters as you type them. For example, `TypeText` needs some text as a required parameter. IntelliSense displays information about the text parameter as you continue typing (See Figure 3.14).

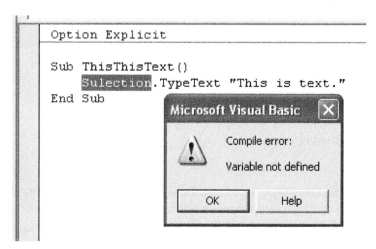

```
(General)

    Option Explicit

    Sub ThisThisText()
        Selection.TypeText |
                    TypeText(Text As String)
```

Figure 3.14. IntelliSense displaying the parameter list

If you type a dot and nothing shows up, something is wrong. Chances are the item is not a recognized object, is not properly instantiated, or is misspelled.

Error Handling

One of the absolutes in the programming is that mistakes are going to happen. Even when recording macros, the recording engine is not perfect, and mistakes can be introduced through no fault of your own. So handling mistakes is important.

The first step is to understand the three types of errors: compile, run-time, and logic.

Compile errors

Compile errors prevent the code from running. A compile error might be caused by a misspelled word (such as entering Sulection instead of Selection in the previous example), or incorrectly bracketing a function or call (such as not matching Sub with End Sub). These are usually the easiest errors to find and fix, since the compiler finds them for you (See Figure 3.15).

```
    Option Explicit

    Sub ThisThisText()
        Sulection.TypeText "This is text."
    End Sub
```

Microsoft Visual Basic [X]

⚠ Compile error:

Variable not defined

OK   Help

Figure 3.15. Compile error in the IDE

The one complication is that VBA is an interpreted language, which means errors aren't always found until the system tries to execute them. In the previous example, if ThisIsText was never called, the misspelling of *Sulection* would never be noticed. The workaround for this in VBA is to select **Debug|Compile Project** in the IDE. This will flag compile errors for you.

Runtime errors

Runtime errors occur during the course of execution when a statement cannot be carried out. Examples of runtime errors include: trying to reference an object that does not exist, dividing by zero, or accessing the tenth item in an array of only nine items.

Unlike compile errors, runtime errors cannot be evaluated until the code is actually run. For example, suppose a macro has the user enter a value, say the number of days in a grading period. If the user enters the value zero and the macro then attempts to divide by that value, a runtime error will occur (See Figure 3.16). Runtime errors are harder to find than compile errors. The best prevention is to anticipate possible errors. For example, always check values typed by a user before using them, and then warn the user or bypass the operation if the value is inappropriate.

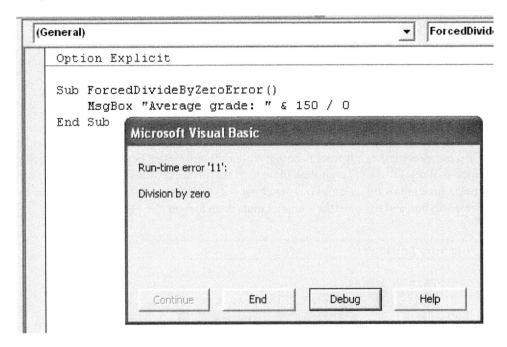

Figure 3.16. Runtime error – divide by zero

Logic errors

Logic errors prevent the code from doing what you intended it to do. Logic errors are technically not coding errors, since the code may both compile and run. That is, the code executes correctly, but doesn't do what you intended it to do.

For example, suppose your code counts the number of times a user presses a particular key, but you forgot to include a statement that adds one to the counter each time the key is pressed. The code does exactly what you told it to do, but not what you intended. This is the hardest kind of error to detect and fix.

Debugging

"Debugging" is the process of looking for and fixing errors. The methods used for debugging are not limited to finding problems; you can use the same techniques to look at the code while it's running. For example, you can keep track of values as the program runs to be sure you're getting the correct results at the correct time. Debugging capabilities are built into the IDE.

Stepping through code

Debugging is all about controlling the execution of your code. This starts with executing code one line at a time. Procedure 3.13 illustrates how debugging works:

Procedure 3.13. Debugging example

1. Type or paste Example 3.7 into the IDE.

```
Sub ADebugExample()
    Dim i As Long
    For i = 1 To 10
        Debug.Print i * i
        DoEvents
    Next i
End Sub
```

Example 3.7. Debug code sample

2. Place the cursor anywhere within the macro.

3. Select **Debug|Step Into**. The macro declaration line (the one starting with Sub) will become highlighted.

4. Select **Debug|Step Into** again. The highlighting moves down to the next executable line, in this case the next line. The highlighted statement will be executed next. The process of going line-by-line is called "stepping through code."

5. Keep selecting **Debug|Step Into** until all the code runs. At any point along the way you can skip this line-by-line approach and select **Run|Continue** to run the remaining lines without interruption.

Watching variables

By stepping through code one line at a time, you can watch variables as they change. This allows you to check your progress, confirm that statements do what you think they should do, and even change the code. Procedure 3.14 shows how to look at variables during debugging.

Procedure 3.14. Watch a variable using the IDE

1. Type or paste Example 3.7 into the IDE.

2. Place the cursor anywhere within the macro.

3. Select **Debug|Step Into**. The macro declaration line (the one starting with Sub) becomes highlighted.

4. Select the variable i, anywhere in the code, and right click on it. This displays a debugging pop-up menu.

5. Select **Add Watch...** The **Add Watch** dialog will display. Click **OK** to accept all the defaults. A **Watches** window pane will display in the IDE (by default, the window pane will appear at the bottom of the screen). The **Expression** column displays i and next to it in the Value column is its current value, zero (see Figure 3.17).

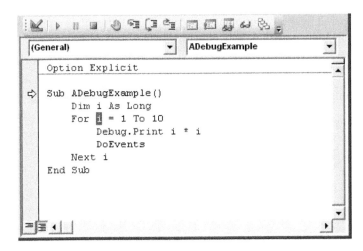

Figure 3.17. Debug panels with variable i equal to zero

6. Select **Debug|Step Into** twice; an alternate way of selecting this is with **F8**. The value automatically changes to 1.

7. You can repeat these steps as needed. The **Watch** variables dynamically change in the display each time the variable changes. To stop the code during this process, select **Run|Reset**. As confirmation, the highlighted line becomes unhighlighted.

Line 4 in Example 3.7 is the Debug statement. Debug.Print displays the results of executing the code that follows in the **Immediate** window. In this case, the code is i * i or i^2. Procedure 3.15 shows how this works.

Procedure 3.15. Debug using Debug.Print

1. Type or paste Example 3.7 into the IDE.

2. Select **View|Immediate Window (CTRL-G)** to open the **Immediate Window**. This displays near the **Watch** window pane. This window pane is a display area for debug statements.

3. Place the cursor anywhere within the macro.

4. Select **Debug|Step Into**. The macro declaration line (the one starting with Sub) becomes highlighted.

5. Click **F8** three more times, until after the Debug statement. As soon as that line is executed, the **Immediate** window displays the results of that statement, in this case 1.

6. Click **F8** until you pass the Debug statement again. The next display will be 4, followed by 9, and so on (see Figure 3.18).

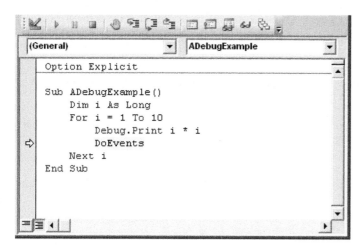

Figure 3.18. Results of the Debug.Print **statement**

Setting breakpoints

While stepping through code is useful, in the previous example you were interested in one specific line, and it took pressing **F8** several times to get there each time. Of course, there's a faster and easier way to stop only at certain points, and that's by setting a breakpoint. Procedure 3.16 shows how this works.

Procedure 3.16. Set a breakpoint

1. Type or paste Example 3.7 into the IDE.

2. Click in the left margin of the code after the Debug statement; that's the DoEvents line (see the highlighted line in Figure 3.19). A red dot will appear. This is the breakpoint.

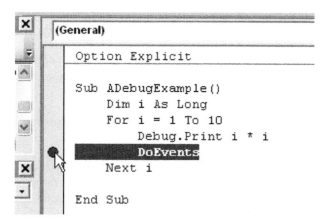

Figure 3.19. Code with breakpoint set

3. Select **View|Immediate Window (CTRL-G)** to open the **Immediate** Window, if it's not already opened.

4. Select **Run|Run Sub/User Form**. This executes the code until it reaches the breakpoint. The value of $i*i$ will display in the window; 1 for the first loop ($i=1$), 4 for the second loop ($i=2$), and so.

5. Select **Run|Continue**. This is the same menu option as **Run|Run Sub/User Form**, but it is labeled differently when the code is already running.

Procedure 3.17 presents a more convenient way to run all this code by using the **Debug** toolbar.

Procedure 3.17. Set a breakpoint using the Debug toolbar

1. Right click in the empty space in the toolbar area. The **Toolbar** pop-up menu will display.

2. Select **Debug**. This will display a small toolbar (See Figure 3.20), which you can position wherever you like it.

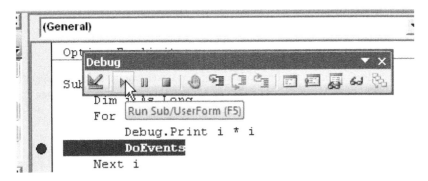

Figure 3.20. Debug toolbar

This toolbar contains menu items to run, step through, or view variables. There are tool tips that display information for each menu item.

Summary

Macros in Word are useful in many ways. You can combine individual functions of the Word interface into one macro, then modify it to further hone the procedure. You can also share macros with others.

Creating macros isn't difficult, although many users see it as arcane or complex programming. It can be as simple as recording your actions from the user interface.

The full power of macros can be seen when you modify the code to introduce features not available through the ribbon. In later chapters, you will see how to have a macro prompt for information, make decisions, and go through a document or a folder of documents looking for hyperlinks, bookmarks, specific words, or formatting. The possibilities are endless.

4

Find and Replace

It may seem odd to consider Find and Replace as an automation technique. Find has to be one of the most frequently used features in any application. It's among the first features users go to, and it would seem to need little explanation.

The dialog in its basic form has only two controls: A text box and a **Find** button. This apparent simplicity can be deceiving. By the end of this chapter you will see how useful and robust Find and Replace can be for document processing.

This chapter starts with an overview of Find and Replace, including procedures for improving its usefulness. It then introduces wildcards, which help you find patterns, and shows how wildcards can automate complex Find and Replace problems. The chapter concludes with an introduction to regular expressions, a vastly more powerful version of wildcards.

The Find Dialog

In its simplest form, Find and Replace is intuitive. CTRL-F displays the **Find** dialog (as does **Home|Editing|Find**). Enter some text and click the **Find** button to locate that text within the document. Replace is equally obvious. You specify the text to find and new text to replace it with.

GoTo Option

The **Find and Replace** dialog box has a third option: **GoTo**, which allows you to find non-text locations such as fields, footnotes, and tables. Click the **GoTo** tab of the **Find** dialog to see the options. For example, selecting **Table** in the **Go to what** list on the left side and then clicking **Next** selects the next table after the current insertion point.

Many of the **GoTo** options include additional specifications particular to the type of object. For example, selecting **Comment** lets you see the next comment from any reviewer. You can also specify a reviewer by name using the **Enter reviewer's name** drop-down list.

Related to **GoTo** is another feature that also finds similar objects: **Browse Object**. This feature (consisting of three icons) can be found under the down scroll bar. You can also access it by pressing ALT-CTRL-Home (see Figure 4.1).

Figure 4.1. Two views of the Browse object

Browse Object also finds non-text locations and shares many features with the **GoTo** dialog, but there are some differences. For example, **Go To** can find more types of objects, including equations and embedded objects, and it offers you more control. You can skip past objects, going for example to the third or twelfth object.

Browse Object may provide some convenience. The **Browse Object** search capability ties into the **Find** dialog's last search. You can then can use the **Browse Object|Find Next** button (the downward pointing double arrow icon) to repeat the last find, or the **Previous Find** button (the upward pointing double arrow icon) to also repeat the last find but in upwards in the document.

Find and Replace Techniques

Efficient use of Find and Replace depends on your ability to find the exact text you need in the first place and then replace it with the correct replacement text. We will explore several techniques to precisely and flexibly do both.

The most common case for using Find and Replace is simply to enter the exact text to find and the exact text to replace it with. Here are two simple approaches.

The Boilerplate Approach

This approach uses text such as **[USERNAME]**, **[ISSUEDATE]**, or **[AMOUNTDUE]** to create a "template" with fields that can be replaced later (see Example 4.1).

```
Dear [USERNAME],
The book you checked out on [ISSUEDATE] is currently overdue.
The balance due is [AMOUNTDUE].
```

Example 4.1. Find and Replace – boilerplate approach

You can customize a new document quickly by opening the template and using Find and Replace to insert the appropriate information for a particular client.

The Three-Step Approach

There may be times when you need to switch two values. For example, if you need to switch all instances of "John Q Public" with "John Doe," you can use a three-step process with a temporary placeholder. Procedure 4.1 shows how to do this.

Procedure 4.1. Three-step find and replace

1. Find "John Q Public" and replace all with "!TEMPNAME!". There's nothing special about "!TEMPNAME!", any placeholder can be used, as long as it's unique in the document.

2. Find "John Doe" and replace all with "John Q Public"

3. Find "!TEMPNAME!" and replace all with "John Doe".

This technique is used later (see the section titled "Converting a Text File" (p. 46)).

Special Characters

Find and Replace allows you to find non-textual items including special characters like paragraph marks, tabs, white space, or symbols. The easiest way to find special characters is through the **Find** dialog. In the **Find** dialog, click **More** and then click **Special** to display a list of special characters. Then select the character you need from the Special menu (see Figure 4.2). The list changes slightly depending on whether you are inserting content into the **Find what** field or the **Replace with** field.

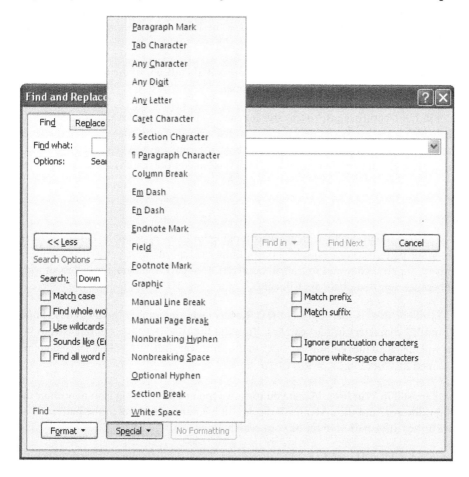

Figure 4.2. The Special menu of the Find dialog

Regardless of how special characters display in the menu, the **Find what** and **Replace with** text boxes represent them as a series of letter codes proceeded by the caret (^). For example, a paragraph mark is "^p" and a tab is "^t". You can also type these character sequences directly, instead of using the **Special** menu. For example, you could locate a manual page break (^m) and delete it by replacing it with nothing, or create a tab-delimited file by replacing all commas with tabs (^t).

You are not limited to the items in the list. Characters can also be specified by a numeric code. Each character has an assigned number from the ASCII, Extended ASCII, ANSI, or Unicode encoding tables. There is an ASCII/Extended ASCII table in Appendix C. Because of the size of the Unicode standard (thousands of characters), Appendix C does not include any Unicode tables. You can find the Unicode tables, plus other excellent resources, at http://unicode.org.

To use special characters in the **Find** dialog, enter the character information in one of the following formats:

- **ASCII Character Encoding:** ^*nnn,* where *nnn* is the character code in ASCII decimal format.

- **ANSI Character Encoding:** ^0*nnn,* where 0 is zero and *nnn* is the character code in ANSI decimal format.

- **Unicode Character Encoding:** ^u*nnnn,* where u is the letter u and *nnnn* is the four digit hexadecimal character code.

For example, the capital letter "A" is represented by the ASCII code 65, so the find text is "^65". Clicking **Find Next** locates the next "A" in your document.

By default, Word's Find feature is case insensitive for the 26-character roman alphabet, letters A-Z and a-z, whether you use letters or character codes. The previous example – finding the letter "A" by specifying "^65" in the **Find what** field – finds both the uppercase "A" (ASCII value of 65), and lowercase "a" (ASCII value of 97). Checking **Match Case** makes the search case sensitive. With this option set, a search for ^65 will only locate an uppercase "A."

Wildcards

Up until now, we have known exactly what we were looking for in every example. However, often you need to look for patterns. For example, a part number is typically a structured sequence of letters or numbers. Suppose you want to find all occurrences of part numbers, regardless of what the exact numbers are. For that, there are wildcards.

Wildcards are symbolic tokens that represent text. Readers who remember the DOS days know about the "*" and "?" characters in file searches. Running the DIR *.DOC command from the command line will match all files ending in .DOC. In the same way, DIR REPORT?.xls matches spreadsheets named REPORT1.xls or REPORT9.xls.

These wildcards are still in Windows. When you use any **Open** or **Save** dialog, you may enter the file name using wildcards, and the system will display all file names that match the pattern. You can fill in more or less information to refine your search.

Word has expanded wildcards greatly in recent releases. Table 4.1 lists the wildcards currently available in Word.

Table 4.1. Wildcards in Word

Symbol	Meaning	Example
?	Matches any single character.	C?t matches *cat*, *cut*, and *cot*.
*	Matches any string of characters.	t*g matches *taking*, and *thug*.
<	Matches the start of a word.	<track matches *tracking* but not *untracking*.
>	Matches the end of a word.	track> matches *untrack* but not *tracking*.
( )	Placeholder tags. These group letters.	See the section titled "Placeholder Tags" (p. 44).
[]	Matches any single character within the brackets.	[Bb]r[aeiou]*> matches *Brahms* and *brain*.
[-]	Matches any single character within the range. For example [0-9] matches the numeral zero through nine.	th[b-m]*> matches *thicken* and *thirst*, but not *thanks* or *three*.
[!x-z]	Excludes that range of characters from being matched.	th[!b-m]*> matches *thanks* and *three*, but not *thicken* or *thirst*.
{x}	Matches exactly x occurrences of the previous character or expression	bo{2}* matches the *boo* in *bamboozle* and *book*.
{x,}	Matches x or more occurrences of the preceding character or expression	o{2,}d> finds at least two occurrences of the letter *o* followed by *d* at the end of a word. Matches *wood*, but not *method*. (123){2,} matches *123123* inside *41231235*.
{x,y}	Matches x to y occurrences of the previous character or expression	10{1,3} matches 10, 100, and 1000.
@	Matches one or more occurrences of the previous character or expression.	o@d> matches *method* and *wood* (pattern at the end of the word). This is the same as o{1,}d>.
\	Escapes a wildcard character	* matches the asterisk (*) character and does not act as a wildcard.

Procedure 4.2 shows how to use a wildcard search

Procedure 4.2. Wildcard search

1. Open the **Find** dialog (CTRL-F).

2. Click **More**.

3. Check **Use wildcards**. Now, text typed into the **Find what** text box will be interpreted as wildcards.

As a simple example, enter th? in the **Find what** text box and click **Find Next**. This simple example is also very broad, locating the next occurrence of th plus any next character, such as "the", "tha" within "that", and "th "(space) from "with ".

Wildcards come with a few qualifications:

► You might think that * (the asterisk by itself) would select the entire document (after all, * "Matches any string of characters"). In practice, however, the lone asterisk will locate only the next single character. For example:

  • <* matches a single character at the start of a word.

  • <*> matches whole words.

  • * matches a single character.

► Characters are case sensitive. There's no toggle to change this, but you can work around this limitation using groupings (for example, [Aa] matches an upper or lower case a).

Examples of Wildcard Searches

Wildcard searches have to be done carefully, which is perhaps one reason they are not used as much as they could be. Here are some examples using the following five-character part numbers:

PN003, PN451, SN567, and RD328

PN451
> The basic case. You know the part number exactly. Finds PN451, but nothing else.

PN???
> Matches PN003, PN451. The PN is explicitly stated and three single character wildcards are used.

?N???
> Matches PN003, PN451, and SN567. The N in the second position is explicitly stated and the other four positions are single character wildcards.

[PR]????
> Matches three of the four, except SN567. The brackets specify any one, but only one, of the enclosed characters as a valid match. This matches the uppercase P or R in the first position. Unfortunately, this might also find *Plato*, or *Refel*. In fact, the previous choices are likely to have incidental matches, too. The more you know about the pattern (in this case P and R are specified), the better you can craft a search. At any rate, this search needs to be more specific.

[PRS][ND]???
> Matches all four. It can still match words, although in English, that's unlikely. Even so, a more restrictive search is better. Using a ? wildcard may be fine, but in this case, you know those three characters are digits. Use that knowledge to hone your searches.

[PRS][ND][0-9][0-9][0-9]
> Matches all five characters in each of the four part numbers. This is a good search. It's unlikely to find any incidental matches given the odd construction of the part number format. The

last three bracket sets still match only one character each, but instead of the explicit values that `[PRS]` matches, these match a range, in this case any character between zero and nine inclusive. A range could also be a set of letters such as `[a-z]` or `[A-Z]` as well as crossing between different cases such as `[M-d]`.

`[PRS][ND][0-9]{3}`

Matches all five characters in each of the four part numbers.. This is a more concise version of the previous search. The final part of this search, `{3}`, requires the immediately preceding pattern, `[0-9]`, be matched exactly three times.

Here are some other common searches:

`[0-9]{3}-[0-9]{2}-[0-9]{4}`

Matches Social Security numbers, such as 123-45-6789. Here, the hyphens make good markers, since that pattern is unlikely to be part of an incidental match, and the SSN format generally uses hyphens.

`[A-Z][A-Z]`

Matches postal codes. Actually, this pattern matches two upper case letters so it's not absolute and may also get incidental matches. `[A-Z]{2}` also works.

`[0-9][0-9][0-9] [0-9][0-9][0-9] [0-9][0-9]`

This should match phone numbers. But, this pattern returns the error message "The **Find What** text contains a Pattern Match which is too complex." Wildcard searches can have no more than seven groupings. This is a limitation imposed by Word.

`[\([0-9]{3,4}[!0-9]{1,2}[0-9]{3}[!0-9]{1,2}[0-9]{4}`

This is a better search for phone numbers and will find common variations such as (425) 555 3453, 425 555-3453, (425)-555-3453, 425.555.3453. Of course, there are many potential patterns for phone numbers in the United States and many more when you consider other countries.

`\([0-9]@\)`

Finds the (425) in the phone number (425) 555 3453. Since parentheses are wildcard characters, you need the backslashes to match the literal '(' and ')' characters.

`<[A-Za-z0-9]@\@[A-Za-z0-9]@.[A-Za-z]{3,4}`

Finds e-mail addresses, sort of. There is a limited set of suffixes, for example `.com`, `.net`, and `.org`, but this search would match any three or four letter suffix. It would also miss the six letter suffix `.museum`.

`<[A-Z]*,[^32^t^s]{1,}[A-Z]{2}[^32^t^s]{1,}[1-9]{1}[0-9]{4}`

Finds the city portion of a mailing address, such as *Houston, TX 77058*, and multiple word cities like *New York, NY 10112*, and *Salt Lake City, UT 84116*. This pattern assumes each address starts on a new line. Keep in mind that wildcards aren't perfect and multiple word city names can throw off accurate results.

`\<b\>`

Finds the markup tag `<b>`. The backslash symbols escape the angle brackets, treating them as literal characters and not the wildcard symbols for the start and end of a word.

Wildcards can also help match groups of letters:

The
> Finds the exact occurrence of *The*. `[Tt]he` finds either *the* or *The*. These occurrences can be inside words.

`[SPACE]the[SPACE]`
> The space before and after the pattern (represented by "[SPACE]", or the character produced by the **Space** bar) looks for just that, single spaces before and after "the," essentially identifying it as a word within a sentence.

`<the>`
> This is a better version of the previous search. The open bracket specifies that the pattern must occur at the start of a word, and the closed bracket specifies that it must occur at the end. Unlike the previous example, which looks for a space character (as if you pressed the space bar), this search defines a word as being preceded and followed by any whitespace, including non-breaking spaces, tabs, line feeds, and mathematical spaces.

`<*>`
> Finds any word. The open bracket finds the start of the word, and the close bracket finds the end of the word. It even knows that a period shouldn't be part of the word. That means this will match each part of a compound phrase such as *google.com* as a separate word, in this case *google* and *com*.

`\<([!\<\>]@)\>[!\<\>]@\</\1\>`
> Finds well formed XML tags, although not if they are nested or break across multiple lines.

Search patterns can get confusing. With a complex search, it's better to start small. Match a portion of the text first, then keep adding and testing portions until it's just right.

Placeholder Tags

Placeholder tags allow you to reuse parts of a found pattern in a replace. Each search term enclosed in parentheses is a text group. Each text group can be referenced by its position in the search string. You use a backslash symbol coupled with a single digit number, like `\1` or `\2`, to reference the placeholder in the replace string. The number after the backslash identifies which placeholder you want to reference.

For example, in the search pattern "`(Christopher) (Marlowe)`," the replace placeholder `\1` refers to `Christopher`, and `\2` refers to `Marlowe`. To reverse a name, for example to change names in a list from "first last" to "last, first," the search pattern would be `(<*>) (<*>)^13`, the replace statement would be `\2, \1^13` with the comma separator added for good measure (see Figure 4.3). Placeholder statements work only with wildcards and text grouping, and only up to nine statements.

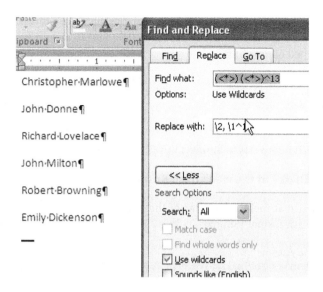

Figure 4.3. Find and replace using placeholders

 The metacharacter ^13 is often used like a paragraph mark, but be aware that ^p and ^13 are not identical. Word's paragraph mark (^p) contains the formatting information for the preceding paragraph and ^13 does not. The main difference is that text created outside of Office may use ^13 (sometimes referred to as a "fake paragraph") and could cause formatting inconsistencies. The problem is that ^p is not supported in wildcard searches; ^13 is. A good general rule would be to find and replace all ^13 values with ^p after importing text created outside of Office.

Placeholder Examples

The following two examples use placeholder tags to swap date formatting information. Example 4.2 converts a date formatted in the British style (d/m/yy or d/m/yyyy) to the American format (m/d/yy or m/d/yyyy). The same find and replace will also convert the American format to the British format.

Find What: `([0-9]{1,2})/([0-9]{1,2})/([0-9]{2,4})`
Replace with: `\2 \1 \3`

Result: 12/7/1941 converts to 7/12/1941

               9/11/2001 converts to 11/9/2001

Example 4.2. Switch date formats between British and American format

Example 4.3 changes a date in a format that includes the day of the week from the British format (Sunday, 25 July 2011), to the American format (Sunday, July 25, 2011). The find strings in Example 4.3 and Example 4.4 need to be typed on one line.

Find What:

```
(<[MTWFS][ondayueshrit]{2,7},)( [0-9]{1,2})
( [JFMASOND][anuryebchpilgstmov]{2,8})( [12][0-9]{3}>)
```

Replace with:

```
\1\3\2,\4
```

Result: Sunday, 25 July 2011 converts to Sunday, July 25, 2011

Example 4.3. Switch date formats with day of the week from British to American style

Example 4.4 changes date using a format that includes the day of the week from the American format (Sunday, July 25, 2011) to the British format (Sunday, 25 July 2011).

Find What:

```
(<[MTWFS][ondayueshrit]{2,7},)
( [JFMASOND][anuryebchpilgstmov]{2,8})
( [0-9]{1,2}),( [12][0-9]{3}>)
```

Replace with:

```
\1\3\2\4
```

Result: Sunday, July 25, 2011 to Sunday, 25 July 2011

Example 4.4. Switch date formats with day of the week from American to British style

Multiple Searches

Wildcards give you an impressive Find and Replace mechanism, but in practice, you may need a series of Find and Replace operations to get the result you want.

Converting a Text File

Some applications write text files using a paragraph return at the end of every line (and two paragraph returns to separate paragraphs). This is annoying if you want to paste the text into a Word document and have it wrap correctly. For example, consider Example 4.5, which contains a portion of Mark Twain's *A Connecticut Yankee in King Arthur's Court*.[6]

```
CHAPTER I¶
¶
CAMELOT¶
¶
"Camelot--Camelot," said I to myself.   "I don't seem to remember¶
hearing of it before.   Name of the asylum, likely."  ¶
¶
It was a soft, reposeful summer landscape, as lovely as a dream, ¶
and as lonesome as Sunday.   The air was full of the smell of¶
flowers, and the buzzing of insects, and the twittering of birds, ¶
and there were no people, no wagons, there was no stir of life, ¶
nothing going on.   The road was mainly a winding path with hoof-prints¶
in it, and now and then a faint trace of wheels on either side in¶
the grass--wheels that apparently had a tire as broad as one's hand. ¶
```

Example 4.5. Excerpt from *A Connecticut Yankee in King Arthur's Court*[6]

Knowing the structure of the document is key to the conversion process. Notice several aspects of this text:

► Each line ends with a paragraph mark.

► Each paragraph ends with two paragraph marks.

► Chapter titles are consistently named using the word "CHAPTER" and a roman numeral.

Each of these aspects is consistent throughout the story. As a result, this is a good candidate for automation. Procedure 4.3 shows how to perform this conversion.

Procedure 4.3. Convert text line endings to Word style

1. Copy the text in Example 4.5 to a Word document. You can find the text at the Project Gutenberg website[1] or at the companion web site for this book[2].

2. Perform the following Find and Replaces (using **Replace All**) with wildcards turned off. The idea is find two consecutive paragraph marks and replace them with a unique tag that doesn't occur anywhere else in the document, then find single instances of the paragraph mark and turn them into spaces, and finally turn the unique tag, (!paragraph!) back into a single pilcrow (the paragraph marker symbol).

Find what	Replace with	Comments
^p^p	!paragraph!	The **Replace with** text must be unique in the file.
^p		Replace ^p with a single space
!paragraph!	^p	

 Each of these replacements may take a while, given the number of items in each search.

3. Turn wildcards on.

4.

Find what	Replace with	Comments
CHAPTER [IVX]*^13	Style Heading 2	No replace text is specified; the replacement will the style itself; see notes below.

To use a style as a replacement value:

a. In the **Find** dialog, click the **More|Format** button and select the **Style** menu item.

This will display the **Find Style** dialog box

[1] http://www.gutenberg.org/cache/epub/86/pg86.txt
[2] http://xmlpress.net/wordsecrets.html

b.   Choose the style (**Style Heading 2** in this instance) from the list and then click **OK**. The style name appears below the **Replace with** text box.

 To remove all formatting, including the selected style, click the **No Formatting** button. Also, you can use these steps in the **Find what** text box to search for text with a particular style.

This step marks all the chapter titles as **Heading 2**.

5.   One last change I like to make is optional but replaces two spaces after a sentence with one space.

Find what	Replace with	Comments
(?) [SPACE] [SPACE]	\1 [SPACE]	Set the style to **No formatting**.

Of course, you could also record any of these examples as a macro. That reduces all the tedious work, such as making sure the phrase [SPACE] really gets replaced with a space character. You can also run the macro many times with only a single command if you have a lot of text files to convert.

Cleaning Up Word's Bloated HTML

Word produces notoriously bloated HTML. For example, open a new Word document, type or paste in some text, and save that document as HTML (save using the **Web Page** and **unfiltered** options is best for this demonstration). Open that document with Notepad to view the HTML code as plain text, and then cut and paste it back into a Word document (you'll need Word's Find and Replace capabilities, something a browser or Notepad doesn't have, for this procedure). You will see something like Example 4.6. Note the copious mark up, even in this simple case.

```
<p class=MsoNormal><span style='font-size:10.0pt;line-height:115%;
font-family:"Courier New";mso-fareast-font-family:"Times New Roman"'>
So saying, he gave the spur to his steed <span class=SpellE>Rocinante
</span>, heedless of the cries his squire <span class=SpellE>Sancho
</span> sent after him, warning him that most certainly they were
windmills and not giants he was going to attack. He, however, was
so positive they were giants that he neither heard the cries of
<span class=SpellE>Sancho</span>, nor perceived, near as he was,
what they were, but made at them shouting, &quot;Fly not, cowards
and vile beings, for a single knight attacks you.&quot;<o:p></o:p>
</span></p>
```

Example 4.6. HTML exported by Word

Using a series of Find and Replaces, you can clean this up. Copy the code from the Notepad file and paste it back into a Word document, then with wildcards turned on do the following:

Find what	Replace with	Comments
\<p*\>	<p>	Removes all attributes (class=MsNormal and so forth) from every paragraph tag (<p>).
\<span*\>		Removes every opening <span> tag.
\</span\>		Removes every closing </span> tag.
\<o:p\>		Removes every opening <o:p> tag.
\</o:p\>		Removes every closing </o:p> tag.
\<head\>*\</head\>		Removes the <head\> tag with any embedded Microsoft styles.

Afterwards, you'll have something close to Example 4.7.

```
<p>So saying, he gave the spur to his steed Rocinante, heedless of the
cries his squire Sancho sent after him, warning him that most certainly
they were windmills and not giants he was going to attack. He, however,
was so positive they were giants that he neither heard the cries of
Sancho, nor perceived, near as he was, what they were, but made at them
shouting, &quot;Fly not, cowards and vile beings, for a single knight
attacks you.&quot;</p>
```

Example 4.7. Cleaned up HTML

Spell Checking an HTML/XML File

There may be times when you'd like to spell check an HTML or XML document. The problem is that the tags themselves will throw off the check to the point of frustration. One solution is to have Word ignore all the tags. Procedure 4.4 shows how to do this.

Procedure 4.4. Spell check an HTML or XML file

1. Open an HTML or XML document in Word or paste an example into a Word document.

2. In the find dialog, with wildcards turned on, search for \<*\>, then set the font to red and turn off spell checking:

   a. In the **Replace** dialog, click **More**, if it's not already opened.

   b. Click **Format|Language** and make sure **Do not check spelling or grammar** is checked. That checkbox has three states and the check mark must be showing.

   c. In the **Find** dialog, click the **More|Format** button and select the **Font** menu item. This displays the **Find Font** dialog box.

   d. Choose the color red from the **Font color** list and then click **OK**. The style name will appear below the **Replace with** text box.

3.   Click **Replace All**.

 Given the possible number of tags, their combinations, or errors in enclosing tag, some coding may not be caught this way. Making the text red doesn't do anything other than help you see which areas were changed. The search, which finds all tags, is marked and excluded from the spell check.

---

4.   You may need to recheck this several times and reapply the grammar so the misspellings show. To do this:

    a.   Click the **Microsoft Office** button, then click **Word Options**.

    b.   Click **Proofing**, and near the bottom, click the **Recheck Document** button.

    c.   Click **OK** to close the screen and reset the text.

Converting a Database

Taking advantage of the placeholder tag, you can format a simple XML database. For example, suppose you have a comma separated address book with entries like Example 4.8. You can reformat the entries into an XML file with a series of relatively simple replacements. This case assumes a consistently formatted file with six comma separated fields.

```
Jarvis,Richard,13544 Pleasant Orchard Ln,Tombstone,AL,77654
Jenkins,Thomas,342 W. Woodwall,Springfield,IA,43212
Elbow,Phil,5522 325th St. NE,Seattle,WA,90815
```

Example 4.8. Address book text file

The conversion (see Procedure 4.5) takes place in three parts: Preparing the data, converting it, and then cleaning it up. Preparing the data puts brackets around each field. If your formatting is better than this example, this step may not be needed.

Procedure 4.5. Converting a simple database to XML

1.   Open the sample document (`Convert_A_Database.docm[8]`) in Word or type/paste Example 4.8 into a Word document.

2.   In the **Find** dialog, with wildcards turned on:

Find what	Replace with	Comments
,	] [	Sets up most fields with a set of brackets, such as [Richard]
([!^13]{1,})	\1]	Add brackets for the last field of each line, which doesn't have a comma.
(<[!^13]{1,})	[\1	Add brackets to the first field of each line.

3. Place the cursor in the first position and use the following parameters for a **Replace All**.

Find What: (\ [*\]) (\ [*\]) (\ [*\]) (\ [*\]) (\ [*\]) (\ [*\])

Replace with: [SPACE][SPACE][SPACE]<UserName>\2 \1<UserName>^13
                   [SPACE][SPACE]<StreetAddress>\3</StreetAddress>^13
                   [SPACE][SPACE]<CityState>\4, \5 \6</CityState>^13

 The **Replace with** string is shown above as three separate lines, but in the **Find** dialog, the string must be entered as one line without a break or spaces between lines.

The [SPACE] characters are optional although later they will make the final XML code easier to read.

The **Find what** pattern creates six text groups, each with a placeholder, that **Replace** depends on. Crafting the right replacement codes may take a moment, or several tries, but the payoff is worth it.

4. Add <MailingAddress> tag around address:

Find What: (*\</CityState\>^13)

Replace with: <MailingAddress>^13\1</MailingAddress>^13

After you do that you get an XML formatted file where each address that looks like Example 4.9.

```
<MailingAddress>
  <UserName>[Richard] [Jarvis]<UserName>
  <StreetAddress>[13544 Pleasant Orchard Ln]</StreetAddress>
  <CityState>[Tombstone], [AL] [77654]</CityState>
</MailingAddress>
```

Example 4.9. Database converted to XML

This is good start but there are two mistakes to fix, which I will address in the next section.

You can convert an entire database in only a few actions without any programming. But this is a book about automation; doing things in one action. The previous example provides a good case for recording a macro, since you can perform all the actions from the keyboard. Procedure 4.6 and Procedure 4.7 demonstrate writing a macro and then modifying its code to fix errors or add features.

Procedure 4.6. Create a macro to automate database conversion

1. Start a document with the text in Example 4.8.

2. In the **Developer** tab, click **Record Macro**, name it ConvertDataToXML, and store it in Document1. Click **OK**.

3.   Repeat Procedure 4.5.

4.   In the **Developer** tab, click **Stop Recording**. This saves the recorded macro.

5.   To test, re-paste the original three lines into document, replacing everything already there and run the macro. The result should look like Example 4.9.

This is a good start, but as in the real world, there are mistakes in the code. Here are two of them:

▸ The closing <UserName> needs a forward slash.

▸ The brackets need to be removed

Correcting the first mistake is simple enough and can be done in the code editor. The last one is more troublesome since you can't modify a recorded macro other than in the code editor; you can't re-record the wrong portion of it. You could re-generate the macro and erase this version. But in this case, we'll just patch the existing code.

First, Procedure 4.7 addresses the typographical error.

Procedure 4.7. Edit a macro to fix a typographical error

1.   Open the IDE by clicking the **Developer** tab and clicking the **Visual Basic** button. The editor displays.

2.   In the **Project** window, expand **Project (Document1)|Modules** and double click **NewMacros**. The code displays.

3.   Scroll down through the code until you see:

    "<UserName>\2 \1<UserName>^13
    <StreetAddress>\3^13
    <CityState>\4,\5 \6</CityState>^13"

4.   Change `<UserName>` to be `</UserName>`.

5.   Click **Save (File|Save)** of the **Save** icon in the tool bar.

The last mistake requires another macro. Record one more and call it `DeleteBrackets`. Without changing the document, start the macro, show the **Replace** dialog, do the following, and then stop recording:

Find what	Replace with	Comments
[\ [\]]		Replace [\ [\]] with nothing

The `DeleteBracket` code displays at the bottom of the IDE code window. To implement the patch, you need to call this newly created macro. At the end of `ConvertDataToXML`, insert a call to `DeleteBrackets`. The result will look like line 7 of Example 4.10.

```
1  ...
2          .MatchAllWordForms = False
3          .MatchSoundsLike = False
4          .MatchWildcards = True
5      End With
6      Selection.Find.Execute Replace:=wdReplaceAll
7      DeleteBrackets 'Added call here
8  End Sub
```

Example 4.10. Patching the `ConvertDataToXML` macro

Save the file again. (You should always save before running a macro; if there is a bug, or the macro hangs the computer, you will have to force the IDE or Word to quit, and any unsaved changes will be lost.)

Test again by re-pasting Example 4.8 into the document, replacing everything already there, and running the macro. All the changes should show up.

Calling Routines

This following section gets into advanced practices, so if you feel this is inapplicable to your needs, skip it and go to the next section.

In the previous example, it would have been better to re-record the macro rather than patching it. In the long run, clean code is always best. It is easier to debug, to read six months later, and to modify. However, this example demonstrates how to call one macro from another. In this case, our macro called Word or Office functions, but you can also call your own macros.

A good demonstration of this is the previous HTML example (see the section titled "Cleaning Up Word's Bloated HTML" (p. 48)). Example 4.11 displays the relevant portion of the `Find` routine:

```
 1  Selection.Find.ClearFormatting
 2  Selection.Find.Replacement.ClearFormatting
 3  With Selection.Find
 4      .Text = "\<p*\>"
 5      .Replacement.Text = "<p>"
 6      .Forward = True
 7      .Wrap = wdFindContinue
 8      .Format = False
 9      .MatchCase = False
10      .MatchWholeWord = False
11      .MatchAllWordForms = False
12      .MatchSoundsLike = False
13      .MatchWildcards = True
14  End With
15  Selection.Find.Execute Replace:=wdReplaceAll
```

Example 4.11. Portion of the `Find` routine

This procedure requires a series of five replacement steps. If you recorded this and looked at the generated code, you would see it takes a brute force approach and includes the Find code five times. That's an awful lot of repetition. To some extent the amount of code the macro runs isn't an issue (even for a large file this code runs quickly), but maintaining a large macro can be difficult.

In fact, the only things that change are lines 2 and 3. And even then only a small part of the code changes: the "`<p>`" and "`\<p*\>`" pairings change to new tags.

It would be much more convenient to explicitly set the replacement text pairing. You can do this by writing your own routines. Procedure 4.8 shows how this works.

Procedure 4.8. Creating your own routine

1. Create a new document.

2. Paste the text sample from Example 4.5 (p. 46) into it. Open the IDE.

3. Right click on the name **Project (Document2)**, selecting **Insert|Module**. This opens a new code module.

4. Paste the code in Example 4.12 into the new module.

5. Run `RemoveHTMLTags` from the **Macros** dialog of the **Developer** tab.

```
Option Explicit

Sub RemoveHTMLTags()
    ReplacementText "\<p*\>", "<p>"
    ReplacementText "\<span*\>", vbNullString
    ReplacementText "\</span\>", vbNullString
    ReplacementText "\<o:p\>", vbNullString
    ReplacementText "\</o:p\>", vbNullString
End Sub

Private Sub ReplacementText(findtext As String, replacetext As String)
    Selection.Find.ClearFormatting
    Selection.Find.Replacement.ClearFormatting
    With Selection.Find
        .Text = findtext
        .Replacement.Text = replacetext
        .Wrap = wdFindContinue
        .MatchWildcards = True
    End With
    Selection.Find.Execute Replace:=wdReplaceAll
End Sub
```

Example 4.12. Remove HTML tags code example

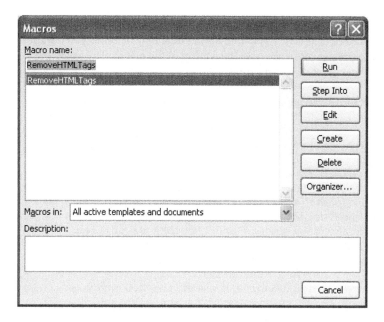

Figure 4.4. The Macros dialog for `RemoveHTMLTags`

This code is cleaner is several ways. The most important is that if you need to delete additional tags, you can just add similar lines to `RemoveHTMLTags`. For example, if you wanted to change the font, you could add a line at the bottom (see Example 4.13).

```
Sub RemoveHTMLTags()
    ReplacementText "\<p*\>", "<p>"
    ReplacementText "\<span*\>", vbNullString
    ReplacementText "\</span\>", vbNullString
    ReplacementText "\<o:p\>", vbNullString
    ReplacementText "\</o:p\>", vbNullString
    ReplacementText "Times New Roman", "Comic Sans MS"     ❶
End Sub
```

Example 4.13. Font change added to `RemoveHTMLTags` **macro**

❶   This line replaces the *Times New Roman* font with *Comic Sans MS*.

This code is much shorter than what would have been generated if you recorded the macro. The macro recorder does an excellent job generating code, but it creates more code than you really need.

You may have noticed that `ReplacementText` did not appear in the **Macros** dialog. The `Private` label in the definition of that call prevents it from being displayed in the **Macros** dialog. The function can only be called from `RemoveHTMLTags`, so there's no sense displaying it to the user.

User Interaction

In the earlier examples, two things are clear. First, a lot of work gets done with little effort. In the HTML case, you can format several thousand lines of code in a few seconds by invoking a single macro. Second, only predefined items were changed. In other words, there were no decisions to make. This creates simple macros, but not very versatile ones. There may be times you'll want to specify what to change or exert greater influence over the control of the macro. The following examples allow you to control a macro while it is running.

Take the case of looking for acronyms in a document. Example 4.14 is from a military document laden with acronyms:

```
a. Exercise COCOM of AMC, MSC, and SDDC in times of peace and war.
d. Submit to the SECDEF, through the CJCS, the DUSD (LM&R), and
such other officials, for approval any changes to transportation,
fiscal, procurement, or other DOD policies to implement this regulation.
(4) Provide management support for Service-unique or theater-assigned
transportation assets, to include pre-positioned ships, to the
Secretaries of the military departments and the CDRs of unified
commands at the direction of the SECDEF, or upon request of the
Service Secretary, CDR, or CCDR concerned.
C. INDIVIDUAL MISSIONS, ROLES, AND RESPONSIBILITIES
(6) Establish and maintain relationships between the DOD and the
commercial transportation industry (in coordination with the
Department of Homeland Security (DHS)/United States Coast Guard
(USCG), Department of Transportation [DOT]/Maritime Administration
[MARAD], Federal Aviation Administration [FAA], and the National
Transportation Safety Board) to promote the seamless transition
from peace to war and improve interfaces between the DOD and
industry.
```

Example 4.14. Document containing many acronyms

For simplicity, assume an acronym is three or more consecutive uppercase letters. The wildcard search is < [A-Z] {3,}. Be aware that there will be some false positives (for example, INDIVIDUAL, MISSIONS, ROLES, and RESPONSIBILITIES will be incorrectly identified as acronyms).

```
Sub FindAcronyms()
    Dim findRange As Range
    Set findRange = ActiveDocument.Range

    findRange.Find.ClearFormatting
    findRange.Find.MatchWildcards = True

    Do While findRange.Find.Execute(findtext:="<[A-Z]{3,}") = True
        findRange.Select
        DoEvents
    Loop
End Sub
```

Example 4.15. The `FindAcronyms` macro

As a practical matter, the code in Example 4.15 doesn't do anything worthwhile, aside from highlighting each acronym briefly. However, from an automation point of view this is an important macro. It introduces Find's Do While loop. As long as there is something for the Find statement to locate, it keeps going. In this example, it finds every occurrence of three or more consecutive uppercase letters, quite good considering it's only two lines (Do While...Loop). The work is done inside the loop. Example 4.16 uses a loop to create a list of all acronyms in the document.

```
Sub FindAndStoreAllAcronyms()
    Dim targetDocument As Document        ❶

    Application.ScreenUpdating = False ❷

    Dim sourceDocument As Document
    Set sourceDocument = ActiveDocument

    Dim findRange As Range
    Set findRange = sourceDocument.Range

    findRange.Find.ClearFormatting
    findRange.Find.MatchWildcards = True

    Do While findRange.Find.Execute(findtext:="<[A-Z]{3,}") = True
        If targetDocument Is Nothing Then
            Set targetDocument = Documents.Add
        End If

        findRange.Select

        targetDocument.Range.InsertAfter findRange.Text
        targetDocument.Range.InsertParagraphAfter

        DoEvents
    Loop

    If Not targetDocument Is Nothing Then
        targetDocument.Paragraphs.Last.Range.Delete
        targetDocument.Range.Sort
    End If

    Application.ScreenUpdating = True        ❸
End Sub
```

Example 4.16. The FindAndStoreAllAcronyms macro

This function, FindAndStoreAllAcronyms, finds every string in your document that matches the wildcard search, <[A-Z]{3,}. Some additional notes:

❶   The new code creates a document (targetDocument) for the terms if at least one is found..

❷❸   The two ScreenUpdating calls turn off the application's ability to show changes on the screen (False) at the beginning of the function, and then back on (True) at the end. This prevents any awkward updates or flickers while the macro is running. Afterwards, turning screen updating back on performs only one update, showing the final result. While you are developing or debugging the code, you may want to leave screen updating enabled so you can see the changes on the screen.

Example 4.16 finds acronyms, but it also finds things that aren't acronyms. Therefore, you need to make some decisions. Example 4.17 lets you do that. For each term found, it asks you if you want to record the term or not (or quit the macro). Paste this code into the same module as the other routines and run AskToStoreAllAcronyms.

```
Sub AskToStoreAllAcronyms()
    Dim targetDocument As Document

    Dim sourceDocument As Document
    Set sourceDocument = ActiveDocument

    Dim findRange As Range
    Set findRange = sourceDocument.Range

    findRange.Find.ClearFormatting
    findRange.Find.MatchWildcards = True

    Do While findRange.Find.Execute(findtext:="<[A-Z]{3,}") = True      ❷
        findRange.Select

        Select Case MsgBox(prompt:="Save the term '" & _                ❶
                findRange.Text & "'?", _
                buttons:=vbQuestion + vbYesNoCancel, _
                Title:="Save This Term?")
        Case vbYes
            If targetDocument Is Nothing Then
                Set targetDocument = Documents.Add
            End If

            targetDocument.Range.InsertAfter findRange.Text
            targetDocument.Range.InsertParagraphAfter

        Case vbNo
        Case vbCancel
            Exit Do

        End Select

        DoEvents
    Loop

    If Not targetDocument Is Nothing Then
        targetDocument.Paragraphs.Last.Range.Delete
        targetDocument.Range.Sort
        targetDocument.Activate
    End If
End Sub
```

Example 4.17. The AskToStoreAllAcronyms Macro

Here are some coding notes:

❶ The Msgbox call, usually used to just display information, asks the user to keep or skip the selected term or to quit the macro. In this case, Msgbox returns one of three values, vbYes, vbNo, or vbCancel. The subsequent Select statement handles each case individually.

❷ Each loop, and here it's a Do While ... loop, should include a DoEvents call. This relinquishes control from the macro to the operating system for a moment and allows the operating system to do things like update the screen. However, the main purpose is to prevent you from being locked out if you unintentionally get into an endless loop.

When you run the AskToStoreAllAcronyms macro, you will end up with a second document that contains the collected acronyms sorted, with duplicates removed.

Macros to Create Hyperlinks

You can automate the creation of almost anything; the next example automates the creation of hyperlinks to reference sections.

Example 4.18 is a short excerpt from a municipal code. It includes a structured, numbered outline with references in the text to other sections. We want to link all references to the corresponding numbered paragraph. If the document were longer, then manually creating the links would be prohibitive, both to initially set up and then to maintain. Three macros and two supporting macros complete the task.

3.22.110 Fire Prevention and Suppression Contracts.

(Amended by Ordinance Nos. 321245, 054344, and AC43245-1, effective July 9, 1987.) The Commissioner In Charge of Fire And Rescue and the City Auditor hereby are authorized to enter into contracts under the provisions of the State Rural Fire Protection District Act.

3.22.120 Renewal Notices.

(Amended by Ordinance No. 1123456, effective Feb. 30, 1968.) On or near February 8 of each year the Auditor shall mail to each individual, organization and political subdivision then under contract with the City for fire suppression and/or fire prevention, letter stating the dollar amount the City will charge for renewal of the contract in the next succeeding fiscal year. This amount will be computed by the formula in Section 3.22.110.

3.22.150 Use of Fire Boats for Pumping Water Out of Boats and Barges.

(Amended by Ordinance No. 55432, effective December 16, 1967.) Upon the approval of the Chief of Fire And Rescue and of the Commissioner In Charge, the fire boats of Fire And Rescue may be used for the purpose of pumping out water from boats and barges which ply the county rivers.

Example 4.18. Text for hyperlink example

Analyzing this document reveals several things:

► The numbering is consistent and predictable. It looks like there are only three sets of numbers for section headers in the format of ##.##.###. Although in the complete document the numbers can get as low as 1.1.1 and as high as 12.1.220, the format is still consistent.

► The section numbers always start at the beginning of a line. Technically, they always follow a preceding paragraph mark, which is a good reference for writing a search pattern.

► The section numbers are bolding. Again, that makes for a good flag for a search pattern.

This text is consistent, and therefore, an excellent candidate for automation. Now, you need a strategy.

► First, you need something to link to. This anchor must be a bookmark. Since we have consistently formatted section numbers, we can derive a bookmark name directly from the section number (see Example 4.19 (p. 60)).
► Second, you need to place the bookmarks (see Example 4.20 (p. 61)).
► Finally, you to create links back to the bookmarks (see Example 4.21 (p. 61)).

Begin by opening a document and pasting or typing in the contents of Example 4.18

Next we need to name the section number anchors. The anchor names will be based on the section number, of course, but anchor names can't start with a number and can't contain a period. We get around both of these limitations by formatting the names like this: fp3pt22pt160. This name refers to section 3.22.160. The fp is the for "fire prevention," and pt is short for "point."

The anchor names should be unique to this linking system to differentiate them from other anchors. The routine is declared as Private, since it's only called from other routines and there's no need to display it on the user's **Macro** dialog list. Example 4.19 creates a bookmark name in a standardized format.

```
Private Function CreateName(rangeString As String) As String
    On Error GoTo MyErrorHandler
    Dim newBookMark As String
    newBookMark = rangeString

    'Remove the paragraph mark
    newBookMark = Mid(newBookMark, 2)
    newBookMark = Replace(newBookMark, ".", "pt")
    newBookMark = "fp" & newBookMark

    CreateName = newBookMark

    Exit Function

MyErrorHandler:
    MsgBox "CreateName" & vbCrLf & vbCrLf & _
           "Err = " & Err.Number & vbCrLf & _
            "Descripion: " & Err.Description
End Function
```

Example 4.19. Macro to create a bookmark name

Example 4.20 creates the bookmark. It uses a `Find` loop looking for all section numbers. When it finds one, it creates the name using the `CreateName` macro and then inserts that bookmark. The `wildcardSearch` variable will be discussed in more detail later.

```
Public Sub MakeBookMarks()
    On Error GoTo MyErrorHandler

    Dim sourceDocument As Document
    Set sourceDocument = ActiveDocument

    Dim findRange As Range
    Set findRange = sourceDocument.Range
    findRange.Find.ClearFormatting
    findRange.Find.MatchWildcards = True

    Dim wildcardSearch As String
    wildcardSearch = "([0-9]{1,2}.[0-9]{1,}.[0-9]{1,})"
    findRange.Find.Font.Bold = True

    Dim newBookMark As String
    Do While findRange.Find.Execute(findtext:=wildcardSearch)
        findRange.Select
        newBookMark = CreateName(findRange.Text)
        sourceDocument.Bookmarks.Add newBookMark, findRange
        DoEvents
    Loop

    Exit Sub

MyErrorHandler:
    MsgBox "MakeBookMarks" & vbCrLf & _
    vbCrLf & "Err = " & Err.Number & vbCrLf & _
    "Description: " & Err.Description
End Sub
```

Example 4.20. Macro to create bookmarks

Example 4.21 creates the links. This example uses `Find` to locate a section number sequence. Once found, it creates the name using the `CreateName` macro, and then using that name, creates the link. The `wildcardSearch` variable will be discussed in more detail later.

```
Public Sub MakeLinks()
  On Error GoTo MyErrorHandler

  Dim sourceDocument As Document
  Set sourceDocument = ActiveDocument

  Dim findRange As Range
  Set findRange = sourceDocument.Range
  findRange.Find.ClearFormatting
  findRange.Find.MatchWildcards = True

  Dim wildcardSearch As String
  wildcardSearch = "([0-9]{1,2}.[0-9]{1,}.[0-9]{1,})"
```

```
findRange.Find.Font.Bold = False

Dim newBookMark As String
Do While findRange.Find.Execute(findtext:=wildcardSearch)
  findRange.Select
  newBookMark = CreateName(findRange.Text)
  sourceDocument.Hyperlinks.Add _
      Anchor:=findRange, SubAddress:=newBookMark
  findRange.Start = findRange.End + 1
  DoEvents
Loop

Exit Sub

MyErrorHandler:
  MsgBox "MakeReferences" & vbCrLf & vbCrLf & _
    "Err = " & Err.Number & vbCrLf & _
    "Description: " & Err.Description
End Sub
```

Example 4.21. Macro to create links

MakeLinks (Example 4.21) and MakeBookMarks (Example 4.20) are almost identical, with the exception of the part inside the Do While...Loop, where all the work is done. This kind of redundancy is usually discouraged, but in this case, it makes for a cleaner example and is easier to maintain should you want to change one routine or the other.

A fourth routine (Example 4.22) deletes all the anchors and hyperlinks so you can start over.

```
Public Sub DeleteBookMarks()
    On Error GoTo MyErrorHandler

    Dim sourceDocument As Document
    Set sourceDocument = ActiveDocument
    Dim i As Long

    Dim myBookMarks As Bookmark
    For i = sourceDocument.Bookmarks.Count To 1 Step -1
        If InStr(sourceDocument.Bookmarks(i).Name, "fp") > 0 Then
            sourceDocument.Bookmarks(i).Select
            sourceDocument.Bookmarks(i).Delete '
        End If
        DoEvents
    Next i

    Dim myHyperlink As Hyperlink
    For i = sourceDocument.Hyperlinks.Count To 1 Step -1
        If InStr(sourceDocument.Hyperlinks(i).Name, "fp") > 0 Then   ❶
            sourceDocument.Hyperlinks(i).Range.Select
            sourceDocument.Hyperlinks(i).Delete
        End If                                                        ❷
        DoEvents
    Next i
```

```
    Exit Sub

MyErrorHandler:
    MsgBox "DeleteBookMarks" & vbCrLf & _
            vbCrLf & "Err = " & Err.Number & _
            vbCrLf & "Description: " & Err.Description
End Sub
```

Example 4.22. Delete bookmarks

❶❷ The statement If InStr(sourceDocument.Hyperlinks(i).Name, "fp") > 0
makes sure only these hyperlinks are deleted and not any others in the document. If you want
to delete all hyperlinks, remove that statement and the End if statement three lines down.
If the document has to be updated, it may be best to delete the existing bookmarks and hyperlinks first, and then regenerate them all.

To test this application, run MakeBookMarks and MakeLinks, in that order. If you need to
recheck the document or want to start over, run DeleteBookMarks to clean up.

One variation is to write a new macro that runs all three together. Example 4.23 does just that.

```
Public Sub MakeNewReferences()
    On Error GoTo MyErrorHandler

    DeleteBookMarks
    MakeBookMarks
    MakeLinks

    Exit Sub

MyErrorHandler:
    MsgBox "MakeNewReferences" & vbCrLf & _
    vbCrLf & "Err = " & Err.Number & vbCrL & _
    "Description: " & Err.Description
End Sub
```

Example 4.23. Run all bookmark and link procedures

Regular Expressions

Wildcards give you an impressive flexibility for Find and Replace. However, there is an even more
powerful feature along the same lines. Regular expressions (or regexp) are similar to wildcards,
but vastly expand the options. They are used instead of wildcard searches. These extensions come
at a price, and crafting a regular expression search is not for the faint of heart. There is a complete
study within computer science about regular expressions. This overview is just that, an overview,
and not meant to be an in-depth exploration.

Superficially, regular expressions are similar to wildcards in that they use meta-characters to represent classes of searches. The symbols are different, but many of the concepts are the same. For
example, you can still find patterns at the beginnings of words. Regular expressions, however, go
well beyond Word's wildcards. Table 4.2 lists a few of the options.

Table 4.2. Regular Expression Symbols

Symbol	Meaning	Example
Any character	Matches the character exactly except for the following special characters: `[\^$.|?*+().`	`Cat` matches the literal *Cat* anywhere in a word.
\ (backslash) followed by a special character	A backslash causes any of `[\^$.|?*+(){}` to be interpreted as a literal.	`\(425\)` matches *(425)* but not *425*.
\n, \r and \t	Matches a line feed (LF), carriage return (CR), or tab, respectively.	`\.\t` matches a period followed by a tab.
[]	Starts and ends a character class or grouping. Matches any single character within the brackets.	`c[aeiou]t` matches *cat*, *cut*, and *cot*, but not *chat* or *clot*.
\d, \w, and \s	Matches any digit, character, or whitespace, respectively.	`425-555-\d\d\d\d` matches any phone number in the 425-555-xxxx exchange.
{x}, {x,y}	{x} matches the immediately preceding expression x number of times. {x,y} matches the immediately preceding expression at least x number of times but no more than y number of times.	`\d{1,5}` matches any five digit number, such as the zip code in *Beverly Hills 90210*. \d{5,5} matches only five digit numbers. 425-555-\d{4,4} matches any phone number in the 425-555-xxxx exchange.
?	The preceding character is optional.	`\(?425\)?` matches any of *425, (425)*, or *(425*
.	Matches any single character except line feed and carriage return	`te.t` matches *text*, *test*, and *tent*
|	Matches the pattern before or after each pipe (|). Allows a single match among multiple choices.	`grey|gray` matches either *grey* or *gray*.
()	Groups the combination into a single term.	`\.(com|net|org)` matches suffixes any of `.com`, `.net`, or `.org`. `[Gg]ray|[Gg]rey` matches Gray, gray, Grey, or grey.

Procedure 4.9 shows how to use regular expressions to match all of the phone number patterns shown in Example 4.24 using a single search.

```
(425) 555 3453,
425 555 3453,
425-555-3453,
(425) 555-3453,
(425) 555 3453
```

Example 4.24. Telephone number strings.

Regular expressions operate differently from wildcards, so you have to introduce the feature explicitly as a Word add-in. This can't be done as a recorded macro, but only through code.

Procedure 4.9 shows how to use regular expressions in a macro.

Procedure 4.9. Using regular expressions in a macro

1. Open the IDE

2. Click **Tools|References**.

3. Scroll down to **Microsoft VBScript Regular Expressions 5.5** (not **Microsoft VBScript Regular Expressions 1.0**). This is the library file containing the calls for the regular expressions.

4. Check this item.

5. Click **OK**.

6. Open a Word document and paste or type in Example 4.25.

```
1  Sub FindPhoneNumbersWithregularExpressions()
2    'Tools|References|Microsoft VBScript Regular Expressions 5.5
3    Dim regEx As RegExp
4    Set regEx = New RegExp
5    regEx.Pattern = "\(?\d{3}\)?[\s.-]\d{3}[\s.-]\d{4}"
6    regEx.IgnoreCase = False
7    regEx.Global = True
8
9    Dim Matches As MatchCollection
10   Set Matches = regEx.Execute(ThisDocument.Range.Text)
11
12   Dim Match As Match
13   For Each Match In Matches
14     ThisDocument.Range(Match.FirstIndex, _
15       Match.FirstIndex + Len(Match.Value)).Font.Color = _
16         RGB(255, 0, 0)
17     DoEvents
18   Next
19 End Sub
```

Example 4.25. The `FindPhoneNumbersWithregularExpressions` macro

The important difference is that rather than calling a simple `Find` directly, you must first create a regular expression object. Lines 2 through 6 in Example 4.24 create and initialize a regular expression named `regEx`. Lines 8 and 9 create a new variable, called `Matches`, and sets its value to the result of the regular expression search.

The result is a list of all the matches found in the current document. The remaining code goes through the matches and highlights them in red.

Summary

Find and Replace is a commonly used feature, and many users know about its specialized features. Combining them in new ways, along with carefully crafted searches, unleashes its true power. Macros further enhance Find and Replace by adding capabilities not available from the user interface alone.

5

Fields, Form Fields, and Content Controls

This chapter introduces fields, explains their intent, and describes some new ways of using them. Programming is not required, but I will discuss using fields as part of recorded macros and programmatic solutions. VBA code examples will show how to get more out of fields.

Fields

Fields let you insert dynamic information into a document; they are a kind of information placeholder. Some fields change over time (such as the current date), some depend on location (such as page *x* of *y*), and some remain constant once set (such as the date a document was created or the name of the author). Some fields let you perform Excel-like calculations, and others can be even more complex, for example calculating the day of the week for a particular date.

Many fields are already installed (there are about 85 predefined fields), and many have additional options or custom formatting. These combinations alone might meet your needs. With additional customization and macros, you can likely meet nearly any need.

Inserting Fields

You can insert fields in one of four ways: the **Ribbon**, the **Field** dialog box, keyboard short cuts, and as custom fields. The last two are the primary focus of this chapter.

The Ribbon

The most common and quickest way to create a field is through the **Ribbon** (see Figure 5.1). The choices are directly on the **Ribbon** or presented in a gallery. Many of the fields in the **Ribbon** aren't identified as fields. For example, all of the **Insert|Header and Footer** panel items are fields, but no one ever thinks of them as such. Clicking on a page number, though, clearly reveals them as fields with the field modification options.

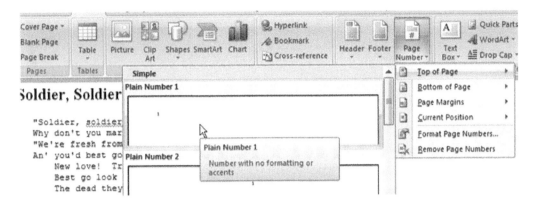

Figure 5.1. Inserting fields through the Ribbon.

Field dialog

Another way to insert a field is through the **Fields** dialog. Click **Insert|Text|Quick Parts|Field**. This displays the **Field** dialog (Figure 5.2). There are no galleries, as with the **Ribbon**, but this dialog presents all the fields.

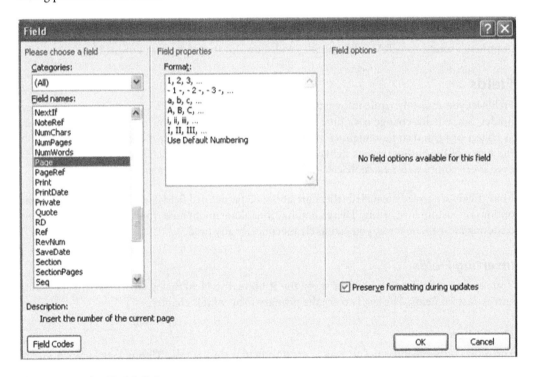

Figure 5.2. The Field dialog.

The left side scroll list (**Fieldnames**) displays all the available fields. If seeing all of them at one time is confusing, you can select from the **Categories** drop-down list to see only those belonging to a specific category. Clicking on a **Field** name displays additional information. Some fields have properties that change the basic display of the field and/or options, which supplement the field information.

Customizing fields

Many fields can be customized by providing additional information or setting configuration switches. The customization can be accomplished in one of two ways: **Field properties/field options** and **Field codes**.

Field properties/field options provides a graphical way of completing field information (see Figure 5.2). The **Field properties** and **Field options** are presented in two sections of the **Field** dialog when you select a field from the **Field names** list.

Not all fields will have both sets, and some fields will have neither. When the latter is the case, you may be able to use **Field codes**, or there may be no configurable options at all. For example, the **Page** field (see Figure 5.2) only has Field properties, which relate to the format of the page numbers. It does not have any additional options, which is indicated by the statement **No field options available for this field.**

When the option sets display, select the configuration you want by selecting items from any or all the options presented. In Figure 5.2, you may select one of the format options. In some cases, a default is already highlighted. Clicking **OK** accepts the configuration and places the field into the document.

Field codes present a textual way to provide field information (see Figure 5.3). All of the options are represented as text or a token (usually a letter indicating one of the options); these can be thought of as parameters, or arguments, for the field code. Field codes are the way fields display in the document when expanded to **Toggle Field Codes**. Click the **Field Codes** button to present this option, also referred to as **Advanced field** properties. In some cases, additional options may be available by clicking the **Options** buttons. If this button is inactive, then no more options are available. Clicking **OK** accepts the configuration and places the field into the document.

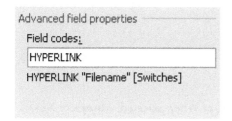

Figure 5.3. Advanced field properties menu

 Even with Word help and Microsoft's online references, many fields are poorly documented. Therefore, I suggest you explore the **Field properties/field options** and **Field codes** to discover the full range of configuration options. A good online reference is the Microsoft document, *Field Codes in Word*[9]. You may also want to search the Internet for information.

For some fields, it may be better to use the **Ribbon** option, if one exists. For example, the **Field** dialog presentation for **Citation** lists no properties or options, even though both exist. In this case, use the **References|Citations** and **Bibliography Ribbon** panel, which does have supporting dialogs for properties and options.

Some fields have defaults. That is, Word assigns an initial value to some properties and/or options. These are smart defaults, or Word's best guess as to what the initial value should be. In some cases, Word bases the default on the selected text; in others, Word predetermines it. Figure 5.4 is an example of smart defaults. DOCPROPERTY has one required parameter. The value Author is provided automatically, but you can change it if you need to.

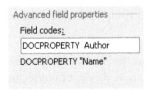

Figure 5.4. Smart defaults

 Word's Help resources and guidance with field codes can be inconsistent, and both the explicit help (**Microsoft Office Word Help [F1]** in the menu bar) and the implicit help (text in the **Field** dialog box) can be inconsistent, too. For example, the **Page** field defaults to the Roman numeral format, even though that choice is not highlighted in the choices list. In contrast, **AutoTextList**, which also has a default value, has *None* highlighted.

Inserting customized fields

To insert a field, select the properties and options, and then press **OK**. The field will be inserted at the cursor location and will replace the current selection, if there is one. The field displays in the document according to the preferences set in the **Office** icon|**Word Options**|**Advanced, Show Document Content** options. By default, the field blends into the document seamlessly, using the style of formatting at that selection. Procedure 5.1 shows how to control field highlighting

Procedure 5.1. Control field highlighting

1. Click the **Office** icon, and then select **Word** Options.

2. Click **Advanced** in the left column.

3. In **Show document content**, select **Field shading** of **When Selected**, **Always**, or **Never**.

For example, while developing a report, you may want all the fields shaded so you can easily see and modify them. In that case, select **Always**. When you deliver the report, you can change the highlighting to **Never**, so readers can focus on the content and not the format.

Keyboard

Another way to insert a field is as a keyboard short cut. You cannot insert all fields this way, but some are predefined:

► Date Field: **ALT-SHIFT-D**
► Time Field: **Alt-SHIFT-T**
► Page number field: **Alt-SHIFT-P**
► Insert ListNum field: **CTRL-Alt-L**

In addition, you can record a macro and assign it to a keyboard equivalent. When making your own fields or updating existing ones, the keyboard method becomes more important. See the section titled "Custom Fields" (p. 78) for additional information about writing your own fields.

Field Management

In addition to inserting and deleting fields, you can manage them.

Updating Fields

Although fields are designed mostly to present dynamic information, that is, information that can change automatically, they do not update automatically.

Field types

There are three types of field, each of which has well-defined events that determine when it updates.

- ► **Cold:** The field doesn't update, because it's an informational marker only. Some fields, such as XE (mark index entry) or Author (the author's name), are not supposed to update. XE doesn't display anything, it just flags an index entry, and although Author does display a name, a document's author doesn't typically change.

- ► **Warm:** A warm field can be updated and does return a result or display a value. Warm fields must be explicitly updated through a qualifying event (see the section titled "Update events" (p. 72)).

  For example, although you can add new paragraphs and outline items to a document, a table of contents field will not pick up those new paragraphs until a qualifying event takes place.

- ► **Hot:** A hot field can be updated and does return a result. Hot fields automatically update when the field changes, so that no explicit update event is needed. Hot fields are also updated during a print, print preview, or pagination event. Examples include: SYMBOL (inserts a symbol based on a character code) and ListNum (maintains a list numbering sequence). Other hot fields include AUTONUM, AUTONUMLGL, AUTONUMOUT, BARCODE, and EQ.

Most fields can also be marked as Invalid (see Figure 5.5). Invalid is not a field type, but rather a flag indicating an error has occurred, such as a grammar, format, or logic error. An invalid field never updates until the error has been corrected. The field also displays a brief error message, reminding you something is wrong.

Error! Reference source not found.

No bookmark name!

Zip code not valid!

Figure 5.5. Errors in fields

Update events

For warm fields, there are certain events that cause an update. The list of events is greatly simplified since Word 2003, although which fields are updated for a particular event is still not always clearly documented. The following events can cause an update:

Explicit updates

You can explicitly update fields at any time. To force one or more fields to update:

Procedure 5.2. Force field(s) to update

1. Select the field or fields.

2. Click **F9** or right click and then select **Update Field**.

Some fields present an update dialog. For example, the table of contents field displays an **Update Table of Contents** dialog with some field-specific options, but a date field immediately updates the date with no dialog displayed. You can update multiple fields with one **F9** action by selecting a range that contains more than one field. In this instance, each field updates individually and you may get more than one dialog. Taken to an extreme, all the fields can be manually updated by selecting the entire document (**CTRL-A**) and then selecting **F9**. Fields in the header and footers do not update this way. As an alternative to selecting the document, use Print Preview (**Print/Print Preview section**) to update all the links.

Opening a document

Opening the document updates fields in the header and footer. It does not generally update fields in the main body. However, this does cause a pagination event, and fields associated with pagination will be updated.

Fields with links in them can be set to update or not when the document is opened. This applies to all links in the document.

Procedure 5.3. Force fields with links to update on document open

1. Click the **Office** icon, and then select **Word Options**.

2. Click **Advanced** in the left column.

3. In **General**, check or uncheck **Update automatic links at open**.

Opening a document in print layout view

Opening the document in print layout view updates fields in the header and footer. This also causes a pagination event, and fields associated with pagination will be updated.

Switching to print layout view or print preview

Switching to print layout view updates fields in the header and footer. This causes a pagination event, and fields associated with pagination will also be updated. In addition, the following fields also update automatically: DATE, TIME, PAGE, PAGEREF, PRINTDATE (only if the document is actually printed), REF (to any bookmark or cross reference), SECTIONPAGES, STYLEREF, and SEQ.

Printing a document

Printing a document updates some of the fields and also causes a pagination event, so fields associated with pagination will be updated. In addition, the following fields also update automatically: DATE, TIME, PAGE, PAGEREF, PRINTDATE (only if the document is actually printed), REF (to any bookmark or cross reference), SECTIONPAGES, STYLEREF, and SEQ. Other fields may be updated during printing. Procedure 5.4 shows how to automatically update those fields.

Procedure 5.4. Setup to update files before printing

1. Click the **Office** icon, and then select **Word Options**.

2. Click **Display** in the left column.

3. In **Printing Options**, check or uncheck **Update fields** before printing.

Pagination events

Opening the document in print layout view updates fields in the header and footer. This also causes a pagination event, and fields associated with pagination will be updated.

Converting a Field to Text

If you no longer need a field to be dynamic, you can convert it to normal text. This removes the field and replaces it with text containing the value of the field. Procedure 5.5 shows how to convert a field. Once converted, the only way to go back to a field is to create the field again.

Procedure 5.5. Convert field to text

1. Select the field or fields you want to convert.

2. Press **CTRL-SHIFT-F9**

Locking Fields

Even though fields were meant to be interactive or dynamic, there may be instances when you need them to be static. If you want to retain a field, but keep the value from changing during an update, you can lock it (see Procedure 5.6).

Procedure 5.6. Lock a field

1. Select the field or fields.

2. Press **CTRL-F11**.

The only way to tell if a field is locked is to see if the **Update Field** menu item is disabled or if the field value doesn't change after an update.

Procedure 5.7 shows how to unlock a field.

Procedure 5.7. Unlock a field

1. Select the field or fields.

2. Press **CTRL-SHIFT-F11**.

Viewing Field Codes

Field codes look like programming code. You can view the field codes and even modify them directly. Procedure 5.8 describes how to show the field codes for a single field.

Procedure 5.8. Show field codes for one field

1. Select the entire field. It's best to select the entire field since toggling the field codes expands only the selected part of the field. In simple cases, for example if there is only a single field, this may not matter much. In more complex cases, for example, when a field is made up of two or more embedded fields, it would take several extra steps to complete the process.

2. Either press **SHIFT-F9**, or right click the selection and select **Toggle Field Codes**.

Procedure 5.9 shows how to change the view for all fields in document.

Procedure 5.9. Show field codes for all fields

1. Click the **Office** icon, and click **Word Options**.

2. Click **Advanced** in the left pane.

3. In the **Show document content** area, check **Show field codes instead of their values**.

Macros and VBA

Macros may be used to manipulate fields. This provides versatility in choosing which fields to manipulate and how to change them. You can use macros to add and delete fields and control their content.

Updating fields with macros

You can update fields with macros. Example 5.1 updates all the fields in a document.

```
'Recorded macro
Sub Macro1()
    Selection.WholeStory
    Selection.Fields.Update
End Sub
```

Example 5.1. Update all fields in a document

Example 5.1 only updates fields in the main body of the document and not those in the headers or footers. Updating fields in headers and footers will be addressed in a moment. Example 5.1 does not present any dialogs during the update. For instance, when individually updating the table of contents field or selecting the range and using **F9**, each table of contents displays the **Update Table of Contents** dialog with two options (page numbers only, which is the default, or the entire table) that you have to pick from.

Example 5.1 is a recorded macro and is a good example of the limitations of generated code. The main limitation is that it uses `Selection` to pick the document range to work on. If you already had a selection picked, running this code would lose your selection, and if the active document changes before the update statement runs, the wrong document may be updated. Example 5.2 is better; it is handwritten, but simpler, safer, and shorter.

```
Sub BasicFieldsUpdate()
    ActiveDocument.Fields.Update
End Sub
```

Example 5.2. Handwritten macro to update fields

Actually, Example 5.2 only updates some of the document, the main body. A document is a series of parts, called "stories." There are 17 types of stories, which usually is not large consideration in Word programming. Most of the time you're affecting only the main story (such as Example 5.2), in which case you don't have specify the story type. Updating fields is one time when you need to specify the story type. Example 5.3 updates fields in the body, header, and footer, which are three of the common stories to update.

```
Sub FieldsUpdateBodyHeadersFooters()
    On Error Resume Next ❶
    ActiveDocument.Fields.Update
    ActiveDocument.StoryRanges(wdPrimaryFooterStory).Fields.Update
    ActiveDocument.StoryRanges(wdPrimaryHeaderStory).Fields.Update
End Sub
```

Example 5.3. Update fields in the body, header, and footer

❶   This line, `On Error Resume Next`, is an example of an error handling statement. It directs the program to ignore any errors it encounters and continue to the next line. In general, this is not a good approach; you should handle errors as they occur. But, if one of the sections does not have a field to update, that will generate an error. Since this situation does not represent a real problem, there's no reason to handle the error, and it can be ignored.

Example 5.4 shows a more complete routine that finds all the fields in all the stories, but in a different manner.

```
Sub UpdateAllFields()
    Dim currentDocument As Document
    Set currentDocument = ActiveDocument

    Dim myField As Field
    Dim myStory As Range
    For Each myStory In currentDocument.StoryRanges        ❶
      For Each myField In myStory.Fields         ❷
        myField.Update
      Next myField
    Next myStory
End Sub
```

Example 5.4. Update all fields in `myStories`

❶   This `For Each` statement goes through each of the story types.
❷   This `For Each` statement goes through each field in one story part. If there are no fields, the `Update` statement is never run, and therefore, no error is generated.

Updating specific fields

You can specify which fields to update in several ways. For instance, Example 5.5 updates only the warm fields in the main story, which is the default story type.

```
Sub UpdateWarmFields()
    On Error GoTo MyErrorHandler

    Dim currentDocument As Document
    Set currentDocument = ActiveDocument

    Dim myField As Field
    For Each myField In currentDocument.Fields
        If myField.Kind = wdFieldKindWarm Then myField.Update
    Next myField

    Exit Sub

MyErrorHandler:
    MsgBox "UpdateWarmFields" & vbCrLf & vbCrLf & _
        "Err = " & Err.Number & vbCrLf & _
        "Description: " & Err.Description
End Sub
```

Example 5.5. Update only warm fields

Programmatically updating one specific field is difficult. Although each field can be uniquely identified by its ID, that ID is hard to track and is a long and awkward number to use or to remember. It would be convenient and consistent if you could give fields friendly names. While you cannot do this directly, you can create a bookmark to hold the field and then access the field using the bookmark name. Procedure 5.10 shows how to do this.

Procedure 5.10. Create field with bookmark

1. Insert a field. This example uses a time field. Select **Insert|Text|Quick Parts|Field|Time**, choose one with seconds (such as M/d/yyyy h:mm:ss am/pm), and click **OK**.

2. Select the field by highlighting it.

3. Insert a bookmark, **Insert|Links|Bookmark**. This displays the **Bookmark** dialog.

4. In the **Bookmark name** field enter an easy to remember or useful name. For this example, use MyUpdateTime.

5. Click **Add**.

Example 5.6 updates a field that has been bookmarked.

```
Public Sub UpdateNamedField()
    On Error GoTo MyErrorHandler

    Dim currentDocument As Document
    Set currentDocument = ActiveDocument

    Dim myBookmark As Bookmark
    'There must be a bookmark named 'MyUpdateTime'
    Set myBookmark = currentDocument.Bookmarks("MyUpdateTime")
    myBookmark.Range.Fields(1).Update
    Exit Sub

MyErrorHandler:
    MsgBox "UpdateNamedField" & vbCrLf & vbCrLf & _
            "Err = " & Err.Number & vbCrLf & _
            "Description: " & Err.Description
End Sub
```

Example 5.6. Update field that has been bookmarked

Deleting fields

You can delete fields with macros. Example 5.7 deletes all the fields in the document.

```
Sub DeleteAllFields()
Dim currentDocument As Document
Set currentDocument = ActiveDocument

Dim currentField As Long
Dim myField As Field
Dim myStory As Range
  For Each myStory In currentDocument.StoryRanges
    For currentField = myStory.Fields.Count To 1 Step -1
      myStory.Fields(currentField).Delete
    Next currentField
  Next myStory
End Sub
```

Example 5.7. Delete all fields in a document

Notice that this code counts backwards from the number of fields in the story down to one. Fields are kept in an internal list. Deleting the last item first preserves the integrity of the list. If you delete items starting at the beginning of the list, the list could be improperly updated internally, possibly hanging or crashing Word.

Custom Fields

If you find that the default ways of inserting fields don't meet your needs, you can insert custom fields and handcraft your own sequences. Fields follow a general pattern, here directly displayed as field codes:

```
{ Fieldname Properties Optionalswitches }
```

▸ **Fieldname:** The name of the field. The complete list of field names is displayed in the **Field Names** list of the **Field** dialog.

▸ **Properties:** Parameters or command names that are specific to that field. Not all fields have properties. If they exist, properties may be required or optional.

▸ **Optionalswitches:** Additional settings or modifications to the basic features. Not all fields have switches.

▸ **Spaces.** When constructing fields, spaces between parts are ignored and are generally not required. That is, you can insert any number of spaces you need to make the field code more readable. An exception is that a space is needed after the equal sign (=) of an IF test.

For example, the following three fields generate the same value:

```
{ = 512.45 \* DOLLARTEXT \* UPPER }
{=512.45 \*DOLLARTEXT \*UPPER }
{=512.45\*DOLLARTEXT\*UPPER }
```

The last example still evaluates correctly even though there are no spaces at all between the parameters.

Example 5.8 displays the code for a simple field, with Figure 5.6 displaying the results.

```
{ = 512.45 \* DOLLARTEXT \* UPPER }
```

Example 5.8. Display code for simple field

FIVE HUNDRED TWELVE AND 45/100

Figure 5.6. Results of running Example 5.8

Example 5.8 converts the number 512.45 into a textual representation. This macro has four parts:

▸ **Brackets.** The brackets ({ }) indicate this a field. You must use the **Field** dialog or **CTRL-F9**. Simply typing brackets will not work.

▸ **Mathematical Function.** The equal sign (=) indicates that this is a mathematical function.

▸ **Mathematical Equation.** *512.45* is the mathematical part of the equation. This could be an equation such as 2+2 or more a more complex calculate, but the end result is the same, an equation that evaluates to a single number.

▸ **Optional Switches.** *DOLLARTEXT and *UPPER are optional switches. *DOLLARTEXT displays the value as a text string in the language specified by the Windows regional setting.

*UPPER converts the text string to uppercase characters. Each function has its own set of switches, and some functions may not have any switches. A complete list of switches is available through Word's online help.

Creating Custom Fields

To create a custom field, press **CTRL+F9**. This will insert the field at the cursor, as shown in Figure 5.7.

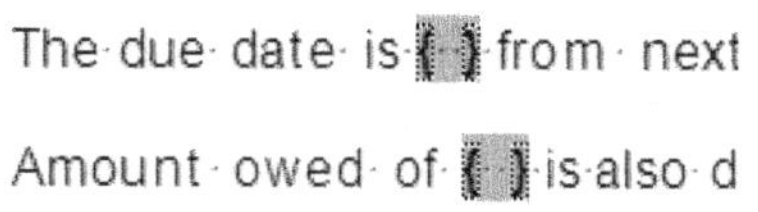

The·due· date· is·{ }·from· next

Amount· owed· of· { }·is·also· d

Figure 5.7. Custom field brackets inserted into text

You then insert the contents of the field between the curly brackets (**CTRL+F9** inserts the brackets). For example, you could type { = 5 + 5 } or { DATE \@ "M/d/yyyy" }.

Another way of creating a field is to type the text first, then create the brackets. Enter and select the text you want to be in the field, then press **CTRL+F9**. This converts the selected text into a field. To try this, type the text, =5+5, select it, and then press **CTRL+F9**.

Converting =5+5 to a field wouldn't seem all that helpful since the value is static (5+5 will always equal 10). But you can use fields within fields to make this interactive.

It doesn't matter where the parameter values come from as long as they're the correct data type (for example, number or string). That means you can use another field to get the information you need. For example, you can add five to the page count with { = { NUMPAGES } + 5 }. To enter a nested field, just type **CTRL+F9** with the cursor at the desired place inside the outer field.

As a more practical example, writers might display the price of their articles, say 15¢ a word, using the {NUMWORDS} field:

{ ={NUMWORDS} * .15 }

A dollar sign format in front of it completes the presentation:

{ = { NUMWORDS } * .15 \# "$,0.00;" }

For an article of 546 words, the result is $81.90. You can find a full list of formatting options in Word's online help.

It would be nice if this field updated with each character typed, but VBA does not support that. You either need to explicitly update the fields by typing **F9** or wait for an automatic update such as printing or opening the document. Microsoft Excel users expect cells and formulas to update automatically when a source value changes. However, Word fields do not do that.

Field Functions

There is a set of built-in functions that can be used in fields. A complete list is available through Word's online help for `=` `(formula)` `field`. For example, if you want to calculate the average of three numbers, use: { `= AVERAGE(95, 86, 91)` }. To calculate the sum of three numbers, use: { `= SUM(1, 2, 3)` }.

Here is another way to calculate averages: { `= (SUM(95, 86, 91)) / (COUNT(95, 86, 91))` }. This uses three functions: SUM, COUNT (the number of items in the set), and division (`/`). You can use the results of a function or other fields as parameters for other functions.

Logical Operators

Fields can use logical operators to make decisions. Logical operators compare two values and return either TRUE or FALSE. Word supports three operators:

▸ **AND:** If both statements are TRUE, AND will return TRUE. Word uses 1 to represent a true statement and 0 for a false statement, so { `= AND(1, 1)` } returns TRUE.

▸ **OR:** If either of the two statements is TRUE, OR will return TRUE, otherwise it will return FALSE. { `= OR(0, 1)` } is TRUE since the second statement is true.

▸ **NOT:** Reverses the return value from TRUE to FALSE, FALSE to TRUE. { `= NOT(1)` } is FALSE.

These operators are useful in IF statements. IF statements return the value of a statement depending on the value of a logical condition. The general format is:

```
{IF logicalcondition  truestatement  falsestatement}
```

If the *logicalcondition* evaluates to TRUE, then *truestatement* executes, otherwise *falsestatement* executes. In other programming languages this is often notated as:

```
IF logicalcondition THEN truestatement ELSE falsestatement
```

For example, {`if 1 = 1 "This statement is true" "This statement is false"` } returns the result, "`This statement is true`", because the logical condition, 1 = 1 is TRUE. For IF statements, the spaces around the equal sign are required; you'd get an *Error! Unknown op code for conditional* error message if they were not present.

If statements can be nested, although you have to be careful crafting them. Here is an example:

```
{ If 1 = 1 {If 2 = 2 {If 3 = 3 "3=3" "3<>3"} "2<>2} "1<>1"}
```

This example may seem absurd but it clearly shows the parts. It is best to build nested If statements one step at a time, as shown in Procedure 5.11.

Procedure 5.11. Craft a nested If statement

1. Begin with:

    ```
    {If 1 = 1 truestatement "1<>1"}
    ```

2. Then replace `truestatement` with `{If 2=2 truestatement "2<>2"}` to get:

    ```
    {If 1 = 1 {If 2 = 2 truestatement "2<>2"} "1<>1"}
    ```

3. Replace `truestatement` again, this time with:

    ```
    {If 3 = 3 "3=3" "3<>3"}
    ```

The result will be:

```
{If 1=1 {If 2=2 {If 3=3 "3=3" "3<>3"} "2<>2"} "1<>1"}.
```

Created this way, it doesn't seem as intimidating.

These statements lack one critical aspect. So far, they all use fixed data. There's little point evaluating `1 = 1` since it always has the same result, and therefore, makes no decision. You can use variables, bookmarks, or table cell information to provide dynamic information.

For example:

```
{ IF {DOCUMENTPROPERTY Author} = "Robert"
      "Robert is the author" "Robert is not the author" }
```

This compares the document's author (from the document properties) and the string "Robert" to display the corresponding message. A better approach when using strings would be:

```
{ IF {DOCPROPERTY Author \*UPPER} = "ROBERT"
      "Robert is the author" "Robert is not the author" }
```

`\*UPPER` forces the value of the Author property to be upper case. String comparisons are case sensitive, that is, "A" is not the same as "a." Using `\*UPPER` to force everything to be uppercase makes sure that this test will evaluate to TRUE, even if the value of the Author property is "Robert" or "robert".

Here's another example, this time with a more complex field. The field code prints a note about Joseph Heller's birthday, but only if the field is on the first page and only then if *Catch-22* is the paper's title. The final version looks like this:

```
{If {PAGE} = 1
    {If {TITLE} = "Catch-22"
        {If { DATE  \@ "MMMM yy"} = "May 1"
            "This is Joseph Heller's birthday"
            "Nothing important happened on this day."}
        "This is not the right book."}
"This is not the cover page"}
```

Procedure 5.12 crafts this one step at a time, with each step replacing the *truestatement* with additional codes.

Procedure 5.12. Craft a complex nested IF statement

1. `{If {PAGE}=1 truestatement "This is not the cover page."}`

2. `{If {PAGE}=1 {If {TITLE} = "Catch-22" truestatement`
    `    "This is not the right book."}`
    `"This is not the cover page."}`

3. `{If {PAGE} = 1`
    `    {If {TITLE} = "Catch-22"`
    `        {If { DATE  \@ "MMMM yy"} = "May 1"`
    `            "This is Joseph Heller's birthday"`
    `            "Nothing important happened on this day."}`
    `        "This is not the right book."}`
    `"This is not the cover page"}`

Using Bookmarks with Fields

You can define your own bookmarks and use them in fields. Example 5.9 asks the user if the document is going to be long. If an answer is provided and the user clicks **OK**, the bookmark IsLong-Document is created and the response stored there.

```
{
 {ASK isLongDocument "Is this a long document?"\d Yes}
 {IsLongDocument}
}
```

Example 5.9. Macro to prompt user about length of document

Example 5.9 uses the ASK field. The field prompts users with an input box, allowing them to provide input, and then creates a bookmark if it doesn't exist or updates the bookmark if it does exist with that response. In the listing, ASK is the field name, IsLongDocument is the bookmark it will create, the prompt is "Is this a long document?,", and the default answer, which is optional, is "Yes" noted by \d Yes.

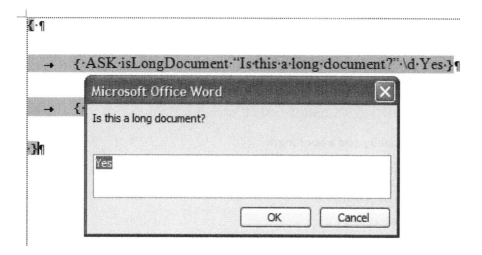

Figure 5.8. Input box from Example 5.9

The example also shows that you can split the code over several lines. This is convenient when crafting long or complicated fields, so you can see the breakdowns better. However, if the field leaves a result, as this one does, there might be some formatting issues. For example, in this case the result will include an extra space. If there are issues, be sure to condense everything after making the field.

Combining the logic statements from the Logical Operators section with field construction, you can make the following IF statement:

```
{If {PAGE} > 1 "Page Number: {PAGE}"
    {ASK IsCorrect "Is this page 1?" \d Yes }}
```

This field tests if you are on page one. If you are, the code prompts the user to confirm that. If you are after page one, then it displays the page number.

This can also be used as a workaround for Word's formatting of the **First Page Special** option for placing page numbers.

Creating Bookmarks

Bookmarks in Word have two uses. First, they identify a location or selection within a document. In this respect, they come close to being what most think a physical and traditional bookmark is; perhaps a piece of paper stuck in a book to mark the place where you stopped reading. Second, they are also a variable that contains information. Typically they contain a small amount of information; metadata or information about the running of a document. For example, a previous example used a bookmark to record if the document was going to be long or not (IsLongDocument, in Example 5.9).

There are two ways to create your own bookmarks: fields and the bookmark dialog

Creating a Bookmark Using Fields

You can use fields like ASK, where a bookmark is required. If a bookmark doesn't exist, ASK creates one; if a bookmark does exist, then ASK overwrites it with a new value.

Using the Bookmark Dialog

Procedure 5.13 shows how you can manually add a bookmark.

Procedure 5.13. Manually add a bookmark

1. Click **Insert|Links|BookMark**. This displays the **Bookmark** dialog.

2. Enter a name in **Bookmark name**.

3. Click **Add**.

The bookmark will be created at the current insert point. If you have selected a range, the bookmark will represent the entire range.

Procedure 5.14 shows how you can manually delete a bookmark.

Procedure 5.14. Manually delete a bookmark

1. Click **Insert|Links|BookMark**. This displays the **Bookmark** dialog.

2. Click on a bookmark name in the **Bookmark name** list.

3. Click **Delete**.

4. Click **Close**.

Procedure 5.15 displays a **Hidden Bookmarks** checkbox. Checking this displays any hidden bookmarks, but does not delete them.

Showing or Hiding Bookmarks

Procedure 5.15 shows how to display the bookmark locations in a document:

Procedure 5.15. Show hidden bookmarks

1. Click the Office logo and click **Word Options**.

2. Click **Advanced**.

3. In the **Show document content** section, check **Show bookmarks**.

4. Click **OK**.

Using Bookmarks

The following example (Figure 5.9) shows how you use bookmarks in fields. The document author manually created two bookmarks (*ItemCost* and *SalesTax*) in the document and typed in their values. The field calculates the final cost of the item.

Cost·of·item:··$120¶

Sales·tax:8%¶

Total·cost:·${·=·ItemCost·*·(1+(SalesTax/100))·\#·"0.00"}¶

Figure 5.9. Setting up fields for calculating sales tax

When updated, Figure 5.10 shows the expected results.

Cost·of·item:··$120¶

Sales·tax:8%¶

Total·cost:·$129.60¶

Figure 5.10. Updated fields for calculating sales tax

Other examples include:

```
© {CREATEDATE \@ "yyyy"} by {AUTHOR}
```

Displays the notice, "© 2011 by James Joyce". Of course the value for the predefined bookmark AUTHOR is used. The CREATEDATE function, which shows the creation date for the file is used since it does not change. Some authors like showing the range of a copyright:

```
© {CREATEDATE \@ "yyyy"} - {DATE \@ "yyyy" } by {AUTHOR}
```

This displays "© 2001 - 2011 by James Joyce."

One problem with this code is that when CREATEDATE and DATE are the same year, you will get a result like, "© 2011 - 2011." To solve that problem, use an IF statement as in Example 5.10:

```
{ IF { CREATEDATE \@ "yyyy"} = { DATE \@ "yyyy"}
   "© { CREATEDATE \@ "yyyy"} by { AUTHOR }"
   "© { CREATEDATE \@ "yyyy"} - { DATE \@ "yyyy" } by { AUTHOR }"
}
```

Example 5.10. Avoid duplicate copyright date

This displays: "© 2011 by James Joyce," if the two dates are the same, or "© 2001 - 2011 by James Joyce," if they are not.

Instead of using your name, you could use the company name. Example 5.11 shows that you can create, set, and use bookmarks as you need them. Here, the bookmark MyCompanyName is created and assigned the value "MegaBigCorporation." Once a legitimate value is entered or calculated, that bookmark can used anywhere in the document and even referenced from fields in other documents. Example 5.11 changes the logic a bit, putting the IF statement just around the CREATE-DATE. This makes a slightly smaller example, though maybe a bit harder to read.

```
© { IF { CREATEDATE \@ "yyyy"} <> { DATE \@ "yyyy"}
   "{ CREATEDATE \@ "yyyy"} - "}{ DATE \@ "yyyy"} by { MyCompanyName }"
```

Example 5.11. Insert copyright

This displays: "© 2011 by MegaBigCorporation."

Example 5.12 shows a way to handle conditional text. You can display different text based on how the reader responds to a question or what the current value of the bookmark IntendedAudience is. Here, the user is asked who the audience is, and the response determines what file will be included. This example assumes two files, army.txt and other.txt, are located in the C drive root.

```
{ ASK  IntendedAudience "Who is the intended audience?" \d "Army" }
{ IF IntendedAudience = "Army"
   { INCLUDETEXT  "c:\\army.txt " \* MERGEFORMAT }
   { INCLUDETEXT  "c:\\other.txt" \* MERGEFORMAT }
}
```

Example 5.12. Conditional text in field

Example 5.13 is similar, but expanded to include three cases and a new file, navy.txt.

```
{ ASK  IntendedAudience "Who is the intended audience?" \d "Army" }
{ IF IntendedAudience = "Army"
   { INCLUDETEXT  "D:\\My Documents\\Army.docm" Army }
   { IF IntendedAudience = "Navy" ❶
      { INCLUDETEXT  "c:\\navy.txt" \* MERGEFORMAT }
      { INCLUDETEXT  "c:\\other.txt" \* MERGEFORMAT }
   }
}
```

Example 5.13. Conditional text in field expanded

Creating Complex Fields

Fields don't have to be small or trivial. Indeed, complex math and logical statements can occur inside the brackets. Be warned though. Although fields provide some flexibility, they are not a robust programming language. There is no error checking or debugging support, so tracking down problems can be frustrating and costly. For some features, such as time/date calculations and math, you might want to consider other options, including VBA.

Example 5.14 shows what is possible in a complex field. This field takes the current date and offsets it by a number of days (stored in the variable Delay, which is set to 14 days). When updated, the field displays the new date.

```
{QUOTE
{SET Delay 14}
{SET a{=INT((14-{DATE \@ M})/12)}}
{SET b{={DATE \@ yyyy}+4800-a}}
{SET c{={DATE \@ M}+12*a-3}}
{SET d{DATE \@ d}}
{SET jd{=d+INT((153*c+2)/5)+365*b+INT(b/4)-
       INT(b/100)+INT(b/400)-32045+Delay}}
{SET e{=INT((4*(jd+32044)+3)/146097)}}
{SET f{=jd+32044-INT(146097*e/4)}}
{SET g{=INT((4*f+3)/1461)}}
{SET h{=f-INT(1461*g/4)}}
{SET i{=INT((5*h+2)/153)}}
{SET dd{=h-INT((153*i+2)/5)+1}}
{SET mm{=i+3-12*INT(i/10)}}
{SET yy{=100*e+g-4800+INT(i/10)}}
"{mm}-{dd}-{yy}" \@ "dddd, MMMM d, yyyy"}
```

Example 5.14. Complex field example

This code is unusual and represents the oddities of time and date calculations. In contrast, Example 5.15 does about the same thing using VBA.

```
Sub Adddate()
    On Error GoTo MyErrorHandler

    Dim startTime As Date
    startTime = InputBox(prompt:= _
        "What is the starting date in dd/mm/yyyy format?", _
        Default:=Now)

    Dim endTime As String
    endTime = InputBox(prompt:= _
        "What is the number of hours, minutes & seconds to add?", _
        Default:="1:30:00")

    Dim timeArray As Variant
    timeArray = Split(endTime, ":")

    Dim BmkNm As String
    BmkNm = "TimeStamp"
    ActiveDocument.Bookmarks.Add BmkNm

    Dim NewTxt As String
    NewTxt = "End time: " & DateAdd("s", (timeArray(0) * 3600) + _
        (timeArray(1) * 60) + (timeArray(2)), startTime)

    Dim BmkRng As Range
    Set BmkRng = ActiveDocument.Bookmarks(BmkNm).Range
    BmkRng.Text = NewTxt
    'ActiveDocument.Bookmarks.Add BmkNm, BmkRng

    Exit Sub
```

```
MyErrorHandler:
    MsgBox "Adddate" & vbCrLf & vbCrLf & "Err = " & Err.Number & _
        vbCrLf & "Description: " & Err.Description
End Sub
```

Example 5.15. Complex field example using VBA

Fields in Tables

Tables and table cells can be used as a data source for fields. Tables and cells in Word share a close relationship to Excel. Many of the same functions can be used in both. For instance, the cells have the same naming scheme. There are columns, numbered with the first at the left and continuing through the right. Rows are numbered top down. Therefore, the first cell is in row 1, column 1 (R1C1). In the same way, columns are lettered starting the left. The first cell can also be addressed as A1.

The following examples use math functions. Although the examples are in tables, these functions are not restricted to tables. Fields can use bookmarks from almost anywhere in the document.

The math functions ignore everything except numbers. For example, if you create field that adds the two strings "Jack is 36 years old" and "Jack drives a 4 by four," the calculation will throw away everything except the numbers and return 40 (the sum of 36 and 4).

The formulas – you may recognize them as fields – work in the same way. Figure 5.11 shows a table with simple formulas.

10	20	{ = A1 + B1 }
15	25	{ = SUM(LEFT) }
{ = A1+ A2 }	{ =SUM(ABOVE) }	{ = SUM(LEFT) }

Figure 5.11. Table with formulas expanded

Figure 5.12 is the same table with the fields updated.

10	20	30
15	25	40
25	45	70

Figure 5.12. Table with updated formulas

You can explicitly reference cells from inside or outside a table. One way is to bookmark part of the cell in the normal way. Figure 5.13 shows a bookmark in the second cell (R1C2) named Cell2. The figure also shows two fields, one expanded and the other updated, displaying the bookmark Cell2.

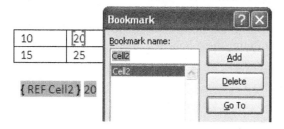

Figure 5.13. Bookmark within a table

Another way is to bookmark the entire table and make cell references to that. Figure 5.14 shows the entire table bookmarked as Table1. It also shows two fields, one expanded and the other updated, referring to the bookmark Table1 B1

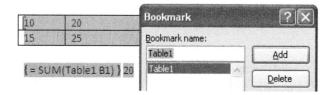

Figure 5.14. Table bookmarked as "Table1"

The field { = SUM(Table1 B1) } displays 20, the value in the bookmarked table named Table1 at column B, row 1.

Likewise, you could reference an entire row ({ = SUM(Table1 1:1) } totaling 30, or column ({ = SUM(Table1 B:B) } totaling 45.

Programming Fields

As with automation in general, if you do an action once, you're likely to need to do it again, and many of these fields can be re-created through recording them as a macro. In other words, if you need help with coding fields, record a macro and look at the finished code in the IDE. If you need more flexibility, you can always hand code or hand modify the solutions.

Example 5.16 displays the contents of all the fields in the **Immediate** window of the IDE (click **CTRL-G** to see that window in the IDE before running the code).

```
Public Sub DisplayFieldCodes()
    On Error GoTo MyErrorHandler

    Dim currentDocument As Document
    Set currentDocument = ActiveDocument

    Dim myField As Field
    For Each myField In currentDocument.Fields
        myField.Select
        Debug.Print myField.Code.Text
        DoEvents
    Next

    Exit Sub

MyErrorHandler:
    MsgBox "DisplayFieldCodes" & vbCrLf & vbCrLf & _
            "Err = " & Err.Number & vbCrLf & _
            "Description: " & Err.Description
End Sub
```

Example 5.16. Display contents of all fields in the Immediate window

This example displays the contents of each field in the **Immediate** window of the IDE. This approach isn't ideal. One problem is that the brackets may not show up at all if they're nested on separate lines. Another problem is that field brackets that appear inside a field do not have a textual representation in this window, and so show up as an undefined character (I use an empty box, "□" below to represent the undefined character). For example, a field defined as one of the logic fields we used earlier:

{if 1=1 {if 2 = 2 {if 3 = 3 "3 = 3" "3<>3"} "2<>2"} "1<>1"}

shows up as:

IF 1 = 1 □ if 2 = 2 □ if 3 = 3 "3 = 3" "3<>3" □ "2<>2" □ "1<>1"

Example 5.17 lists all the bookmarks, along with their values in a separate document.

```
 1 Public Sub CollectBookMarks()
 2   On Error GoTo MyErrorHandler
 3
 4   Dim currentDocument As Document
 5   Set currentDocument = ActiveDocument
 6
 7   Dim targetDocument As Document
 8   Set targetDocument = Nothing
 9
10   Dim myBookmark As Bookmark
11   For Each myBookmark In currentDocument.Bookmarks
12
13     If targetDocument Is Nothing Then
14       Set targetDocument = Application.Documents.Add
15       targetDocument.Range.InsertAfter "Bookmarks for " & _
16         currentDocument.Name
17       targetDocument.Range.InsertParagraphAfter
18       targetDocument.Range.InsertParagraphAfter
19       targetDocument.Paragraphs(1).Range.Style = "Heading 1"
20       targetDocument.Sections(1).Footers(wdHeaderFooterPrimary). _
21         Range.Text = "Bookmarks for " & currentDocument.Name & _
22         vbTab & "Page " & _
23         targetDocument.Range.Information(wdActiveEndPageNumber) & _
24         " of " & _
25         targetDocument.Range.Information(wdNumberOfPagesInDocument)
26     End If
27
28     targetDocument.Range.InsertAfter myBookmark.Name & vbTab & _
29       myBookmark.Range.Text
30     targetDocument.Range.InsertParagraphAfter
31
32     DoEvents
33 Next
34
35 If Not targetDocument Is Nothing Then
36   'deletes the last paragraph mark; for cosmetic purposes only.
37   targetDocument.Paragraphs.Last.Range.Delete
38 End If
39
40     Exit Sub
41
42 MyErrorHandler:
43     MsgBox "CollectBookMarks" & vbCrLf & vbCrLf & _
44     "Err = " & Err.Number & vbCrLf & _
45     "Description: " & Err.Description
46 End Sub
```

Example 5.17. List all bookmarks and values in a separate document

Lines 13 through 25 aren't directly related to fields or bookmarks but show how to format a document. The code adds a title (as a Heading 1) and footer and page numbers, should the document get long.

A more interactive example, Example 5.18, shows the user a dialog that can change the bookmark values on the fly. You will be prompted at each bookmark to either keep the current value (press **Cancel** or **OK**) or enter a new value (type in the new value and click **OK**).

```
Public Sub EasyChanger()
  On Error GoTo MyErrorHandler

  Dim currentDocument As Document
  Set currentDocument = ActiveDocument

  Dim tempRange As Range
  Dim myBookMark As Bookmark
  For Each myBookMark In currentDocument.Bookmarks
    myBookMark.Select

    Dim bookmarkName As String                                    ❶
    bookmarkName = myBookMark.Name

    Dim inputboxReturn As String
    inputboxReturn = InputBox(prompt:="Current value: " & _
      myBookMark.Range.Text, Title:=bookmarkName)
    If inputboxReturn <> vbNullString Then
      Set tempRange = myBookMark.Range
      tempRange.Text = inputboxReturn

      currentDocument.Bookmarks.Add bookmarkName, tempRange      ❷
    End If

    DoEvents
  Next

  Exit Sub

MyErrorHandler:
    MsgBox "EasyChanger" & vbCrLf & vbCrLf & _
           "Err = " & Err.Number & vbCrLf & _
           "Description: " & Err.Description
End Sub
```

Example 5.18. Dialog to change bookmark values on the fly

To change a bookmark value is a little more involved. The existing bookmark has to be deleted and a new one, with the same name, created in the same location.

❶   The variable bookmarkName stores the name temporarily.
❷   The Bookmarks.Add statement restores the bookmark.

Using Find with Fields

You can use the **Find** dialog to edit fields by finding and modifying text within brackets. It can also locate the field brackets, but cannot insert them. The fields have to be toggled (so you can see the field codes) prior to using **Find**. Other than that, just enter the text you want to find or replace.

For example, suppose you want to delete the *MERGEFORMAT switch we used in Example 5.12 and Example 5.13 (p. 86). This switch preserves the formatting of the surrounding text, but in practice, it's generally unnecessary and can cause formatting problems. This option is controlled by the **Preserve Formatting During Updates** checkbox in the **Field** dialog.

Procedure 5.16 shows how to delete this text in all of the document's fields.

Procedure 5.16. Delete text in all document fields

1. Select the entire document (**CTRL-A**).

2. Expand the fields. Either right click somewhere in the highlighted text and select **Toggle Field Codes** or press **ALT-F9**. Make sure the field codes are visible.

3. Press **CTRL-F** to show the **Find** dialog, selecting the **Replace** tab or **CRTL-H** to go to the **Replace** tab directly.

4. In **Find what**, enter: *MERGEFORMAT. In **Replace with** enter nothing (leave blank).

5. Click **Find**. This selects the next occurrence of the Find what text.

6. Click **Replace** or **Replace All**.

If you need to do this frequently, make it a macro. Example 5.19 is the recorded macro, although some unneeded lines of code have been removed.

```
Sub CleanUpFields()
    ActiveWindow.View.ShowFieldCodes = True
    Selection.Find.ClearFormatting
    Selection.Find.Replacement.ClearFormatting
    With Selection.Find
        .Text = " \* MERGEFORMAT "
        .Replacement.Text = ""
    End With
    Selection.Find.Execute Replace:=wdReplaceAll
    ActiveWindow.View.ShowFieldCodes = False
End Sub
```

Example 5.19. Recorded macro to delete text in all document fields

Creating Fields with VBA

The recorded macro does a good job generating code for fields. For simple fields, defined as having a single set of field brackets, the matter is straightforward. For example, if the modified date field looks like this:

```
{ DATE \@ "dddd, MMMM dd, yyyy" }
```

The result will look like this: Thursday, April 29, 2011.

The VBA recorder produces Example 5.20. To record this macro, select **Insert|Text|Quick Parts|Fields**, selecting Date. In the Date formats list, select the date in the following format: Thursday, April 29, 2011. As confirmation, the picture format ("dddd, MMMM dd, yyyy") displays in the text box.

```
Sub Macro2()
' Macro2 Macro
  Selection.Fields.Add Range:=Selection.Range, _
  Type:=wdFieldEmpty, Text:="DATE  \@ ""dddd, MMMM dd, yyyy"" ", _
  PreserveFormatting:=True
End Sub
```

Example 5.20. Macro for modified date field, from macro recorder

This code is as optimized as anyone can do by hand. For more complex fields, the programming gets more complex. Using the macro recorder may be the easiest way to automate complex fields, but the code isn't exemplary or efficient. For example, during the recording session, you have to move the current insert point (the **Selection**), to the new position in the field (using the arrow keys) and insert a new field manually. In general, it's not a good idea to use Selection as a VBA navigation means. Example 5.21 is a more complex field that implements a basic number guessing game.

```
{ QUOTE { ASK MysteryNumber "Try to guess the mystery number." }
  { IF { = MysteryNumber } = 1
      "You guessed the mystery number."
       "No, that isn't the mystery number, but try again."
  }
}
```

Example 5.21. Number guessing game

Example 5.22 is a recorded macro that creates this field:

```
Sub MysteryNumberGuess()
  Selection.Fields.Add Range:=Selection.Range, Type:=wdFieldEmpty, _
    Text:="QUOTE  A ", PreserveFormatting:=True
  Selection.MoveLeft Unit:=wdCharacter, Count:=1, Extend:=wdExtend
  Selection.Fields.ToggleShowCodes
  Selection.MoveRight Unit:=wdCharacter, Count:=1
  Selection.MoveLeft Unit:=wdCharacter, Count:=18
  Selection.TypeBackspace
  Selection.Fields.Add Range:=Selection.Range, Type:=wdFieldEmpty, _
    Text:="ASK  MysteryNumber ""Guess the mystery number:"" ", _
    PreserveFormatting:=True
  Selection.MoveRight Unit:=wdCharacter, Count:=1, Extend:=wdExtend
  Selection.Fields.ToggleShowCodes
  Selection.MoveRight Unit:=wdCharacter, Count:=17
  Selection.Fields.Add Range:=Selection.Range, Type:=wdFieldEmpty, _
    Text:="IF MysteryNumber = 3 ""You guessed the mystery number." & _
    " ""No, that isn't the mystery number but try again.""", _
    PreserveFormatting:=True
  Selection.MoveLeft Unit:=wdCharacter, Count:=1, Extend:=wdExtend
  Selection.Fields.ToggleShowCodes
  Selection.MoveRight Unit:=wdCharacter, Count:=2
  Selection.MoveLeft Unit:=wdCharacter, Count:=1, Extend:=wdExtend
  Selection.Fields.Update
End Sub
```

Example 5.22. Number guessing game – recorded macro

Recording fields as a macro is a tricky task. Don't be surprised if it takes you several attempts. In particular, the `Selection.MoveLeft` and `.MoveRight` statements cause some inconvenience, since the insert point must be moved precisely.

Another thing to note is that the statement `Selection.Fields.ToggleShowCodes` could also have been written as: `Selection.Fields.ToggleShowCodes = True`. Some functions have a default parameter – a parameter value that the function will use if you do not provide a value. In this case, the default value is `True`. It's best to be explicit about these things and state the value. In the programming community, there are many who don't like default values, since they can change between releases. In practice, since there are so many default values, it's not always possible to include them all. In fact, unless you check every statement, you're not going to catch them all.

Field Shortcut Summary

Table 5.1 maps field keyboard shortcuts with the matching VBA command.

Table 5.1. Field shortcut summary

You want to...	Key strokes	VBA command
Update selected field(s)	**F9** or **ALT-SHIFT-U**	*object*.Fields.Update
Insert field brackets	**CTRL-F9**	*object*.Fields.AddRange:=RangeObject
Toggle all fields.	**ALT -F9**	View.ShowFieldCodes = True|False
Toggle selected fields.	**SHIFT-F9**	
Convert selected field to plain text	**CTRL-SHIFT-F9** or **CTRL-6**	*object*.Fields.Unlink
Lock fields.	**CTRL-F11** or **CTRL-3**	*object*.Fields.Locked = True
Unlock fields.	**CTRL-SHIFT-F11** or **CTRL-4**	*object*.Fields.Locked = False
Go to next field down.	**F11**	Selection.NextField.Select
Go to next field up.	**SHIFT-F11**	Selection.PreviousField.Select
Update text linked from the field to the original document.	**CTRL-SHIFT-F7**	Selection.Fields.UpdateSource
Run GOTOBUTTON or MACROBUTTON to the field that displays the results.	**ALT+SHIFT+F9**	Selection.Fields(1).DoClick
Insert the date in default format	**ALT+SHIFT+D**	Selection.Fields.AddRange:=Selection.Range, Type:=wdFieldDate

Form Fields

Form fields are placeholders for information provided or filled in by the user of the document. Many users know these better as "form controls," which are related to the blanks that users fill in when completing forms. Although that's part of it, there's more to them. Word offers three types of form fields: legacy controls, content controls, and Active X controls. The combined set allows a wide range of capabilities, but can be confusing.

▶ **Legacy controls:** As the name implies, legacy controls are carried over from previous versions of Word, specifically Word 97 and later. They still work and have a place in current versions of Microsoft Office. The legacy controls function exactly as they did in previous versions. You can place them in documents, and if you then protect the form, they can take input from users while preventing changes to the document in non-form areas. You can save the control information, and only the control information, to a comma-separated file, and export it to databases.

▶ **Content controls:** Office 2007 introduced Content Controls, taking legacy form fields and bookmarks to the next level. It is important to understand that they were not meant as replacements for legacy controls. For starters, they can only be used in Word 2007 and later, not in previous versions of Word. Unlike legacy controls, they cannot saved information separately to a file, making data collection by conventional means difficult.

On the other hand, they do offer several advantages:

- They support XML. This allows data binding – the ability to tie data to and from an external data source. XML is out of scope for this book. Consult your IT department or programming staff for additional information.

- The new controls allow you to better structure your documents. You can more easily protect or prevent changes to areas of the document. In the past, to prevent any part of the document from changing, you had to protect the entire document. With content controls you can specify which areas to protect, from a single character to the entire document. You can also make more effective forms. Content controls go beyond legacy controls by letting you set up a form for users to complete. The new controls include a date picker, although a checkbox control is not included. These controls also blend in better with the document, not being highlighted unless you hover over them.

Both sets of controls support VBA and macros. Legacy controls work as they always have, allowing macros to be run when entering or exiting a field. Custom controls work slightly differently, allowing macros to be run through events, although there is only one event handle for all controls. Therefore, the macro has to determine which control is being invoked.

▶ **ActiveX controls:** ActiveX controls are meant mostly for creating Web forms, but always require VBA to provide any functionality. They have fallen out of favor since ActiveX can be a security risk. They are out of scope for most of this discussion.

You can easily identify the fields (either content or legacy controls) by their look. Table 5.2 shows the two kinds of controls and how the document displays them.

Table 5.2. Legacy and content controls

Content Control	Legacy Field	Action
Full name: Click here to enter text.	Full name:	The field is not selected
Full name: Click here to enter text.	Full name:	The field has the cursor hovering in it.
Full name: Click here to enter text.	Full name:	The field is selected.
Full name: Click here to enter text.	Full name:	The field has the insert point clicked in it. Design Mode is on.

Controls vary in the extent to which they can be customized. Select the control you want to customize and while in Design Mode (**Developer|Controls|Design Mode**), click **Properties**. This displays additional properties for customization.

Legacy Form Fields

The following section explains legacy form fields, with automation and VBA examples.

Creating legacy form fields

For legacy and ActiveX controls, use Procedure 5.17 to place controls.

Procedure 5.17. Create a legacy form field

1. In the **Developer** tab, click **Design Mode** from the **Controls** panel.

2. Place the insert point where you want the control to be. It is customary to place a label in front of each form control. If the control is part of the document content flow, a label won't be necessary.

3. Select the **Legacy tools** icon, which drops down a list of controls (see Figure 5.15). Select the tool you want to place. The new control is placed.

Figure 5.15. Legacy controls on the Developer Tab

You can automate this process. For example, if you record a macro to produce the form field shown in Figure 5.16, the macro recorder generates the code shown in Example 5.23.

Full·name: → |(Enter·Text·here]¶

Figure 5.16. Example of a legacy field

```
 1 Sub Macro1()
 2   Selection.TypeText Text:="Full Name: " & vbTab
 3   Selection.FormFields.Add Range:=Selection.Range, _
 4     Type:=wdFieldFormTextInput
 5   Selection.PreviousField.Select
 6   With Selection.FormFields(1)
 7     .Name = "Text1"
 8     .EntryMacro = ""
 9     .ExitMacro = ""
10     .Enabled = True
11     .OwnHelp = False
12     .HelpText = ""
13     .OwnStatus = False
14     .StatusText = ""
15     With .TextInput
16       .EditType Type:=wdRegularText, _
17         Default:="(Enter Text here)", Format:=""
18       .Width = 0
19     End With
20
21   End With
22 End Sub
```

Example 5.23. Macro to produce form field from macro recorder

You can remove lines 8 through 14 to get the shortened version of Example 5.24:

```
Sub Macro1()
  Selection.TypeText Text:="Full Name: " & vbTab
  Selection.FormFields.Add Range:=Selection.Range, _
    Type:=wdFieldFormTextInput
  Selection.PreviousField.Select
  With Selection.FormFields(1)
      .Name = "Text1"
  With .TextInput
      .EditType Type:=wdRegularText, _
      Default:="(Enter Text here)"
    End With
  End With
End Sub
```

Example 5.24. Shortened version of Example 5.23

The final modification is to add the list items as in Example 5.25:

```
 1 Sub Macro2()
 2   Selection.TypeText Text:="Organization Code: "
 3   Selection.FormFields.Add Range:=Selection.Range, _
 4     Type:=wdFieldFormDropDown
 5   Selection.PreviousField.Select
 6   Selection.FormFields(1).Name = "CompanyDepartment"
 7
 8   Selection.FormFields("CompanyDepartment").DropDown. _
 9     ListEntries.Clear
10   Selection.FormFields("CompanyDepartment").DropDown.ListEntries. _
11     Add Name:="HR"
12   Selection.FormFields("CompanyDepartment").DropDown.ListEntries. _
13     Add Name:="IT"
14   Selection.FormFields("CompanyDepartment").DropDown.ListEntries. _
15     Add Name:="Marketing"
16   Selection.FormFields("CompanyDepartment").DropDown.ListEntries. _
17     Add Name:="Test"
18 End Sub
```

Example 5.25. Added list items

Using legacy form fields

To use legacy form fields, first design the form by placing the form fields in the needed positions. At this point in the form design, the body text – that text which is not a form field – will be normal text and can be edited or changed as you would expect. The form fields will appear highlighted in blue. If you enter text in a form field, the field will go away and be replaced by the text you entered. Procedure 5.18 shows how to preserve the forms and text from being changed in a document.

Procedure 5.18. Protect a document

1. In the **Developer** tab, make sure **Design Mode** is off (the button is not highlighted).

2. Click **Protect Document** in the **Protect** panel.

3. Click **Restrict Formatting and Editing**. This displays the **Restrict Formatting and Editing** panel inside the document area.

4. Check **Using Legacy Form Fields** .

5. Select **Filling in forms** from the drop-down list.

6. Click **Yes, Start Enforcing Protection**.

7. Optionally enter a password. This limits the users who will be able to modify the form itself. If you don't want it password protected, leave the password fields empty.

8. Click **OK**.

The document is now protected and when users click in the document at a location other than a field, the cursor automatically advances to the next available field, ready to enter information.

To unprotect the document, for example if you need to make changes to the form, use the above procedure but click **Stop Protection** in the **Restrict Formatting and Editing** panel. If you created a password when you protected the document, you will be prompted to enter that password to unprotect the document.

Macros and legacy form fields

Legacy form fields have better support for macros than the other fields. One important reason is that they support macros as you enter the field or leave it. This allows you to prepare data before using the field, for example, to make sure sure the right information is present and is in the right format. As you leave a field, you might update the field. This can be a convenient way to deal with any issues you have when trying to update fields.

You can assign macros to fields through their property dialog. To see this dialog, either:

1. Double click the **legacy form** field,

   or

2. Select the control, and then click **Properties** in the **Controls** panel.

This will display the **Field Options** dialog (see Figure 5.17).

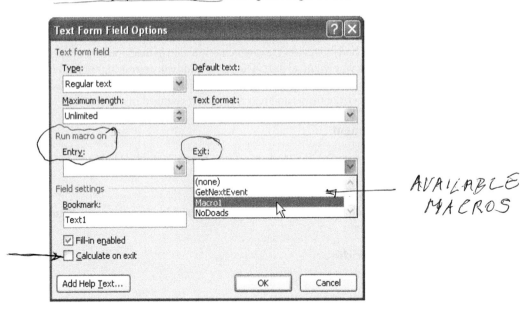

Figure 5.17. Text Form Field Options dialog with Run Macro on Exit drop-down list

Among other options are **Run macro onEntry** and **Run macro onExit**. A drop-down list displays the available macros. These macros may be either from the document template or global templates. Select the one you need. If you leave the option blank or select **none**, a macro will not run on that condition.

As an example, had the Macro1 macro, (the one that updates all the fields in the main story, Example 5.1 (p. 74)) been installed, the drop-down lists would include that macro. Selecting Macro1 as the Exit macro would update all the fields after the user exits the form.

Form fields can also be bookmarks. In this case, the control, a text box (see Figure 5.18), has a bookmark (named *Text1*). The document can immediately use that bookmark for other fields. Suppose the document looked like this, with FORMTEXT referring to the dialog in Figure 5.18.

{ QUOTE "The { REF Text1 * MERGEFORMAT }Report" }

Full Name: { FORMTEXT }

Last Modified { DATE \@ "M/d/yyyy h:mm:ss am/pm" }

Figure 5.18. Using fields as bookmarks

After the user completes the field labeled **Full Name**, the document will update (the UpdateFields macro was selected to run on field exit). The report title now has a valid TEXT1 bookmark to use. In addition, the date will be updated. The finished document looks like Figure 5.19.

The Catch-22 Report

Full Name: Catch-22

Last Modified 4/10/2011 6:15:16 PM

Figure 5.19. Form example with labeled fields

Calculate on exit

Calculate on exit is an option to update form fields without the use of macros. This is helpful where you don't want to write macros for the update, or if your environment restricts macros. Text or values you type in form fields can appear in other fields of the document, such as other Text fields, or REF (reference) fields. It also applies to other fields that are not directly dependent on those source fields, such as Time. However, this update is not automatic. If the document is protected (being treated like a form), those fields do not update. Checking the **Calculate on exit** option updates other fields when one of the referenced fields changes.

As an example, create a document with three fields:

Procedure 5.19. Add Calculate on exit updates

1. Click **Developer|Controls|Legacy Tools**, selecting **Text Form Field**.

2. Double click that field (or right click on the field and choose **Properties**), change the **Type** to **Number** and check **Calculate on exit**. Click **OK**. Notice the default bookmark name will be a serial sequence, such as Text1 or Text2.

3. Insert two more text fields, repeating the two steps above.

4. In the third text field, change the **Type** to **Calculate** and enter the Expression as `=SUM(Text1, Text2)`, or `= (Text1 * Text2)`. Leave **Calculate on exit** unchecked. Click **OK**.

5. Protect the document by selecting **Developer|Protect|Protect Document|Restrict Formatting and Editing**. This displays the **Restrict Formatting and Editing** panel. In that panel, check **Allow only this type of editing in the document**, selecting **Filling in forms**. Click **Yes, Start Enforcing Protection**. You can enter a password, although for this example you don't need to. Click **OK**. This turns the document into a form with only the form fields being editable. The first text field (`Text1`) is automatically selected.

6. Enter a numeric value and click **Tab**. The value for `Text3` changes.

To see how this changes other fields, stop the document protection (in the **Restrict Formatting and Editing** panel click **Stop Protection**).

Procedure 5.20. Add additional fields with Calculate on exit updates

1. Add a REF field (**Insert|Quick Parts|Field**), selecting **REF**. Choose one the bookmarks listed in **Bookmark names**, such as `Text1`. Click **OK**.

2. Add a second field for Time (**Insert|Quick Parts|Field**), selecting **Time**. Choose a time format that displays the seconds such as *mm/dd/yyy h:mm:ss AM/PM*. Click **OK**.

3. Protect the document again.

4. Enter a numeric value in either `Text1` or `Text2` and click **Tab**. The value for `Text3` still changes but also the two new fields update.

Gathering information

An important purpose of a form is to collect and save information. Procedure 5.21 shows how to do this, but note that this process works only with legacy form fields.

Procedure 5.21. Gather information with forms

1. Click the **Office** button, and select **Word Options**.

2. Select the **Advanced** tab in the left pane, then scroll to the **Preserve fidelity when sharing this document** section in the right window.

3. Check **Save form data as delimited text file.** *COMMA-SEPARATED TEXT*

4. Choose **Plain text (.txt)** in the **Save as type** drop-down menu, and then click **OK**. *VALUE*

The legacy form fields will be saved as a comma-separated text value. This format allows you to export the information to Microsoft Excel, or a more formal database, such as a Microsoft Access, Oracle, or MySql database. You can save the forms information as shown in Example 5.26.

```
Sub SaveFormsDataInFile()
    ActiveDocument.SaveAs FileName:="Name.txt", SaveFormsData:=True
End Sub
```

Example 5.26. Macro to save a form

The problem is that this saves to the same file each time and will keep overwriting that file. You could save using different file names, but you might end up with too many files. A better solution would be to save the data to the same file each time, but append the information at the end, as in Example 5.27.

```
Sub SaveAllFormsToOneFile()
    On Error GoTo MyErrorHandler

    Dim currentDocument As Document
    Set currentDocument = ActiveDocument

    ActiveDocument.SaveFormsData = True
    ActiveDocument.SaveAs FileName:="c:\temp.txt", SaveFormsData:=True

    Dim targetDocument As Document
    Set targetDocument = _
        Application.Documents.Open(FileName:="c:\temp.txt", _
        addtorecentfiles:=False)
    targetDocument.Range.Copy
    targetDocument.Close wdDoNotSaveChanges

    On Error Resume Next
    Set currentDocument = Documents.Open(FileName:="c:\combinedlist.txt")
    If Err.Number = 5174 Then
        'File is not there, so create it
        Set currentDocument = Documents.Add
        currentDocument.SaveAs FileName:="c:\combinedlist.txt"
    End If
    On Error GoTo MyErrorHandler

    Dim pasteRange As Range
    Set pasteRange = currentDocument.Range
    pasteRange.Collapse wdCollapseEnd
    pasteRange.Paste

    currentDocument.SaveAs FileName:="c:\combinedlist.txt", _
        fileformat:=wdFormatUnicodeText
    currentDocument.Close wdDoNotSaveChanges

    Exit Sub

MyErrorHandler:
    MsgBox "SaveAllFormsToOneFile" & vbCrLf & vbCrLf & _
        "Err = " & Err.Number & vbCrLf & _
        "Description: " & Err.Description
End Sub
```

Example 5.27. Variation on Example 5.26

Example 5.28 is useful if you run the macro on each file you receive. In a likely scenario, you'll be getting back many files. If you put those files into one folder, you can run Example 5.28, which goes through a folder that you choose, looking for .doc, .docx, or .docm files. It opens each one, collects the field information, and adds it to a single file, here named CollectedForms.txt.

```
Sub GetFromDataFromDocuments()
    On Error GoTo MyErrorHandler

    Dim myFileDialog As FileDialog
    Set myFileDialog = Application.FileDialog(msoFileDialogFolderPicker)

    myFileDialog.Title = "Select the source directory."
    myFileDialog.InitialView = msoFileDialogViewList

    If myFileDialog.Show <> -1 Then Exit Sub

    Dim whichDocumentDirectory As String
    whichDocumentDirectory = myFileDialog.SelectedItems.Item(1)

    Dim whichDocumentList As String
    whichDocumentList = Dir$(whichDocumentDirectory & "\*.doc?")

    Dim targetDocumentName As String
    targetDocumentName = "CollectedForms.txt"

    Dim targetDocument As Document
    On Error Resume Next
    Set targetDocument = Documents.Open(whichDocumentDirectory & _
      "\" & targetDocumentName, False)
    If Err.Number = 5174 Then
        Set targetDocument = Application.Documents.Add
        targetDocument.SaveAs FileName:=whichDocumentDirectory & _
          "\" & targetDocumentName, fileformat:=wdFormatText
    End If
    On Error GoTo MyErrorHandler

    Dim tempFileName As String
    tempFileName = "tempFile.txt"

    'Disables any automatic macros the document may have
    WordBasic.DisableAutoMacros 1

    Dim sourceDocument As Document
    Do While whichDocumentList <> vbNullString

        Set sourceDocument = Documents.Open(whichDocumentDirectory & _
          "\" & whichDocumentList)

        sourceDocument.SaveAs FileName:=tempFileName, _
            fileformat:=wdFormatText, SaveFormsData:=True
        sourceDocument.Close SaveChanges:=wdDoNotSaveChanges
        Set sourceDocument = Nothing

        Set sourceDocument = Documents.Open(tempFileName, False)

        'Write the fields from the source into the target document
        targetDocument.Range.InsertAfter sourceDocument.Range.Text

        'Close the temporary file
        sourceDocument.Close SaveChanges:=wdDoNotSaveChanges
```

```
            Set sourceDocument = Nothing

            'Save the data file
            targetDocument.Save
            whichDocumentList = Dir$()
        Loop
    WordBasic.DisableAutoMacros 0

    MsgBox "Done compiling forms."

    Exit Sub

MyErrorHandler:
    WordBasic.DisableAutoMacros 0
    MsgBox "GetFromDataFromDocuments" & vbCrLf & vbCrLf & _
        "Err = " & Err.Number & vbCrLf & _
        "Description: " & Err.Description
End Sub
```

Example 5.28. Gather field information from files in a folder

Content Controls

This section explains content controls, with automation and VBA examples. Content controls function similarly to legacy controls, but with additional versatility. Content controls can only be used with the Word 2007 (and later) document formats (`.docx` or `.dotm`). Documents created using earlier versions of Word will not have these options available. In that case, the document must be saved into the new format.

The following controls are available:

► **Text:** Content is limited to text. Any text styling or formatting applies to all the text in the control.

► **RichText:** Content is also limited to text. Any range of characters in the control may be styled or formatted independently.

► **Picture:** Specifies a picture or graphic.

► **Drop-down List:** Contents are limited to a single selection from a list of items. In the control's properties dialog, you can manually add the list items.

► **Combo Box:** Contents are limited to a single selection from a list of items, or you can enter another value. In the control's properties dialog, you can manually add the list items.

► **Date Picker:** Contents are a calendar control.

► **Building Block Gallery.** Contents are limited to a single selection from a building block gallery. You can specify which Gallery (Quick Parts, AutoText, Cover Pages, and so on) you want and then any one or all of the categories in that Gallery.

All of these controls have **Properties** associated with them. You can see the properties by selecting the control, or part of it, while in **Design Mode** and then either right clicking on the control and choosing **Properties** or clicking the **Developer|Controls|Properties** button. Some controls may have additional options from the ribbon. For example, double clicking a picture control adds a **Picture Tools** tab in the ribbon.

Each control has a common set of properties:

- **Title:** This is the title or name of the control. The **Title** plays a more prominent role when used with XML.

- **Tag:** This is the tag text associated with the control. The **Tag** plays a more prominent role when used with XML.

- **Content control cannot be deleted:** Checking this option prevents the control from being deleted from the document. The contents of the control may be empty or have no value, but the control will still be present.

In addition, each control may have a unique set of properties. For example, the combo box and drop-down list have a list properties value that lets you add items to the drop-down list. The text and rich text controls have an option to allow multiple paragraphs (using carriage returns).

Creating content controls

Procedure 5.22 shows how to create and place content controls.

Procedure 5.22. Create and place a content control

1. Click **Developer|Controls|Design Mode**.

2. Place the insert point where you want the control placed. For forms, it is customary to have a label before the control. If the control is part of the document content flow, a label won't be necessary.

3. Select the tool you want to place (Figure 5.20). The new content controls are the first seven icons listed. Clicking an icon places the new control.

Figure 5.20. Controls panel of the Developer Tab

Content controls vary in the degree to which they can be customized. Select the control and then click **Properties**. This displays additional properties.

Customizing properties

Procedure 5.23 shows how to customize properties for content controls.

Procedure 5.23. Customize content controls

1. • If you are in design mode, right click in the text or picture area of the control and select **Properties**. This displays the associated **Content Control Properties** dialog box.

- If you are not in design mode, select the control and select **Developer|Controls|Properties**.

2. Check the option or options you want and then click **OK**.

Locking controls, text, and documents

You can lock content controls or any text from being changed in one of two ways: locking a control and protecting the document. Take the case that you have company stationary that has a header, logo, and company address area, along with the body portion of the document. Of course, you would want team members to be able to type their own letters, and thus be able to change the body of the document. You would not want them to change the logo or company address. Both protection methods can accomplish this, but each takes a slightly different approach.

Locking a control

Individual content controls or ranges of text can be locked or prevented from being edited. This allows you to specify distinct areas to protect. You don't have to use content controls for this feature, any text or range can be used.

Locking and unlocking content controls

Any individual content controls may also be locked to prevent changes or editing as show by Procedure 5.24.

Procedure 5.24. Lock and unlock content controls

1. Select the content control you want locked or unlocked.

2. In the properties dialog (Procedure 5.23), check **Contents cannot be edited** to lock the content control, or check **Contents cannot be edited** to unlock it.

An easy way is to see content controls and their groupings is to click **Developer|Controls|Design Mode**. However, this doesn't show whether a control is locked or unlocked.

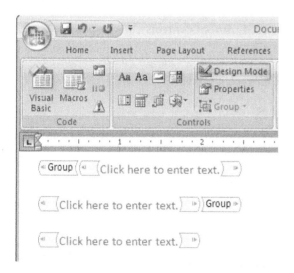

Figure 5.21. Content controls and their groupings

If you attempt to modify text within a locked control, you will see the Word status message display: **This modification is not allowed because the selection is locked**. Likewise, if you click on an individual control, many items in the ribbon will not be active if the control is locked. For example, items in the **Home|Font** panel will be inactive since the text of a control cannot be modified. Also, if you try to delete any selection that has at least one locked content control, the delete will fail and you will see the same message (**This modification is not allowed because the selection is locked**).

Macro To find ranges with locked content controls

Example 5.29 selects each grouped range. Since the ranges cannot be highlighted, only selected, to see each group you may have to step through the code in the IDE debugger.

```
Sub SelectGroupedRegions()
    On Error GoTo MyErrorHandler

    Dim sourceDocument As Document
    Set sourceDocument = ActiveDocument

    Dim myControl As ContentControl
    For Each myControl In sourceDocument.ContentControls
        If myControl.Type = wdContentControlGroup Then
            myControl.Range.Select
        End If

        DoEvents
    Next

    Exit Sub

MyErrorHandler:
    MsgBox "SelectGroupedRegions" & vbCrLf & vbCrLf & _
        "Err = " & Err.Number & vbCrLf & _
        "Description: " & Err.Description
End Sub
```

Example 5.29. Macro to find ranges with locked content controls

Protecting an entire document

Procedure 5.25 shows how to protect an entire document from being edited.

Procedure 5.25. Protect an entire document

1. Select **Developer|Protect|Protect Document|Restrict Formatting and Editing**. This displays the **Restrict Formatting and Editing** panel.

2. Check **Allow only this type of editing in the document**. The drop-down menu becomes active.

3. Select **No changes (Read only)**.

4. Click **Yes, Start Enforcing Protection**. This displays the **Start Enforcing Protection** dialog. If this button is not active, you may be in Design Mode; if so, uncheck that option (**Developer|Controls|Design Mode**). Afterwards, **Start Enforcing Protection** will display.

5. You may want to add a password to prevent others from modifying the form. If you add a password, be sure to record it in a safe place. The password is not recoverable. Leave the password text boxes empty to not assign a password.

6. Click **OK**. The document cannot be changed. You can close the **Restrict Formatting and Editing** panel.

Unprotecting an entire document

Procedure 5.26 shows how to unprotect an entire document from being edited.

Procedure 5.26. Unprotect an entire document

1. Select **Developer|Protect|Protect Document|Restrict Formatting and Editing**. This displays the **Restrict Formatting and Editing** panel.

2. Click **Stop Protection**. If the document has a password, the **Unprotect Document** dialog will display. Enter the password and click **OK**.

Protecting parts of a document

You can protect some parts of a document and allow edits in the rest. Procedure 5.27 shows how to protect parts of document from being edited.

Procedure 5.27. Protect parts of a document

1. Select **Developer|Protect|Protect Document|Restrict Formatting and Editing**. This displays the **Restrict Formatting and Editing** panel.

2. Check **Allow only this type of editing in the document**. The drop-down menu becomes active.

3. Select **No changes (Read only)**.

4. In the document, select the areas or ranges you want to be able to edit. For each region or range selected, from **Exceptions**, select **Everyone**. This allows that area to be edited. The area will be highlighted in light gray and will be enclosed with heavy brackets (these are not the Show Bookmarks brackets). Repeat this step for each region you want to be editable.

5. Click **Yes, Start Enforcing Protection**. This displays the **Start Enforcing Protection** dialog. If this button is not active, you may be in Design Mode; if so, uncheck that option (**Developer|Controls|Design Mode**). Afterwards, **Start Enforcing Protection** will display.

6. You may want to add a password to prevent others from modifying the form. If you add a password, be sure to record it in a safe place. The password is not recoverable. Leave the password text boxes empty to not assign a password.

7. Click **OK**. The document cannot be changed except for the specified areas.

The **Restrict Formatting and Editing** panel shows additional options for seeing the editable areas. The **Highlight the regions I can edit** option faintly highlights the editable region. The **Find Next Region I Can Edit** option selects the next region that can be edited. The **Show All Regions I Can Edit** option selects all the regions that can be edited.

Unprotecting parts of a document

Procedure 5.28 shows how to unprotect parts of a document from being edited.

Procedure 5.28. Unprotect parts of a document

1. Select **Developer|Protect|Protect Document|Restrict Formatting and Editing**. This displays the **Restrict Formatting and Editing** panel.

2. Click **Stop Protection**. If the document has a password, the **Unprotect Document** dialog will display. Enter the password and click **OK**. Afterwards, the document will be unprotected. The document will still show the previously defined editable regions.

Procedure 5.29 shows how to remove an individual editable region.

Procedure 5.29. Remove an editable region from a document

1. Click or select a range anywhere inside that region.

2. Uncheck the owning groups in the **Restrict Formatting and Editing|Exceptions** panel. The highlighting from the region disappears.

Procedure 5.30 shows how to remove all editable regions.

Procedure 5.30. Remove all editable regions from a document

1. Select the entire document.

2. From **Exceptions**, check **Everyone**. Then immediately uncheck **Everyone**.

Making a form

Word allows you to make a form, which is a document that is protected, except for blanks where the user can add information. To make a form, complete a document to your needs, using content controls for the user-provided regions. For example, to add the user's name, provide a text box. Any number of content controls may be added.

Each control should be customized (see the section titled "Locking and unlocking content controls" (p. 107)) to prevent the text and the content control from being edited or deleted. Some content controls may be need to be customized to be useful. For example, the combo box should have list items added for the user to select from. You may also want to consider making the form a template, to make creating copies of the form easier.

To allow only content controls to be edited and protect the remainder of the document, use the document protection feature.

Protecting a form document

Procedure 5.31 shows how to protect a form document.

Procedure 5.31. Protect a form document

1. Select **Developer|Protect|Protect Document|Restrict Formatting and Editing**. This displays the **Restrict Formatting and Editing** panel.

2. Check **Allow only this type of editing in the document**. The drop-down menu becomes active.

3. **Select Filling in forms**.

4. Click **Yes, Start Enforcing Protection**. This displays the **Start Enforcing Protection** dialog. If this button is not active, you may be in Design Mode; if so, uncheck that option (**Developer|Controls|Design Mode**). Afterwards, the **Start Enforcing Protection** will display.

5. You may want to add a password to prevent others from modifying the form itself. If you add a password, be sure to record it in a safe place. The password is not recoverable. Leave the password text boxes empty to not assign a password.

6. Click **OK**. You can close the **Restrict Formatting and Editing** panel.

The document cannot be changed, except for the content controls you added. Clicking in a protected or non-editable region automatically advances the insertion point to the first available editable field. You can navigate from one content control to another by pressing **Tab**. You can also use the **Up** and **Down** arrow keys to navigate.

There are two exceptions. In a rich-text content control, **Tab** does not advance to the next content control. Instead, it inserts the tab character. Also, the **Up** and **Down** arrow keys will not navigate away from a legacy control.

Unprotecting a form document

To unprotect a form document or make the document itself editable again, use Procedure 5.32.

Procedure 5.32. Unprotect a form document

1. Select **Developer|Protect|Protect Document|Restrict Formatting and Editing**. This displays the **Restrict Formatting and Editing** panel.

2. Click **Stop Protection**. If the document has a password, the **Unprotect Document** dialog displays. Enter the password and click **OK**. Afterwards, the document is unprotected.

This stops document protection, although regions within the document may be still **Developer|Controls|Group|Group** protected.

Macros and VBA

Content controls can also be created through macros and VBA. The macro recorder produces efficient code for inserting content controls, as in Example 5.30

```
Sub Macro1()
    Selection.TypeText Text:="Full Name:" & vbTab
    Selection.Range.ContentControls.Add (wdContentControlRichText)
    Selection.ParentContentControl.Title = "Text1"
    Selection.ParentContentControl.Tag = "FullName_ID"
End Sub
```

Example 5.30. Macro to insert content controls

Example 5.31 is a safer, though longer, version of Example 5.30 (it does not use Selection).

```
Sub Macro2()
  Dim currentDocument As Document
  Set currentDocument = ActiveDocument

  currentDocument.Range.InsertAfter "Full Name:" & vbTab

  Dim contentControlRange As Range
  Set contentControlRange = currentDocument.Range
  contentControlRange.Collapse wdCollapseEnd

  Dim myContentControl As ContentControl
  Set myContentControl = _
    currentDocument.ContentControls.Add(Type:=wdContentControlText, _
    Range:=contentControlRange)
  myContentControl.Title = "Text1"
  myContentControl.Tag = "FullName_ID"
End Sub
```

Example 5.31. Safer version of Example 5.30

Gathering information

There is no function to save content controls as you can with legacy controls. As an alternative, Example 5.32 looks for document files in a folder and collects all the content controls in one place.

```
Sub GetFieldsFromDocuments()
  On Error GoTo MyErrorHandler

  Dim myFileDialog As FileDialog
  Set myFileDialog = Application.FileDialog(msoFileDialogFolderPicker)

  myFileDialog.Title = "Select the source directory."
  myFileDialog.InitialView = msoFileDialogViewList

  If myFileDialog.Show <> -1 Then Exit Sub

  Dim whichDocumentDirectory As String
  whichDocumentDirectory = myFileDialog.SelectedItems.Item(1)

  Dim whichDocumentList As String
  whichDocumentList = Dir$(whichDocumentDirectory & "\*.doc?")

  Dim targetDocumentName As String
  targetDocumentName = "CollectedForms.txt"

  Dim targetDocument As Document
  On Error Resume Next
  Set targetDocument = Documents.Open(whichDocumentDirectory & _
                      "\" & targetDocumentName, False)
  If Err.Number = 5174 Then
    Set targetDocument = Application.Documents.Add
    targetDocument.SaveAs FileName:=whichDocumentDirectory & _
    "\" & targetDocumentName, fileformat:=wdFormatText
```

```
   End If
   On Error GoTo MyErrorHandler

   Dim tempFileName As String
   tempFileName = "tempFile.txt"

   'Disables any automatic macros the document may have
   WordBasic.DisableAutoMacros 1

   Dim sourceDocument As Document
   Do While whichDocumentList <> vbNullString

      Set sourceDocument = Documents.Open(whichDocumentDirectory & _
                     "\" & whichDocumentList)

      Dim myContentControl As ContentControl
      For Each myContentControl In sourceDocument.ContentControls
        myContentControl.Range.Select
        targetDocument.Range.InsertAfter """" & _
          myContentControl.Range.Text & ""","

      DoEvents
      Next

   'Close sourceDocument
   sourceDocument.Close SaveChanges:=wdDoNotSaveChanges
   Set sourceDocument = Nothing

   'Some clean up, removing the last comma and adding an extra line return
   targetDocument.Characters(targetDocument.Characters.Count - 1).Delete
   targetDocument.Range.InsertParagraphAfter

   'Save the compiled document
   targetDocument.Save
   whichDocumentList = Dir$()
Loop
WordBasic.DisableAutoMacros 0

'Uncomment this line to see the open file afterwards.
targetDocument.Close wdDoNotSaveChanges

MsgBox "Done compiling forms."

Exit Sub

MyErrorHandler:
  WordBasic.DisableAutoMacros 0
  MsgBox "GetFieldsFromDocuments" & vbCrLf & vbCrLf & _
         "Err = " & Err.Number & vbCrLf & _
         "Description: " & Err.Description
End Sub
```

Example 5.32. Automation approach to saving content controls

A `For Each` loop is used to gather all the content control information from the document. This loop may look familiar by now since it is one of the best ways to go through all the elements of a specific structure, and content controls are no different in that regard.

It becomes difficult to target one exact content control. In the case of bookmarks, for example, you can specify one by name:

```
Debug.Print currentDocument.Bookmarks("SwissBankAccountNum").Range.Text
```

Example 5.33. Specify bookmark by name

This can't be done with content controls. Although each control is assigned a unique numeric ID within the document, you have to track this number, which can be awkward. You can give the control a title, but the title is not forced to be unique. That is, you can have more than one content control with the same title.

```
Public Sub TestContentControls()
  Dim i As Long
  For i = 1 To ActiveDocument.ContentControls.Count
    If LCase$(ActiveDocument.ContentControls(i).Title) = _          ❶
      LCase$("MySwissBankAccount") Then
      Debug.Print ActiveDocument.ContentControls(i).PlaceholderText.Value
      Exit For ❷
    End If
  Next
End Sub
```

Example 5.34. Find a content control by title

If you do give content controls titles, Example 5.34 will find a specific control by title, in this example, `MySwissBankAccount`.

❶   The title is case sensitive. The `LCase$` function calls force the text to be lowercase, making the comparison case insensitive. If you need the comparison to be case sensitive, leave out the `LCase$` function calls.

❷   The `Exit For` statement terminates the `For...Next` loop, so only the first control titled `MySwissBankAccount` will be found. Of course, you could delete that line and the macro would find all the controls with that title.

The title is also case sensitive, so the typical way of handling this (assuming you don't need it to be case sensitive) is to use the `LCase$` statement. This forces the text to lower case, and since both strings will be evaluated as lower case, case isn't going to matter.

Locking Text Outside a Content Control

Procedure 5.33 shows how to lock text that is not contained in a content control.

Procedure 5.33. Lock text outside a content control

1. Select the region you want locked.

2. Select **Developer|Controls|Group|Group**. The selected region is locked. If you try typing in that region, the Word status message displays **This modification is not allowed because the selection is locked**. That message does not display if you paste or cut although the action will have no effect. A locked region has only one indication that it's been grouped and that is if the selected range or insert point has the **Developer|Controls|Group|Group** button dimmed, then selected range is not capable of being ungrouped. Either the selection or part of the selection is not grouped.

Unlocking Text Outside a Content Control

Procedure 5.34 shows how to unlock text that is not contained in a content control.

Procedure 5.34. Unlock text outside a content control

1. Select any range or insertion point within the locked range.

2. Select **Developer|Controls|Group|Ungroup**. The contiguous range that contains the selected area is unlocked.

Summary

Using fields, legacy form fields, and content controls is a convenient way of placing and controlling information. Fields add dynamic content to a document without requiring programming. Legacy field forms allow basic control for users entering information into a document, along with a forms completion capability. Content controls extend form fields with a robustness that gives you better granular control over areas of a document, what content is allowed, and whether those areas can be deleted. All of these can be combined with macros and automation to produce quicker results.

AutoCorrect and AutoText/Building Blocks

AutoCorrect, introduced in Word 95, automatically changes or replaces letters as you type. Most users know AutoCorrect as the feature that fixes (or tries to fix) your spelling. It's unnerving at first to see your typing change, but many get accustomed to it, if not reliant on it. Used in the collective, AutoCorrect encompasses AutoCorrect, which replaces text as you're typing; AutoFormat, which replaces style and formatting; and AutoText, which inserts significant amounts of text.

AutoCorrect, perhaps the best known of these three, can save considerable time and effort. For instance, in a medical report, the term *arteriovenous malformation* may occur many times. Auto-Correct lets you create a shortened form so you don't have to spell the term out repeatedly. You can create a short tag of a few letters, perhaps \am for *arteriovenous* malformation or \mysig for a graphic of your signature. In these two examples, the leading backslash character is not a special marker; it is just a convention to help ensure that the label is unique.

You have to define AutoCorrect replacement terms prior to use, but once defined, the replacement occurs automatically whenever you type the term. The replacement text or graphic will be inserted with the formatting and style in effect at the insertion, or with the replacement's own formatting, as if you had typed the replacement directly.

AutoFormat, and a related set of options, **AutoFormat As You Type,** perform a similar function with formatting. It will replace straight quotes with smart quotes, and *bold* with real bold formatting. **AutoFormat As You Type** goes further and allows you to automatically use bulleted and numbered lists, or convert Internet and network paths with an actual link.

AutoText, renamed in Office 2007 as Building Blocks, allows you to insert an extensive amount of material, such as cover pages, artwork, page layouts, even multiple pages.

AutoCorrect

AutoCorrect uses a list of term pairings. After you type the shortcut, Word replaces it with the full text. Procedure 6.1 shows how to view these pairings.

Procedure 6.1. View AutoCorrect term pairings

1. Click the **Office** icon, and then **Word Options**.

2. Click **Proofing** in the left column.

3. Click the **AutoCorrect Options** button. The **AutoCorrect** dialog displays.

4. Click **AutoCorrect** tab. (see Figure 6.1).

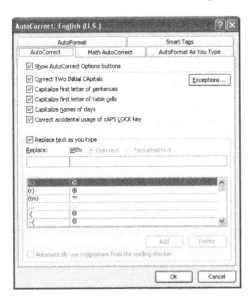

Figure 6.1. The AutoCorrect dialog

Adding Terms

The bottom panel, **Replace text as you type**, displays the pairings. The left column, labeled **Replace**, is the term you can type to trigger the substitution. The right column, labeled **With**, is the term the text is replaced with. By default, there are over 900 of these pairings. Procedure 6.2 shows how to make your own pairing or modify an existing one.

Procedure 6.2. Create AutoCorrect pairings

1. Display the **AutoCorrect** dialog if you have not already done so.

2. Enter the shorthand version in the **Replace** text box. For example, enter \am. If you enter a combination that exists, that entry highlights in the scrolled list.

3. Enter the full text in the **With** text box. Following this example, enter *arteriovenous malformation*.

4. Click **OK**. You could click **Add** instead if you want to keep that dialog up.

You can define both text and graphics with formatting. For text this means the selected text will be replaced with its styling already applied. For graphics, the replacement inserts the selected graphic. Procedure 6.3 shows how to create an entry for formatted text or a graphic.

Procedure 6.3. Create AutoCorrect entry for formatted text

1. Select the text in the document with the desired formatting, or select the graphic.

2. Display the **AutoCorrect** dialog.

3. Enter the shorthand version in the **Replace** text box.

4. The **With** column displays different values.

   a. To use the formatting and style at the insertion point, click **Plain text**.

   b. To retain the formatting (direct or styled), click **Formatted text**

5. Graphics are handled oddly. You can neither paste the graphic into the AutoCorrect dialog nor have the graphic display in the dialog. You must select the graphic before opening the AutoCorrect dialog, then do the following:

   a. Make sure the **Formatted text** button is selected.

   b. Enter a **Replace** value and click **Add**. The text displays an asterisk (*). The graphic retains its size, dimensions, and other characteristics. A graphic noted as **Plain text** is replaced with an asterisk (*).

6. Click **Add** (to keep the dialog box open) or **OK** (to close the dialog box).

Figure 6.2 shows the selected text in the document and the **Display** dialog with the prepared entry.

Figure 6.2. Adding a formatted entry to the AutoCorrect list.

There is no easy way to see all the entries, short of scrolling through the list. Example 6.1 uses a macro to create a document that contains all the entries.

```
Sub ListAutoCorrect()
  On Error GoTo MyErrorHandler

  Dim currentDocument As Document
  Set currentDocument = Documents.Add

  Dim itemCount As Long
  Dim myAutoCorrectEntry As Word.AutoCorrectEntry
  For Each myAutoCorrectEntry In AutoCorrect.Entries
     currentDocument.Range.InsertAfter myAutoCorrectEntry.Name
     currentDocument.Range.InsertAfter vbTab
     currentDocument.Range.InsertAfter myAutoCorrectEntry.Value
     currentDocument.Range.InsertParagraphAfter

     itemCount = itemCount + 1
     currentDocument.Application.StatusBar = "Page " & _
      itemCount & " of " & AutoCorrect.Entries.Count

     DoEvents
  Next

  currentDocument.Paragraphs.Last.Range.Delete

  Dim autoCorrectTable As Table
  Set autoCorrectTable = currentDocument.Range.ConvertToTable()

  autoCorrectTable.Columns(1).PreferredWidth = InchesToPoints(1.2)
  autoCorrectTable.Columns(2).PreferredWidth = InchesToPoints(1.2)
  currentDocument.PageSetup.TextColumns.SetCount NumColumns:=3
  currentDocument.ActiveWindow.ActivePane.View.Type = wdPrintView

  MsgBox "Completed listing AutoCorrect terms."

  Exit Sub

MyErrorHandler:
  MsgBox "ListAutoCorrect" & vbCrLf & _
      vbCrLf & "Err = " & Err.Number & _
      vbCrLf & "Description: " & Err.Description
End Sub
```

Example 6.1. Create a document listing AutoCorrect entries

There are two comments about Example 6.1. First, both a For Each loop and a counter are used. Although it seems redundant (after all, a For Loop using itemCount could have done the same thing), the For Each loop is generally faster. In the case of a small routine such as this, it doesn't matter much, but in general, using a For Each loop is better practice. Second, Word's status bar is used to show the progress. Users like to see things moving on the screen, if for no other reason than to be reassured that something is happening. Typically, you would use a dialog for this, but again, in a small routine and to make a point, this simpler approach is convenient.

Math AutoCorrect

AutoCorrect can only use "simple" objects such as text, graphics, and character-based symbols. Math equations are not considered "simple" objects. Office 2007 introduced the **Math AutoCorrect** feature, which applies the AutoCorrect concept to symbols.

Procedure 6.4. Access the Math AutoCorrect dialog

1. Display the **AutoCorrect** dialog from Figure 6.2.

2. Select the **Math AutoCorrect** tab. The screen looks similar to AutoCorrect except the replacements tend to be symbols.

3. Check the **Use Math AutoCorrect rules outside of math regions** option. Selecting this option allows you to place math symbols anywhere in the document. Having this unselected limits these math symbols to equations.

Otherwise, Math AutoCorrect works the same as text AutoCorrect. That is, you paste or type the symbol in the **With** text box, add a **Replace** marker, and click **Add**.

Example 6.2 lists all the defined Math AutoCorrect symbols, also in a separate document.

```
Sub ListMathAutoCorrect()
  On Error GoTo MyErrorHandler

  Dim currentDocument As Document
  Set currentDocument = Documents.Add

  Dim itemCount As Long
   For itemCount = 1 To Application.OMathAutoCorrect.Entries.Count
     currentDocument.Range.InsertAfter _
       Application.OMathAutoCorrect.Entries(itemCount).Name
     currentDocument.Range.InsertAfter vbTab
     currentDocument.Range.InsertAfter _
       Application.OMathAutoCorrect.Entries(itemCount).Value
     currentDocument.Range.InsertParagraphAfter
     currentDocument.Application.StatusBar = "Page " & _
       itemCount & " of " & _
       Application.OMathAutoCorrect.Entries.Count

     DoEvents
   Next

  currentDocument.Paragraphs.Last.Range.Delete
  currentDocument.Range.ConvertToTable
  currentDocument.Tables(1).Columns(1).PreferredWidth = _
    InchesToPoints(1.2)
  currentDocument.Tables(1).Columns(2).PreferredWidth = _
    InchesToPoints(1.2)
  currentDocument.PageSetup.TextColumns.SetCount NumColumns:=3
  currentDocument.ActiveWindow.ActivePane.View.Type = wdPrintView

  MsgBox "Completed listing Math AutoCorrect terms."
```

```
        Exit Sub

MyErrorHandler:
        MsgBox "ListMathAutoCorrect" & vbCrLf & _
            vbCrLf & "Err = " & Err.Number & _
            vbCrLf & "Description: " & Err.Description
    End Sub
```

Example 6.2. List all defined Math AutoCorrect symbols

Using a macro to add terms

You can use a macro to add your own terms. Using our earlier example, you could define an entry that replaces \am with *arteriovenous malformation*. Using Word's built-in capability to add terms can be awkward. You need to go through the AutoCorrect dialog each time, which requires several steps and interrupts your work flow. Alternately, if a word is marked as a misspelling, you can right click on that term and select the **AutoCorrect|AutoCorrect** options. This method also presents the AutoCorrect dialog, but still requires several steps. A macro can help simplify adding a new AutoCorrect term.

Example 6.3 is a macro for adding terms. To use it, you to select the term in the document, run the macro, and then enter the shortcut text when prompted.

```
Sub AddTermToAutoCorrect()
  On Error GoTo MyErrorHandler

  Dim currentDocument As Document
  Set currentDocument = ActiveDocument

  Dim autoCorrectTerm As String
  autoCorrectTerm = Selection.Text

  Dim inputBoxReturn As String
  inputBoxReturn = InputBox(prompt:="Add the shortcut notation for " & _
    autoCorrectTerm, Title:="Add to AutoCorrect", Default:="\" & _
    Left(autoCorrectTerm, 4))

  If inputBoxReturn = vbNullString Then Exit Sub

  AutoCorrect.Entries.Add inputBoxReturn, autoCorrectTerm

  Exit Sub

MyErrorHandler:
  MsgBox "AddTermToAutoCorrect" & vbCrLf & vbCrLf & _
    "Err = " & Err.Number & vbCrLf & _
    "Description: " & Err.Description
End Sub
```

Example 6.3. Add AutoCorrect terms

You can also do the reverse. Example 6.4 attempts to find the shortcut notation for the current text selection.

```
Public Sub ListBuildingBlocks()
  On Error GoTo MyErrorHandler
  Dim myTemplate As Template
  Set myTemplate = Templates(1)

  Dim targetDocument As Document
  Set targetDocument = Documents.Add

  Dim currentBuildingBlockType As Long
  For currentBuildingBlockType = 1 To myTemplate.BuildingBlockTypes.Count
    InsertText targetDocument, currentBuildingBlockType & ") " & _
    myTemplate.BuildingBlockTypes(currentBuildingBlockType).Name & _
    " (" & _
    myTemplate.BuildingBlockTypes(currentBuildingBlockType). _
      Categories.Count & ")"

    Dim j As Long
    For j = 1 To myTemplate.BuildingBlockTypes(currentBuildingBlockType). _
      Categories.Count
     InsertText targetDocument, vbTab & _
    myTemplate.BuildingBlockTypes(currentBuildingBlockType). _
      Categories(j).Name & " (" & _
      myTemplate.BuildingBlockTypes(currentBuildingBlockType). _
     Categories(j).BuildingBlocks.Count & ")"

      Dim k As Long
      For k = 1 To myTemplate.BuildingBlockTypes(currentBuildingBlockType). _
        Categories(j).BuildingBlocks.Count
       InsertText targetDocument, vbTab & vbTab & _
      myTemplate.BuildingBlockTypes(currentBuildingBlockType). _
        Categories(j).BuildingBlocks(k).Name
      DoEvents
     Next k
    DoEvents
   Next j

   DoEvents
  Next

  MsgBox "Done."

  Exit Sub

MyErrorHandler:
  MsgBox "ListBuildingBlocks" & vbCrLf & vbCrLf & _
  "Err = " & Err.Number & vbCrLf & "Description: " & _
  Err.Description
End Sub

Private Sub InsertText(whichDocument As Document, whichText As String)
  On Error GoTo MyErrorHandler
```

```
    whichDocument.Range.InsertAfter whichText
    whichDocument.Range.InsertParagraphAfter

    Exit Sub

MyErrorHandler:
    MsgBox "InsertText" & vbCrLf & vbCrLf & _
    "Err = " & Err.Number & vbCrLf & _
    "Description: " & Err.Description
End Sub
```

Example 6.4. Find AutoCorrect shortcut notation for current selection

To use the code, select the term in the document and run the macro. If there is a match between the selected text and an AutoCorrect entry, the term and the replacement key will display. Otherwise, you will be informed that no match exists.

VBA, Macros, and AutoCorrect

Recorded macros cannot be used to invoke AutoCorrect. For example, although it might seem like after running Example 6.5 AutoCorrect will replace the word with *story*, it will not.

```
Sub Macro2()
    Selection.TypeText Text:="story "
End Sub
```

Example 6.5. Incorrect AutoCorrect macro

AutoText and Building Blocks

AutoText provides the ability to insert larger blocks of text, such as pages of text, complete with graphics and bookmarks. Revised in Office 2007, AutoText is now part of the Quick Parts collection, specifically the Building Blocks gallery. Making it part of Building Blocks makes sense since it is commonly used to create parts of a document from blocks of content, such as blocks for the header, salutations, body text, closings, and footers.

AutoText doesn't exist as a separate feature anymore, although the AutoText entries from earlier Word versions are still available through the Building Blocks Organizer dialog, and there still is a label called **AutoText**. Microsoft deprecated the AutoText calls in VBA and the macro recorder so that macros recorded with AutoText functions will not work. In all other respects, AutoText can be treated like Building Blocks.

There are two key differences between AutoText/Building Blocks and AutoCorrect.

► AutoText/Building Blocks can insert a much larger amount of material. The insertion can be a word, page, several pages, or an entire report, and can include styling information and footnotes.

► Inserting Building Blocks is not automatic, like AutoCorrect is. Rather, you have to choose explicitly to make the insertion. Because of this explicit action, some users prefer AutoCorrect for smaller inserts.

Word 2003 users will be disappointed that a pop-up marker (AutoComplete display) no longer displays. In Word 2003, after typing the first four characters of the text, a tool tip-like marker will be displayed, which indicates that an insertion is available. Clicking **Enter** completed the process (see Figure 6.3).

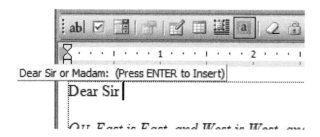

Figure 6.3. Word 2003's AutoText reminder

Word 2007 does not have that reminder, so users have to remember that one is available. This may look like an oversight on Microsoft's part, but given the sheer number of Building Blocks available, this solution is actually the cleanest of the designers' options.

Using AutoText

The following is a brief overview on using AutoText/Building Blocks. Despite the changes that happened between Word 2003 and Word 2007, the two work similarly. They still insert text (and potentially lots of it). In addition to the predefined selections, you can define selections of your own.

To start, it's important to understand that Word stores AutoText/Building Blocks in templates and not in the document itself. The text becomes available only when you attach the template that contains it. There are several ways to attach a template.

Adding Templates

You add templates through the **Templates and Add-Ins** dialog (**Developer|Templates|Document Template**). There are two kinds of templates: document templates and global templates.

Document template

A document template contains the available formatting and style information. It can also contain other material, including Building Blocks and macros. A document template is always assigned automatically when you create a document, by default using the file `Normal.dotm`. If you want another template attached instead, you can explicitly add it through the **Document Template** text box using the **Attach** button. However, if the document was created directly from a template (such as by double clicking on a template), that source template is defined as the document template. Regardless, only one template can be defined as the document template.

The default location for templates is typically *installdrive*:`\Documents and Settings\`*username*`\Application Data\Microsoft\Templates`, where *installdrive* is the drive Office was installed on, and *username* is the user's network ID name. For example, a typical path might look like this: `C:\Documents and Settings\Robert\Application Data\Microsoft\Templates`.

Global template

A global template can be used in addition to the document template. These are not "attached" as the document template is, and they will not cause format or style information to be transferred when the file is moved or copied. Any number of global templates can be explicitly or implicitly added. To explicitly add a global template, click the **Add** button of the **Global Templates and Add-Ins** panel, in the lower part of the dialog, and navigate to the template.

You can also implicitly add a global template so that it will load automatically by saving the template file in the Word Startup Folder: *installdrive*: `\Documents and Settings\`*username*`\Application Data\Microsoft\Word\STARTUP`, where *installdrive* is the drive the Windows system was installed on, and *username* is the user's network ID name.

Both of these folders can be redefined to a new location. If you need to verify these locations, click the Office icon|**Word Options|Advanced|General|File Locations**.

Document building blocks template

Some Building Blocks can be stored in a special template, `Building Blocks.dotx`. This template can not be loaded as a conventional template. However, all the Building Blocks are available to the opened documents and represent a global cache. To move the Building Blocks to another computer, copy it from *installdrive*: `\Program Files\Microsoft Office\Office12\Document Parts\1033` to the same location on the other computer. Looking through the **Quick Parts Organizer** dialog items (**Insert|Text|Quick PartsBuilding Blocks Organizer**), you can see how many are defined in `Building Blocks.dotx`.

Inserting Text

There are three ways to insert text for use with AutoText/Building Blocks.

Building Block organizer

The Building Block Organizer dialog (**Insert|Text|Quick Parts**, see Figure 6.4) provides the complete list of available items. As you highlight an item, it displays in the preview screen on the right side. To insert a Building Block from the list, double click the item or highlight it and click **Insert**.

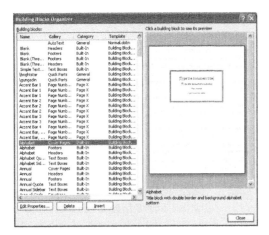

Figure 6.4. The Building Blocks Organizer dialog.

Quick Parts Selection

You can make a selection from the Quick Parts gallery (**Insert|Text|Quick Parts**, see Figure 6.5). Building Blocks that have been saved as the Quick Parts type will be displayed in a gallery before the remaining menu items. It's possible that no selections have been saved as Quick Parts, so there may not be a gallery drop-down list. If there is a gallery selection, you can insert the Quick Part by choosing it from the gallery list directly. Some users don't like saving items as Quick Parts since displaying them in a gallery slows down the menu as well as cluttering it.

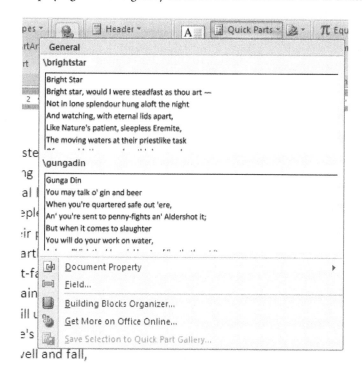

Figure 6.5. Custom added AutoText in the Quick parts menu.

Entering the Name

As you see from the Building Block Organizer dialog (**Insert|Text|Quick Parts**, see Figure 6.4) each building block has a name. You can insert the building block by not using the Building Block Organizer dialog or the Quick Parts gallery. Instead, in the document you can type the building block name, selecting that name or having the cursor in the name, and then pressing **F3**.

You must be careful to enter enough of the AutoText/Building Blocks name to uniquely identify it. For example, *Pu* is not enough to make any default building blocks uniquely identifiable since there are several names that begin with *Pu*. *Puzzle* would be uniquely identifiable. Some names are more than one word, and those also have to be unique, such as *Puzzle Qu* for *Puzzle Quote*.

Word 2007 and later do not indicate whether an entry is valid or not. If it's not a valid name clicking **F3** displays a message in the status bar: "The specified text is not a valid building block name." If the typed text is not sufficient to be unique (that is, there are two or more entries with that part of the name), the message will be, "The specified text is not a unique building block name. Provide a unique name." In that case either keep typing or select another insertion method.

Defining Building Blocks

Word comes with set of default selections, but you can always add your own. Procedure 6.5 shows how to define a new Building Block:

Procedure 6.5. Define a new Building Block

1. Create at least one example of the material to insert. This can be a graphic, text, element, or page layout.

2. Select the entire example.

3. From **Insert|Text|Quick Parts**, choose **Save Selection to Quick Part Gallery**. This displays the Create New Building Block dialog (see Figure 6.6).

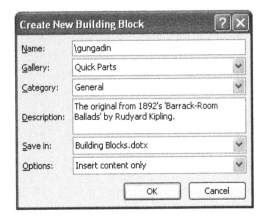

Figure 6.6. The Create New Building Block dialog.

4. Enter descriptive text for the categories:

    ► The **Name** is the text Word uses to identify the replacement name used with the **F3** key to insert the block.

    ► A **Gallery** is a grouping that associates the building block with its function. You may want to remember which grouping it's in; this becomes important when working with macros and VBA code.

    ► **Category** is just a reminder for you. You can create **Categories** as you need them.

    ► **Save in** specifies the template the building block gets stored in. A drop-down menu lists the valid templates that you can store the block in. In some cases a template must already have at least one AutoText/Building Block saved in it before Word will recognize it as a valid **Save in** location. If you think the template is in the correct location, but it is not in the list, you will need to open a document based on that template (by double clicking the template), add an entry, save, and close it. It should then be displayed in the **Save in** drop-down.

    ► **Options** selects how to inset the Building Block. You can keep the default (**Insert Content Only**), which just pastes the building block's items into the insert point, or change it to another selection. For example, selecting **Insert content in its own page** will paste items on a separate, new page.

5.   Click **OK**. The item is now saved.

Macros and VBA

Support for recording macros that include Building Blocks is minimal. To save a few mouse clicks for defining a selection, you might want to record a sequence that saves and names the selection as a Building Block. For example using Procedure 6.5, record a macro starting with Step 3 (after having selected the text), and choosing a different Gallery. The result is Example 6.6, but the operations within the dialog box are not recorded. The saved selection goes into the gallery.

```
Sub DefineAutoText ()
    WordBasic.CreateCommonFieldBlockFromSel Description:=""
End Sub
```

Example 6.6. Recorded macro for saving a Building Block

Example 6.7 is a workaround that creates and names the selected text as an AutoText. As a default it suggests the first three words as the Name. This may not always be want you want, so you are prompted to enter the name yourself. It then adds the AutoText to the attached template.

```
Sub DefineAutoText()
  On Error GoTo MyErrorHandler

  Dim currentDocument As Document
  Set currentDocument = ActiveDocument

  Dim defaultName As String
  If Selection.Range.Words.Count >= 3 Then
    defaultName = Trim(currentDocument.Range( _
    Selection.Range.Words(1).Start, _
    Selection.Range.Words(3).End))
  Else
    defaultName = "(Enter the QuickParts Name)"
  End If

  Dim nameString As String
  nameString = InputBox(prompt:= _
    "Enter a name for this Quick Part", _
    Title:="Define New Quick Part", Default:=defaultName)

  If nameString = vbNullString Then Exit Sub

  Dim myTemplate As Template
  Set myTemplate = NormalTemplate

  Dim myNewBuildingBlock As Word.BuildingBlock
  Set myNewBuildingBlock = _
    myTemplate.BuildingBlockEntries.Add(Name:=nameString, _
    Type:=wdTypeQuickParts, Category:="General", _
    Range:=Selection.Range)
```

```
    Exit Sub

MyErrorHandler:
  MsgBox "DefineAutoText" & vbCrLf & vbCrLf & _
  "Err = " & Err.Number & vbCrLf & _
  "Description: " & Err.Description
End Sub
```

Example 6.7. Macro to create and name selected text as an AutoText

Listing Building Blocks

You can see a list of all the available Building Blocks through the **Building Blocks Organizer** dialog, but there are times when it might be convenient to have a separate list. For that, Example 6.8 creates a list in another document.

```
Public Sub ListBuildingBlocks()
  On Error GoTo MyErrorHandler
  Dim myTemplate As Template
  Set myTemplate = Templates(1)

  Dim targetDocument As Document
  Set targetDocument = Documents.Add

  Dim currentBlockType As Long
  For currentBlockType = 1 To myTemplate.BuildingBlockTypes.Count
  InsertText targetDocument, currentBlockType & ") " & _
  myTemplate.BuildingBlockTypes(currentBlockType).Name & _
  " (" & _
  myTemplate.BuildingBlockTypes(currentBlockType). _
    Categories.Count & ")"

  Dim j As Long
  Dim k As Long
  For j = 1 To myTemplate.BuildingBlockTypes( _
        currentBlockType).Categories.Count
    InsertText targetDocument, vbTab & _
    myTemplate.BuildingBlockTypes(currentBlockType). _
     Categories(j).Name & " (" & _
     myTemplate.BuildingBlockTypes(currentBlockType). _
     Categories(j).BuildingBlocks.Count & ")"

    For k = 1 To myTemplate.BuildingBlockTypes( _
        currentBlockType).Categories(j).BuildingBlocks.Count
      InsertText targetDocument, vbTab & vbTab & _
      myTemplate.BuildingBlockTypes(currentBlockType). _
      Categories(j).BuildingBlocks(k).Name

      DoEvents
    Next k
    DoEvents
  Next j
  DoEvents
  Next
```

```
  MsgBox "Done."
  Exit Sub

MyErrorHandler:
  MsgBox "ListBuildingBlocks" & vbCrLf & vbCrLf & _
    "Err = " & Err.Number & vbCrLf & "Description:  " & _
    Err.Description
End Sub

Private Sub InsertText(whichDocument As Document, whichText As String)
  On Error GoTo MyErrorHandler

  whichDocument.Range.InsertAfter whichText
  whichDocument.Range.InsertParagraphAfter

  Exit Sub

MyErrorHandler:
  MsgBox "InsertText" & vbCrLf & vbCrLf & _
    "Err = " & Err.Number & vbCrLf & _
    "Description: " & Err.Description
End Sub
```

Example 6.8. Create list in another document

Using VBA to Insert an Entry

You can also find text inside a Building Block. Example 6.9 searches for a word or phrase and shows you the name of the block it was first found in. There is a limitation: the text must be in the first 255 characters of the building block. This macro may be helpful if you don't use Building Blocks frequently enough to remember all the text in the blocks.

```
Public Sub FindTextInBuildingBlocks()
  Dim theCount As Long
  Dim myDisplayTemplate As Template
  For Each myDisplayTemplate In Templates
    theCount = theCount + 1
    Debug.Print theCount & ") " & myDisplayTemplate.FullName
    DoEvents
  Next
  Debug.Print " "

  Dim displayString As String
  displayString = vbNullString

  Dim findText As String
  findText = InputBox(prompt:="Enter part of the text to find", _
    Title:="Find Text in Building Block")
  If findText = vbNullString Then Exit Sub

  Dim myTemplate As Template
  Dim templateCount As Long
  For templateCount = 1 To ActiveDocument.Application.Templates.Count
    Set myTemplate = Templates(templateCount)
```

```
      Dim currentBuildingBlockType As Long
      For currentBuildingBlockType = 1 _
        To myTemplate.BuildingBlockTypes.Count

        Dim j As Long
        For j = 1 _
          To myTemplate.BuildingBlockTypes(currentBuildingBlockType). _
            Categories.Count

          Dim k As Long
          Dim myBuildingBlock As BuildingBlock
          For k = 1 _
            To myTemplate.BuildingBlockTypes(currentBuildingBlockType). _
              Categories(j).BuildingBlocks.Count

            Set myBuildingBlock = _
              myTemplate.BuildingBlockTypes(currentBuildingBlockType). _
                Categories(j).BuildingBlocks(k)

            If InStr(myBuildingBlock.Value, findText) > 0 Then
              displayString = displayString & myBuildingBlock.Name & vbCrLf
              Exit For
            End If

          DoEvents
          Next k
        DoEvents
        Next j
        DoEvents
      Next
    Next

    If displayString <> vbNullString Then
        MsgBox "The string '" & findText & _
        "' was  found in the following Building Blocks: " & _
        vbCrLf & vbCrLf & displayString
      Else
        MsgBox "The string '" & findText & "' was not found."
      End If

End Sub
```

Example 6.9. Find name of block containing a word or phrase

Listing All the Quick Parts Entries

To print the names of all the available Quick Parts, run Example 6.10.

```
Public Sub ListBuildingBlockItems()
  On Error GoTo MyErrorHandler

  Dim myTemplate As Template

  Dim targetDocument As Document
  Set targetDocument = Documents.Add

  Dim MyBuildingBlockItem As Long
  Dim myCategory As Long
  Dim myBuildingBlockType As BuildingBlockType
  Dim templateCount As Integer
  For templateCount = 1 To ActiveDocument.Application.Templates.Count
    Set myTemplate = ActiveDocument.Application.Templates(templateCount)
    ActiveDocument.Application.StatusBar = templateCount & _
      " of " & myTemplate.BuildingBlockTypes.Count

    Set myBuildingBlockType = _
      myTemplate.BuildingBlockTypes(wdTypeQuickParts)

    If myBuildingBlockType.Categories.Count < 0 Then
      targetDocument.Range.InsertAfter "Template: " & myTemplate.Name
      targetDocument.Range.InsertParagraphAfter

      targetDocument.Range.InsertAfter vbTab & myBuildingBlockType.Name
      targetDocument.Range.InsertParagraphAfter

      For myCategory = 1 To myBuildingBlockType.Categories.Count
        targetDocument.Range.InsertAfter vbTab & _
        vbTab & myBuildingBlockType.Categories(myCategory).Name & _
        " (" & _
        myBuildingBlockType.Categories(myCategory).BuildingBlocks.Count _
        & ")" & targetDocument.Range.InsertParagraphAfter

        For MyBuildingBlockItem = 1 _
          To myBuildingBlockType.Categories(myCategory).BuildingBlocks.Count
            targetDocument.Range.InsertAfter vbTab & bTab & vbTab & _
            myBuildingBlockType.Categories(myCategory). _
              BuildingBlocks(MyBuildingBlockItem).Name
            targetDocument.Range.InsertParagraphAfter

          DoEvents
      Next MyBuildingBlockItem
      DoEvents
    Next
  End If
  Next

  MsgBox "Completed listing Building Blocks"
  Exit Sub
```

```
MyErrorHandler:
    MsgBox "ListBuildingBlockItems" & vbCrLf & _
        vbCrLf & "Err = " & Err.Number & _
        vbCrLf & "Description: " & Err.Description
End Sub
```

Example 6.10. Print names of all available Quick Parts

Listing All the AutoText Entries

If you want a separate listing of only the AutoText entries, run Example 6.11. It creates a new document and lists the AutoText names.

```
Public Sub SeeAutoText()
  On Error GoTo MyErrorHandler

  Set myTemplate = Templates(1)

  Dim targetDocument As Document
  Set targetDocument = Documents.Add

  theCount = 0
  Dim myAutoText As AutoTextEntry
  For Each myAutoText In myTemplate.AutoTextEntries
    theCount = theCount + 1
    'Debug.Print theCount & ") " & myAutoText.Name

    InsertText targetDocument, myAutoText.Name
    DoEvents
  Next
  MsgBox "Completed listing AutoText"
  Exit Sub

MyErrorHandler:
  MsgBox "SeeAutoText" & vbCrLf & vbCrLf & _
    "Err = " & Err.Number & vbCrLf & _
    "Description: " & Err.Description
End Sub

Private Sub InsertText(whichDocument As Document, whichText As String)
  On Error GoTo MyErrorHandler
  whichDocument.Range.InsertAfter whichText
  whichDocument.Range.InsertParagraphAfter
  Exit Sub

MyErrorHandler:
  MsgBox "InsertText" & vbCrLf & vbCrLf & _
    "Err = " & Err.Number & vbCrLf & _
    "Description: " & Err.Description
End Sub
```

Example 6.11. Create new document and list AutoText names

Sharing AutoText/Building Blocks

After creating the entries you need, the next logical step is to share them with others. All the entries so far have been local to your machine, and need to be in predefined folders. Distributing an updated document that must be stored in a predefined folder on each team member's computer is awkward, and likely prohibitively so. A much more convenient method is to use Word's start-up folder. Remember, any template found here will be used as a global template as well as a Building Blocks source. Procedure 6.6 shows how to use this folder.

Procedure 6.6. Using Word's start-up folder to distribute a Building Blocks template

1. Place the Building Blocks source template in a commonly accessible folder, such as a network share.

2. Open the Word startup folder. This location changes slightly depending on your computer and your version of Windows. Here's how to find the folder. Click the Office logo|**Word Options|Advanced** and click the **Files Location button**. The folder is listed as Start Up. Note that location and open it through the Explorer.

3. Right click and drag the Building Blocks source template to the Start Up folder. Select **Create Shortcuts Here**. This makes a shortcut to the file location. Close all Word documents. When a document is opened, the Building Blocks from that template will be available.

This shortcut method works only with the Start Up folder; it does not work with any other Building Blocks sources in other folders. Once each team member has done this, you can update all team members at one time by changing this one file.

Summary

Building Blocks are designed to help you enter large amounts of data, formatted data, or both as conveniently as possible. They save time, typing, and typos, and along with extensive set of features or combined with VBA, they can form powerful tools.

7

Smart Tags

Smart Tags, introduced in Office XP, are an under-appreciated productivity tool. Smart Tags automatically recognize words or phrases, marking them with a purple underline similar to misspelling or grammar markings. Clicking on the underlined term displays a popup menu of shortcuts to various actions that you can define. Microsoft originally pitched Smart Tags as a way to associate things like customer names, telephone numbers, or stock prices with related information, like a link to a stock page or the Outlook address book. They can also initiate a more complex action, such as adding the selected person's name to a phone list.

Smart Tags can be considered an automation technique since they can help identify large amounts of information quickly and then perform actions on that information. This chapter starts with an overview of Smart Tags and a technical description of their anatomy. This is followed by a description of how to create simple but productive Smart Tags. The chapter concludes with a discussion about deploying Smart Tags to users.

Understanding Smart Tags

To understand what Smart Tags can do, it may be best to see some. Microsoft Office provides a small but representative set of Smart Tags that are included by default from the installation. Procedure 7.1 describes how to show one of these sets.

Procedure 7.1. View a Smart Tag set

1. Start Smart Tags using Procedure 7.3 or Procedure 7.4.

2. Check the tags you want to use. In this example, check **Person Name (English)**. This Smart Tags set is used to recognize people's names.

3. Click **OK** to close the dialog.

4. In the document, enter a person's name, say *John Kennedy*. A purple underline will appear. Given the wide range of possible names, Smart Tags may not detect all of them. For example, it recognizes most American presidents, including *Millard Fillmore* and *Lyndon B. Johnson* (noted here for the relatively uncommon first names) but not *Chester Arthur*, *Grover Cleveland*, or *Dwight D. Eisenhower*.

5. Click on the Smart Tag Action symbol (**i**) to see the available actions (Figure 7.1).

Figure 7.1. Available actions from Smart Tag Action pop-up menu

Smart Tags can also be used with calculations. Procedure 7.2 converts measurements.

Procedure 7.2. Convert measurements with Smart Tags

1. Activate Measurement Converter (Procedure 7.3 or Procedure 7.4, but click **Measurement Converter (Measurement Converter)**). Multiple Smart Tags can be active at the same time, so you don't have to uncheck currently selected ones.

2. Click **OK** to close the dialog.

3. In the document type: `7 miles`.

The Smart Tag now displays the conversion to metric, in this case *11.27 kilometers* (see Figure 7.2). If you select the converted value, Word will replace *7 miles* with *11.27 kilometers* in your text.

Figure 7.2. Result of metric conversion

The list of supported conversions is extensive and includes lengths, volumes, and temperatures. There is a help file with information about conversions in the following locations:

▶ Windows XP/Vista: `C:/Program Files/Common Files/Microsoft Shared/Smart Tag/1033/mcabout.htm`.

▶ Windows 7: `C:/Program Files (x86)/Common Files/Microsoft Shared/Smart Tag/1033/mcabout.htm`.

Managing Smart Tags

Smart Tags have a series of controls that allow different options for display and use.

Turning Smart Tags On or Off

To turn Smart Tags on or off, use one of the following methods (see Procedure 7.3 or Procedure 7.4).

Procedure 7.3. Turn Smart Tags on and off

1. Open a document if one is not already opened. Click **Office icon** and then click **Word Options**.

2. Click **Add-Ins** in the left column.

3. From the **Manage** drop-down list select **Smart Tags**, and then click **Go**. The **AutoCorrect** dialog displays (see Figure 7.3). This displays the same **Smart Tags** dialog information as Procedure 7.4.

4. Check **Label text with Smart Tags** to turn Smart Tags on; uncheck this to turn them off.

5. Check the Smart Tags you want to use; uncheck the Smart Tags you don't want active.

6. Click **OK** to close the dialog.

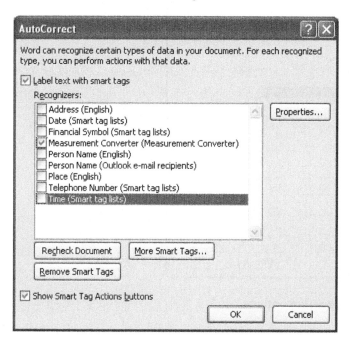

Figure 7.3. Smart Tags dialog add-ins options

Procedure 7.4. Turn Smart Tags on and off – alternate method

1. Open a document if one is not already opened. Click **Office icon** and then click **Word Options**.

2. Click **Proofing** in the left column.

3. Click the **AutoCorrect Options** button. This displays the **AutoCorrect** dialog (see Figure 7.4).

4. Select **Smart Tags** tab.

5. Check **Label text with Smart Tags** to turn Smart Tags on; uncheck this to turn them off.

6. Check the Smart Tags you want to use; uncheck the Smart Tags you don't want active.

7. Click **OK** to close the dialog.

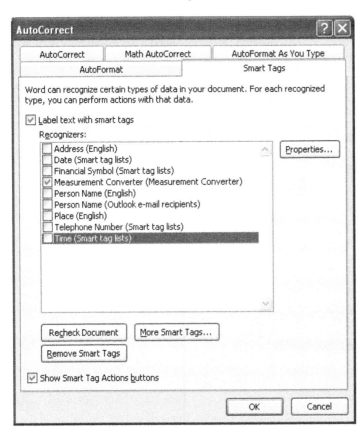

Figure 7.4. Smart Tags dialog proofing options

Showing or Hiding Smart Tag Marks

You can have Smart Tags on but suppress the purple underlines if you find them distracting. The information symbol still displays when you hover the mouse over the text. To turn off the purple underlines, use Procedure 7.5.

Procedure 7.5. Suppress Smart Tags underlining

1. Click the **Office icon** and then click **Word Options**.

2. Click **Advanced**. In the Show document content section, check **Show Smart Tags on or off**.

Showing or Hiding Smart Tag Actions Buttons

You can suppress the display of the information symbol when hovering over the Smart Tagged item. This allows the word or phrase to still be underlined, identifying it as tagged selection but you will be unable to perform the associated actions. To turn off the information marker, use procedure Procedure 7.6.

Procedure 7.6. Turn Off Smart Tags information marker

1. Click the **Office icon** and then click **Word Options**.

2. Click **Proofing**, and then click the **AutoCorrect Options** button. The **AutoCorrect** dialog box displays.

3. Select the **Smart Tags** tab. Check or clear the **Show Smart Tag Actions Button** check box.

Suppressing the information button and hiding Smart Tag purple line would be like having Smart Tags turned off, except Word is still using computer time to find the phrase.

Saving or Discarding Smart Tags

You can save the Smart Tag actions and information within the document. If you think that others will not have the same set of Smart Tags, then embedding them allows others to use those tags. This increases the file size, but you can remove the tagged information at a later time. To save the Smart Tag set in the document, use Procedure 7.7

Procedure 7.7. Save Smart Tag set in the document

1. Click the **Office icon** and then click **Word Options**.

2. Click **Advanced**.

3. Under **Preserve fidelity when sharing this document**, check **Embed smart tags**.

Saving Smart Tags as XML

If you want to save the document as a Web page, the Smart Tags have to be saved as XML. This works for Microsoft Internet Explorer 5 or later, but other browsers may not support this feature. To save the Smart Tag set as XML use Procedure 7.8

Procedure 7.8. Save Smart Tag set as XML

1. Click the **Office icon** and then click **Word Options**.

2. Click **Advanced**.

3. In the **Preserve fidelity when sharing this document** section, check **Save Smart Tags as XML properties in Web pages**.

Removing Download URLs from Smart Tags

Sometimes a Smart Tag will contain private or company URLs. For documents created in Word 2007 you can remove this information from the Smart Tag labels by using the Document Inspector option. To remove proprietary the Smart Tag information use Procedure 7.9.

Procedure 7.9. Remove proprietary Smart Tag information

1. For documents created in Word 2007 or later, use the **Document Inspector** option.

2. Click the **Microsoft Office** icon.

3. Click **Prepare**.

4. Select **Inspect Document**.

5. Check **Document Properties and Personal Information**. Other options may also be selected.

6. Click **Inspect**. This runs the selected tests and then displays the **Document Inspector** dialog.

7. Select and follow screen instructions. For example, if there is personal information, then click **Remove All** to clean the document.

To remove proprietary information from documents created in versions of Word 2003 or earlier, use Procedure 7.10.

Procedure 7.10. Remove proprietary Smart Tag information from Office 2003 documents

1. Click the **Office icon** and then click **Word Options**.

2. Click **TrustCenter**, then click the **Trust Center Settings** button.

3. Click **Privacy Options**.

4. In the **Document-specific settings** section, select or clear the **Remove personal information from file properties on save** check box.

Removing Smart Tags

Procedure 7.11 removes a single type of Smart Tag from a document

Procedure 7.11. Remove a single type of Smart Tags from a document

1. Move the cursor to the tagged text so that the **Smart Tag Actions** button appears.

2. Click the **Smart Tag actions** button, and then click **Remove this Smart Tag**. This removes all occurrences of that specific Smart Tag word from the document.

Procedure 7.12 removes all Smart Tags from a document. This includes Smart Tags you may no longer use and Smart Tags introduced if the document was opened on someone else's computer. You cannot undo this action.

Procedure 7.12. Remove all Smart Tags from a document

1. Click the **Office icon** and then click **Word Options**.

2. Click **Proofing**, and then click the **AutoCorrect Options** button.

3. Click **Smart Tags** tab.

4. Click **Remove Smart Tags**. You will be asked to confirm the removal.

Re-applying Smart Tags

If you removed or stopped the recognition of Smart Tags, you can add them back into the document. This is similar to reapplying a spell check after you've marked the document once. However, only Smart Tags currently installed on your computer will be added back. Smart Tags introduced from another computer will not be added. To add Smart Tags back into a document, use Procedure 7.13.

Procedure 7.13. Reapply Smart Tags

1. Click the **Office icon** and then click **Word Options**.

2. Click **Proofing**, and then click the **AutoCorrect Options** button.

3. Click **Smart Tags** tab.

4. In the **Recognizers** list, check the recognizers you want to use

5. Click **Recheck Document** to refresh and to reapply the Smart Tags you want to keep in your document.

Using Smart Tags

The following are examples of using Smart Tags. For instance, open a document and start Smart Tags. While in the **AutoCorrect** dialog, check **Financial Symbols**. In the document, enter a stock symbol, such as MSFT. After a moment, the Smart Tags purple underline displays (see Figure 7.5).

e·these·galleries·to·insert·tables,·header:
ocks.·"I'll·check·my·MSFT·stock·price,·wh
iate·with·your·current·document·look ·Yc

Figure 7.5. Smart Tags highlighting

Figure 7.6. Smart Tags pop-up menu

Hover over or select the purple underline and the Smart Tag Actions icon displays. Click on that symbol and a pop-up menu displays (Figure 7.6).

Those options are generally in two parts. The first set of controls, down to the first separator line, relate to information about the symbol. Here, you can check the stock price or get information about the company. These actions are defined by the Smart Tag and give Smart Tags their usefulness. The other controls, everything below the first separator line, are about the Smart Tag itself and let you perform actions like turning the Smart Tag on or off.

Making Your Own Smart Tags

There are several ways to create your own Smart Tags without programming or writing any code. The Microsoft Office Smart Tag List (MOSTL) is an XML-based smart list that offers a good deal of flexibility. It is a quick way to create and to test Smart Tags.

With MOSTL, you can have up to 100,000 terms, and if that's not enough, you can use regular expressions. Regular expressions can find detailed and complex text patterns (see the section titled "Regular Expressions" (p. 63) for more).

MOSTL has limitations, and MOSTL-generated tags are not as versatile as programmatically developed ones. For example, MOSTL-based Smart Tags actions are limited to accessing Web sites only. More complex features, such as sharing information with other applications (Procedure 7.1 (p. 137)) or replacing text (Procedure 7.2 (p. 138)) cannot be accomplished with MOSTL tags.

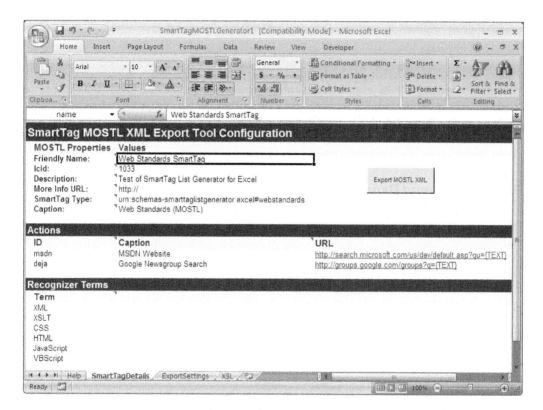

Figure 7.7. `SmartTagMOSTLGenerator.xlt`

Getting Started

The easiest way to start is by demonstrating an idealized MOSTL implementation where the set of terms is static (that is, the set of items to find doesn't need to be frequently updated), and the number of actions is restricted. This kind of implementation, once deployed, can remain on the client machine with little or no maintenance.

Chris Kunick (http://www.officezealot.com) created an Excel spreadsheet, `SmartTagMOSTLGenerator.xlt` (see Figure 7.7), that provides a simple method for creating MOSTL Smart Tags. You can download a version from this book's Web site.[8] The directions provided on the spreadsheet's Help tab are good; read them before you use the tool.

The tool consists of three parts:

▶ **Recognizer terms:** The **Recognizer Terms** part, at the bottom of the screen, is a list of the terms you want recognized. Add the terms, one per row in this section.

▶ **Actions:** The **Actions** part, in the middle of the screen, defines the actions. In the MOSTL version, actions are limited to viewing Web sites or using URLs. The special token {TEXT} gets replaced with the actual term. In this way, you can write a Web search, for example:

```
http://groups.google.com/groups?q={TEXT}
```

So, if the selected text was *Smart Tags*, the URL becomes

```
http://groups.google.com/groups?q=Smart Tags
```

▶ **Smart Tag MOSTL XML export tool configuration:** The **Smart Tag MOSTL XML Export Tool Configuration** panel, at the top, is for administration of the project. The **Friendly Name**, **Description**, **More Info URL**, and **Caption** options are informational and can be filled in as you wish. However, the **Smart Tag Type** requires a different ending, after the pound sign (#), and it should be unique among all the Smart Tag files (just not the one you're currently creating).

File Locations and Deploying Smart Tags

The Smart Tag files must be in certain locations to be recognized. Unfortunately, this means they can't be shared from a common location, such as a company network share. Instead, all Smart Tags and any supporting data files must be located on each user's computer. Simply copying the files there is sufficient, but you must close all Word instances and documents, then restart Word for changes to take effect. The location of Smart Tags files changes with the Windows version:

Windows XP\Vista:

```
C:\Program Files\Common Files\Microsoft Shared\Smart Tag\Lists
```

Windows 7:

```
C:\Program Files (x86)\Common Files\Microsoft Shared\Smart Tag\Lists
```

I will use the notation `%SmartTagFolder%` to identify this location. Replace `%SmartTagFolder%` with the location that matches your version of Windows. Subfolders may be specified in the procedures, for example, `C:\Program Files\Common Files\Microsoft Shared\Smart Tag\Lists\1033`. In that case, the notation would be: `%SmartTagFolder%\1033`.

Some paths may specify a numbered folder, such as `%SmartTagFolder%\Lists\1033`. These folders are language specific (1033 is the internal Windows code for American English). Computers may have a differently named folder depending on the languages set for Windows. They may also have more than one language folder.

To generate a MOSTL list, use Procedure 7.14.

Procedure 7.14. Generate a MOSTL list

1. Double click `SmartTagMOSTLGenerator.xlt`. This creates a new spreadsheet.

2. Use the default values without modification. If you're using the spreadsheet for the first time, check the target directory location. This is the **Directory** cell in the **ExportSettings** tab. This should be the path name from File Locations for your Windows version. `SmartTagMOSTLGenerator.xlt` uses the Windows XP/Vista value by default.

3. Add your terms in the **Recognizer Terms** section of the **SmartTagDetails** tab. The example already has six terms, but you can add your own. Enter one term per row.

4. Click the **Export MOSTL XML** button on the **SmartTagsDetails** tab. The spreadsheet creates a new file (the name is based on the value of `Friendly Name` defined in the **Directory** cell of the application).

5. Quit all instances of Word. Open a document and enter one of the terms. Word displays the Smart Tag information symbol displays, along with the actions.

Writing XML

The real excitement of all this is when you open the file to change the XML. Since these files are XML, you can open the ones that come with Windows for more examples. These can be found starting at `%SmartTagFolder%\Lists` and include the 1033 folder (or the folder for your language code, if you are not using American English).

To look at the code, open the file you just created (`%SmartTagFolder%\Lists\Web Standards SmartTag.xml`) with any text editor (such as NotePad) or a code editor. At this point you may not understand all of the XML elements and attributes; they will be described later. The XML it generates (see Example 7.1) isn't formatted in any useful way:

```
<?xml version="1.0" encoding="UTF-16"?>
<FL:smarttaglist xmlns:FL="urn:schemas-microsoft-com:smarttags:list">
<FL:name>Web Standards SmartTag</FL:name><FL:lcid>1033</FL:lcid>
<FL:description>Test of SmartTag List Generator for Excel
</FL:description><FL:moreinfourl>http://</FL:moreinfourl>
<FL:smarttag type="urn:schemas-smarttaglistgenerator:excel#webstandards">
<FL:caption>Web Standards (MOSTL)</FL:caption><FL:terms><FL:termlist
>XML,XSLT,CSS,HTML,JavaScript,VBScript,</FL:termlist></FL:terms><FL:
actions><FL:action id="msdn"><FL:caption>MSDN Website</FL:caption>
<FL:url>http://search.microsoft.com/us/dev/default.
asp?qu={TEXT}
</FL:url></FL:action><FL:action id="deja"><FL:caption>Google
Newsgroup search</FL:caption><FL:url>http://groups.google.com/groups?
q={TEXT}</FL:url></FL:action>
</FL:actions></FL:smarttag>
</FL:smarttaglist>
```

Example 7.1. MOSTL generated code sample

Example 7.2 contains a more readable form of this file after manually formatting it.

```
<?xml version="1.0" encoding="UTF-8"?>
<FL:smarttaglist xmlns:FL="urn:schemas-microsoft-com:smarttags:list">
  <FL:name>
    Web Standards SmartTag
  </FL:name>
  <FL:lcid>
    1033
  </FL:lcid>
  <FL:description>
    Test of SmartTag List Generator for Excel
  </FL:description>
  <FL:moreinfourl>
    http://www.company-site.cod
  </FL:moreinfourl>
  <FL:smarttag type="urn:schemas-smarttaglistgenerator:excel#webstandards">
    <FL:caption>
      Web Standards (MOSTL)
    </FL:caption>
    <FL:terms>
      <FL:termlist>                         ❶
        XML,XSLT,CSS,HTML,JavaScript,VBScript
      </FL:termlist>
    </FL:terms>
    <FL:actions>
      <FL:action id="msdn">
        <FL:caption>
          MSDN Website
        </FL:caption>
        <FL:url>
          http://search.microsoft.com/us/dev/default.asp?qu={TEXT}
        </FL:url>
      </FL:action>
      <FL:action id="deja">
        <FL:caption>
          Google Newsgroup Search
        </FL:caption>
        <FL:url>
          http://groups.google.com/groups?q={TEXT}
        </FL:url>
      </FL:action>
    </FL:actions>
  </FL:smarttag>
</FL:smarttaglist>
```

Example 7.2. Formatted MOSTL generated code sample

❶   You can add or change terms by changing the contents of the `<FL:termlist>` element. Try this by adding the following terms: "VBA, VB6, Word, Excel," (the comma at the end of the list is optional). Save the file, quit Word, and reopen the document. Enter those terms and they will be underlined.

Here are some rules for term lists:

► Differences in white space are ignored. Spaces, tabs, and carriage returns all convert to a conventional space character. In addition, the interpreter ignores the number of white spaces. Two or more white spaces are treated the same as a single space.

► Terms are case insensitive. The terms *XML* and *xml* convert the same. To include a case sensitive term, use double quotes (""). Anything inside double quotes will be treated literally. Therefore, *"XML"* matches only *XML* and not *xml*. Part of the term can use double quotes. *"e.e." cummings* would match only lower case *e.e.* but any case for *cummings*, such as *e.e. Cummings* or *e.e. cuMMings* but *not E.E. Cummings*.

Using a Term List File

The `<FL:termlist>` element may be used for as many as 5,000 terms, but obviously, handling that many in line will be difficult. For large lists, you can use an external file. This is a separate file of terms that can be maintained independently from the XML. The next section describes the Smart Tags SDK (software development kit), which you will need to use to create a separate file of terms.

Getting the Smart Tags SDK

A software development kit (SDK) is a collection of tools, samples, and documentation required to write software. The Smart Tags SDK includes a detailed explanation of the internals for Smart Tags. While most SDKs are for programmers, which is out-of-scope for this book, this kit is different, since there's so much about XML that doesn't require extensive programming knowledge.

You can download the SDK from Microsoft.[10] or search their site for "Smart Tag Software Development Kit." To install the SDK, open the download installer (`mstagsdk.msi`), then read and accept the license agreement. By default, the SDK installs in the `%SmartTagFolder%\Microsoft Office 2003 Developer Resources` folder. After installing, go to that folder, and open the Tools folder. Inside are two files, `maketrie.exe` (makes the compiled list) and `testtrie.exe` (tests or decompiles a list). These applications are useful, but far from perfect, so, you may occasionally get odd error messages.

Generating the final term list file is broken down into three steps: creating the term list, compiling the term list, and adding the term list.

Creating a term list

To make a term list, create an empty text file using a text editor like Windows Notepad. Add your terms, one term per line, with a maximum 128 characters per line. Terms follow the same rules as described earlier, with the following exceptions, suggestions, and notes:

► As a suggestion, save the file as Unicode. If you're using NotePad, the **Save As** dialog has a third set of options at the bottom, **Encoding**, which defaults to ANSI. You should select **Unicode** (not **Unicode big endian**).

► You may not have duplicate entries or empty lines, including at the end of the list. If you do, you will get an error message when you compile the file.

- ► The terms are case sensitive, even if you use quotation marks around them. That means you'll have to add separate instances of the same term for each combination of upper and lower case characters that you want to match.

- ► This is not a requirement, but when creating the list, consider whether you need to add terms for other variants, like singular and plural forms of the term.

- ► The list should be in alphabetical order. The compiler will sort the terms, but a long list in random order takes additional time.

Example 7.3 is an example of a list created using these rules:

```
Alfred Tennyson
Charles Dickens
e.e. cummings
Miguel de Cervantes Saavedra
```

Example 7.3. Short MOSTL term list

Save the file – giving it a useful name like `DeadPoets.txt` – in the `%SmartTagFolder%\Lists` folder. The path should look like `%SmartTagFolder%\Lists\DeadPoets.txt`.

Compiling a term List

The two test tools are command line applications that must be run in the DOS window, now called the command interpreter. To compile the list, use Procedure 7.15.

Procedure 7.15. Compile a MOSTL list

1. Click **Start|Run** in Windows. This opens the **Run** dialog.

2. Enter **cmd** and click **OK**. The command window opens. Assuming you used the default installation locations, compile the list by entering the following, all on one line, at the command prompt (see Figure 7.8 (p. 151)):

    ```
    "C:\Program Files\Microsoft Office 2003 Developer Resources\
    Microsoft Office 2003 Smart Tag SDK\Tools\maketrie.exe"
    "C:\Program Files\Common Files\Microsoft Shared\Smart Tag\
    Lists\DeadPoets.txt"
    ```

3. It looks formidable but the two parts break down logically. The first (`"C:\Program Files\Microsoft Office 2003 Developer Resources\Microsoft Office 2003 Smart Tag SDK\Tools\maketrie.exe"`) is a path to the tool itself, a file called `maketrie.exe`. The second (`"C:\Program Files\Common Files\Microsoft Shared\Smart Tag\Lists\DeadPoets.txt"`) is the text file just saved above. The new file compiles into the same folder as the text file.

4. Press **Return** to start the compile. Depending on the size of the term list, this may take a while, but for this example, with only four terms, it should be quick. When the command prompt returns, the file is compiled. The tool produces a lot of text that you can ignore.

5. Open the target folder, here `C:\Program Files\Common Files\Microsoft Shared\Smart Tag\Lists`. In addition to `DeadPoets.txt`, there is also a new file called `DeadPoets.bin`. If it doesn't display, force a refresh using **F5** on that active window.

```
C:\WINDOWS\system32\cmd.exe                                    _ □ ×

C:\>"C:\Program Files\Microsoft Office 2003 Developer Resources\Microsoft Office
 2003 Smart Tag SDK\Tools\maketrie.exe" "C:\Program Files\Common Files\Microsoft
Shared\Smart Tag\Lists\DeadPoets.txt"_
```

Figure 7.8. The Windows Command Processor showing the compile orders.

Adding a term list

The last operation is to insert the XML to recognize the term file. This is a one-time operation that you do not need to repeat if you edit and recompile the term list. In the file `Web Standards SmartTag.xml`, replace the lines shown in Example 7.4 with the lines shown in Example 7.5.

```
<FL:terms>
  <FL:termlist>
    XML,XSLT,CSS,HTML,JavaScript,VBScript
  </FL:termlist>
</FL:terms>
```

Example 7.4. Replacing term list with a file (first step)

```
<FL:terms>
  <FL:termFile>
    <FL:filename>
      DeadPoets.bin
    </FL:filename>
  </FL:termFile>
</FL:terms>
```

Example 7.5. Replacing term list with a file (second step)

Quit Word and reopen the document. Type *e.e. cummings* to see the Smart Tags.

Decompiling a term list

To decompile a term list, or see the terms, use Procedure 7.16.

Procedure 7.16. Decompile a MOSTL List

1. Click **Start|Run** in Windows. This opens the **Run** dialog.

2. Enter **cmd** and click **OK**. The command window opens. Assuming you used the default installation locations, enter this at the command prompt (including the quotation marks): **"C:\Program Files\Microsoft Office 2003 Developer Resources\Microsoft Office 2003 Smart Tag SDK\Tools\testtrie.exe" "C:\Program Files\Common Files\Microsoft Shared\Smart Tag\Lists\1033\STOCKS.DAT"**

The `STOCKS.DAT` file is being used here instead of the just-created `DeadPoets.bin`, since the stocks file has more names. The contents of the file will be displayed on the screen. For short files, this may be useable, but to capture the contents to a new file, use:

"C:\Program Files\Microsoft Office 2003 Developer Resources\Microsoft Office 2003 Smart Tag SDK\Tools\testtrie.exe" "C:\Program Files\Common Files\Microsoft Shared\Smart Tag\Lists\1033\STOCKS.DAT" > c:\stocks.txt

This saves the information to a file of your choosing, in this case `c:\stocks.txt`.

Regular Expressions

A term list is good at cataloging words or phrases that you know about ahead of time or can exactly identify. However, there may be times when you don't know the exact word or phrase, such as when you are looking for telephone numbers or part numbers. For those times, there are regular expressions. Unlike word matching, regular expressions match patterns, which can be quite complex.

In brief, a wildcard is a replacement for a character or set of characters. DOS users know the directory `*.doc` command, which lists all the Word documents (`.doc`) in a directory. Window users can use the same syntax in a **Save** or **Save As** dialog to list only specific files. Regular expressions take this several steps further. Instead of just `*`, regular expressions have a wide range of capabilities (see the section titled "Regular Expressions" (p. 63), for a more detailed explanation of regular expressions).

Inside Smart Tags, you can use regular expressions by replacing the `<FL:termlist>` element with the `<FL:re>` element (regular expression) and replacing the termlist with a regular expression (see Example 7.6, lines 2 – 4, and Example 7.7). The regular expression in Example 7.7 (`\d{4}`) matches a four-digit number.

```
1  <FL:terms>
2    <FL:termlist>
3       XML,XSLT,CSS,HTML,JavaScript,VBScript
4    </FL:termlist>
5  </FL:terms>
```

Example 7.6. Replacing a term list with a regular expression (first step)

```
1  <FL:terms>
2    <FL:re>
3      <FL:exp>\d{4}</FL:exp>
4    </FL:re>
5  </FL:terms>
```

Example 7.7. Replacing a term list with a regular expression (second step)

Table 7.1 contains some sample regular expressions. To use these expressions, enclose them in the `<FL:exp>` element.

Table 7.1. Regular expression examples – Smart Tags

Regular expression	Notes
`\d{3}-\d{4}`	Finds a simple phone number, such as 555-5678.
`^4[0-9]{12}(?:[0-9]{3})?$`	Finds a 16 digit VISA card number.
`((\(\d{3}\))|(\d{3}-))?`	Finds more complete phone numbers, with or without the parenthesis, such as (425) 555-1234 and 206 555-1234.
`^[0-9]{3}[\- ]?[0-9]{2}[\- ]?[0-9]{4}$`	Finds a social security number.
`^(\w+\.)*\w+@(\w+\.)+[A-Za-z]+$`	Finds a loosely fitting email address.

VBA and Smart Tags

You can use Smart Tags in macros. Example 7.8 lists the source of each Smart Tag in a document. Open a document that has at least one Smart Tag. If you're reusing a document that previously contained Smart Tags, you might want to delete all the existing ones (see Procedure 7.12 (p. 143)) since they linger even if the original text has been deleted, Open the IDE (using **ALT-F11** as a short cut for the **Developer|Visual Basic** button). In that document's project view, double click **ThisDocument**. Enter the following and run the code:

```
Public Sub SeeSmartTagsSource()
  On Error GoTo MyErrorHandler

  Dim sourceDocument As Document
  Set sourceDocument = ActiveDocument

  Dim mySmartTag As SmartTag
  For Each mySmartTag In sourceDocument.SmartTags
    Debug.Print mySmartTag.Name
  DoEvents
  Next

  Exit Sub

MyErrorHandler:
  MsgBox "SeeSmartTags" & vbCrLf & Err.Number & _
    vbCrLf & Err.Description
End Sub
```

Example 7.8. Finding the MOSTL source file

In the **Immediate** window, a list of Smart Tag names displays. Unfortunately, you can't divine much from this. Most of the useful information hides in XML, which is difficult to get to. But it's not without value. With some creative thinking, you can apply this in different ways. For example, if you had a long document and the Smart Tag identified people's names or acronyms, you could collect all those terms. Example 7.9 does just that, collecting the unique occurrences of the terms and storing them in a new document.

```
Public Sub SeeSmartTags()

  Dim sourceDocument As Document
  Set sourceDocument = ActiveDocument

  Dim nameString As String
  nameString = vbNullString

  On Error Resume Next
  Dim namesCollection As New Collection
  Dim mySmartTag As SmartTag
  For Each mySmartTag In sourceDocument.SmartTags
    namesCollection.Add mySmartTag.Range.Text, mySmartTag.Range.Text
    If Err.Number = 0 Then
    nameString = nameString & mySmartTag.Range.Text & vbCrLf
    End If

    DoEvents
  Next

  If nameString <> vbNullString Then
    Dim targetDocument As Document
    Set targetDocument = Documents.Add

    targetDocument.Range.InsertAfter nameString
  End If
End Sub
```

Example 7.9. Collecting Smart Tag text

If you have different Smart Tags on, or you want to record text from only one specific type, then you need to test the source as in Example 7.10.

```
Public Sub SeeSelectedSmartTags()
  Dim sourceDocument As Document
  Set sourceDocument = ActiveDocument

  Dim nameString As String
  nameString = vbNullString

  Dim smartTagsSource As String
  smartTagsSource = "metricconverter"   ❶
  'smartTagsSource = "PersonName"

  On Error Resume Next   ❹
  Dim namesCollection As New Collection   ❷
  Dim mySmartTag As SmartTag
  For Each mySmartTag In sourceDocument.SmartTags
    If InStr(LCase$(mySmartTag), LCase$(smartTagsSource)) > 0 Then
    namesCollection.Add mySmartTag.Range.Text, mySmartTag.Range.Text   ❸
```

```
    If Err.Number = 0 Then
      nameString = nameString & mySmartTag.Range.Text & vbCrLf
    End If
  End If

  DoEvents
  Next

  If nameString <> vbNullString Then
  Dim targetDocument As Document
  Set targetDocument = Documents.Add

  targetDocument.Range.InsertAfter nameString
  End If
End Sub
```

Example 7.10. Retrieving text from specific Smart Tags

❶   The variable smartTagsSource controls which Smart Tag is used. Two common cases are included in the code, just comment out the one you don't want.

❷   Using Smart Tags for collecting flagged text is considerably faster than using the VBA Find. For starters, Word already marks the text. Second, the Collection object, instantiated here as *namesCollection*, is more efficient than conventional arrays, and can easily filter duplicates.

❸   The Collection object filters duplicates in an odd way. The second parameter, which is optional, is called a "key", and each collection must contain unique keys.

❹   Whenever the macro attempts to add a duplicate entry, the process returns an error. That is why the On Error Resume Next statement is needed; otherwise, it would error out of the routine. This is a good example of a time when you can safely ignore an error.

You can also use the term list text file as a custom dictionary. In many cases, the term list includes words that would otherwise be identified as a misspelling, such as acronyms or part numbers. By attaching it as custom dictionary, the spell check will not flag the terms found in it. This helps with editing because it is hard to see the purple underline with the red spell check underline also showing.

To do this you will have to change the filename DeadPoets.txt to DeadPoets.dic (dictionary). If you're using **Notepad.exe** you can also save the file as Unicode using the **Save As** dialog. After changing the name, you can attach it as a dictionary through the user interface or using Example 7.11.

```
Public Sub AddCustomDictionary()
    On Error GoTo myErrorHandler

    Dim sourcePath As String
    sourcePath = "C:\Program Files\Common Files\Microsoft Shared\" & _   ❶
        "Smart Tag\Lists\"

    Dim myDictionary As Dictionary
    Set myDictionary = Application.CustomDictionaries.Add( _   ❷
        sourcePath & "DeadPoets.dic")

    Exit Sub

myErrorHandler:
    MsgBox "Err: " & Err.Number & vbCrLf & vbCrLf & _
        "Description: " & Err.Description
End Sub
```

Example 7.11. Attaching a custom dictionary from a MOSTL file

❶❷ You may need to adjust the path (sourcePath) and the filename (DeadPoets.dic) for your system.

Example 7.12 shows how to remove a custom dictionary.

```
Public Sub RemoveCustomDictionary()
    On Error GoTo myErrorHandler

    Dim sourcePath As String
    sourcePath = "C:\Program Files\Common Files\Microsoft Shared\" & _
        "Smart Tag\Lists\"

    Application.CustomDictionaries( _
    sourcePath & "DeadPoets.dic").Delete

myErrorHandler:
    MsgBox "Err: " & Err.Number & vbCrLf & vbCrLf & _
        "Description: " & Err.Description
End Sub
```

Example 7.12. Removing a Custom Dictionary

The path name and file name must be correct for your situation. Despite the use of the **Delete** command, this code only removes the file as a custom dictionary, it does not actually delete the file.

XML Reference

This section provides details about each of the Smart Tags elements used in the examples in this chapter. For a complete list, see the Smart Tags SDK, specifically the help file, `stagsdk.chm`. This file is also available online at Microsoft's MSDN site[1]. The SDK also provides additional information and programming guidelines.

You will see in the examples that each element has a prefix. For example, in the element `<FL:name>`, "FL" is the prefix. The prefix identifies a namespace for the tag.

You will see a declaration for the FL namespace as an attribute on the `<FL:smartag-list>` element:

`xmlns:FL="urn:schemas-microsoft-com:smarttags:list"`

For our purposes, as long as you leave the namespace declaration in place on the `<FL:smartaglist>` element, you don't need to worry about namespaces.

The file structure can be loosely defined into two sections: preface and body.

Preface

The preface section is information about the Smart Tag file itself.

`<smartTagList>` element

Required: Yes

The root element required for a valid Microsoft Office Smart Tag List (MOSTL) file. You can use the values from the example for Smart Tags.

Example

```
<FL:smarttaglist xmlns:FL="urn:schemas-microsoft-com:smarttags:list">
    ...
</FL:smarttaglist>
```

`<name>` element

Required: No.

A short description about what the file does. This displays in the MOSTL file only and no place else.

Example

```
<FL:name>
  Web Standards SmartTag.
  Created on the initial product release.
</FL:name>
```

---

[1] http://msdn.microsoft.com/en-us/library/bb190881%28v=office.11%29.aspx

`<caption>` element

Required: Yes.

This is the name that appears in the **Smart Tags** dialog box. There is also a `<caption>` element associated with Actions.

Example

```
<FL:caption>Medical Conditions</FL:caption>
```

`<description>` element

Required: No

A longer string that describes the function of the Smart Tag. This is a substantive and concise description of what the recognizer does. This displays in the MOSTL file only and no place else.

Example

```
<FL:description>
   A list of medical conditions for recognition,
   as well as a set of actions that work with them.
</FL:description>
```

`<moreInfoURL>` element

Required: No.

A URL where a user can find more information about this particular Smart Tag. The user interface does not display the URL.

Example

```
<FL:moreInfoURL>http://www.adatum.com/moreinfo</FL:moreInfoURL>
```

`<LCID>` element

Required: No.

Defines the language of the terms. *1033* is American English. If omitted the language defined by Microsoft Windows is used.

Example

```
</FL:lcid>1033</FL:lcid>
```

Body

The body section contains information about the terms to recognize and defines the actions. The body must contain both a `<terms>` element and an `<action>` element.

`<smartTag>` element

Required: Yes.

Encloses the definitions for the terms and actions. This element has one required attribute.

smartTag type Attribute

Required: Yes

This defines the namespace for the Smart Tag file. A namespace is a label allowing you to uniquely identify and group code. Each Smart Tags file must have a unique namespace. All subsequent Smart Tags files having the same namespace are ignored. A Smart Tag type is specified as *namespace#tagname*. *TagName* can be reused in other Smart Tags files; *namespace* cannot be.

Example

```
<FL:smartTag type="urn:schemas-adatum-com:medical#condition">
```

`<terms>` element

Required: Either `<terms>` or `<re>` is required.

A collection of terms to recognize. This contains the definition of terms recognized by this Smart Tag. The `<terms>` element must contain either a `<termlist>` or `<termfile>` element.

Example

```
<FL:terms>
  <FL:termList>
    allergy, cough, arthritis, headache, migraine,
    heartburn, high blood pressure, digestive disorder,
    cold, thyrotoxicosis, thalassemia,bloating, nausea, bronchitis
  </FL:termList>
</FL:terms>
```

`<termlist>` element

Required: `<termlist>`, `<termfile>`, or `<re>` is required.

Contains a comma-delimited list of terms which will be recognized by this Smart Tag. Also see the *MOSTL Related Exceptions* in the SDK for special cases and certain symbols representation.

Example

```
<FL:terms>
  <FL:termlist>allergy, cough, arthritis, headache, migraine,
    heartburn, high blood pressure, digestive disorder, diarrhea,
    cold, thyrotoxicosis, thalassemia, bloating, nausea, bronchitis
  </FL:termlist>
</FL:terms>
```

`<termfile>` element

Required: Either `<termlist>`, or `<termfile>` is required.

This specifies that a term file will be used, rather than a term list.

Example

```
<FL:terms>
  <FL:termfile>
    <FL:filename>stocks.dat</FL:filename>
  </FL:termfile>
</FL:terms>
```

`<filename>` element

Required: Yes, if `<termfile>` is used.

This is a path to the term file (see the section titled "Creating a term list" (p. 149)).

Example

```
<FL:terms>
  <FL:termFile>
    <FL:filename>stocks.dat</FL:filename>
  </FL:termFile>
</FL:terms>
```

`<re>` element

Required: Either `<terms>` or `<re>` is required.

Contains the definition of regular expressions to be recognized by this Smart Tag.

Example

```
<FL:re>
  <FL:exp>
    (^|\s)((1)(\s|-|\.))?(((\d{3})(\s|-|\.))?(\d{3})(\s|-|\.)(\d{4}\)
  </FL:exp>
</FL:re>
```

`<exp>` element

Required: Yes, if the `<exp>` element is used.

This is a container for a single regular expression.

Example

```
<FL:re>
  <FL:exp>
    (^|\s)((1)(\s|-|\.))?(((\d{3})(\s|-|\.))?(\d{3})(\s|-|\.)(\d{4})
  </FL:exp>
</FL:re>
```

This code attempts to match telephone number patterns. The following examples are successfully matched: 555 1234567, 555 123 4567, 555 123-4567, 555-123-4567, and (555)-123-4567. 5551234567 is not matched.

`<actions>` element

Required: Yes.

Container for the actions associated with the current Smart Tag. This contains a list of new or revised action identifiers.

Example

```
<FL:actions>
  <FL:action id="CompanyInfo">
    <FL:caption>A. Datum Corporation Company Reports</FL:caption>
    <FL:url>http://www.adatum.com</FL:url>
  </FL:action>
  <FL:action id="CompanyHomePage">
    <FL:caption>View A. Datum Website</FL:caption>
    <FL:url>http://www.adatum2.com/home.asp?String={TEXT}</FL:url>
  </FL:action>
</FL:actions>
```

`<action>` element

Required: Yes.

This is the container for a single Smart Tag action. This element has one required attribute called `id`. Each action element must contain at least `<caption>` element (for the screen display) and optionally a `<URL>` element (if you want to associate the term with a Web action).

Example

See the example in the section titled "`<actions>` element" (p. 161).

`<caption>` element

Required: Yes.

Specifies the text for the Smart Tag action menu.

Example

```
<FL:caption>Medical Conditions</FL:caption>
```

id Attribute

Required: Yes, if the action element is used.

This is a string uniquely identifying an action within the context of the current Smart Tag.

Example

See the example in the section titled "`<actions>` element" (p. 161).

`<url>` element

This is a URL which will be launched when the action is invoked. The `{TEXT}` qualifier allows you to pass the term into the URL. This element specifies the URL to activate for an action. The

URL supports a number of tokens that serve as parameters to the HTTP file. These tokens are explained in the *MOSTL Action Special Terms* topic in the SDK.

Example

```
<FL:actions>
    <!-- This is the Web site to connect to.
         For this example, contoso.com is a Microsoft Web site -->
  <FL:action id="urn:schemas-adatum-com:medical#contoso:actionID">
    <FL:url>http://www.google.com</FL:url>
    <FL:caption>Google Actions</FL:caption>
  </FL:action>
</FL:actions>
```

Smart Tag Example

Code Example 7.13 is an example of one of the simplest MOSTL files. Only the required elements are included.

```
<FL:smarttaglist xmlns:FL="urn:schemas-microsoft-com:smarttags:list">
<FL:smarttag type="urn:schemas-smarttaglistgenerator:
    smarttags#msdnsearchterms">
<FL:caption>My MSDN Search</FL:caption>
  <FL:terms>
    <FL:termlist>"XML"</FL:termlist>
  </FL:terms>
  <FL:actions>
    <FL:action id="msdn">
      <FL:caption>MSDN Search Terms</FL:caption>
      <FL:url>http://search.microsoft.com/
        Results.aspx?q={TEXT}</FL:url>
    </FL:action>
  </FL:actions>
  </FL:smarttag>
</FL:smarttaglist>
```

Example 7.13. Simple MOSTL File

This Smart Tag displays in the **Smart Tags** dialog as My MSDN Search and recognizes only one term: All capitalized *XML*. The action is to search Microsoft's MSDN for the term *XML*.

Summary

Smart Tags are an overlooked productivity tool. There is some work getting to them run, and the MOSTL or non-programmatic approach has limited abilities, namely either going to a Web site, or going to a Web site with a single parameter, such as a search term. Yet, they should be considered in some situations. If the term list is well defined, you have a good Web site to reference them from, or if you just want to mark terms, this may be just the thing.

8

Exchanging Data

One of Word's most powerful features is its ability to exchange information with other applications. The most common approach is copying and pasting. You can copy and paste information between any of the Microsoft Office products, and you can cut and paste information from and to other sources, such as other word processors, spreadsheets, image applications, and even compilers.

In a way, we have almost total data transparency in that we may move information around with few limits. But just moving data to a new location isn't always enough. Being able to manipulate data or make it dynamic is becoming equally important.

An important source of dynamic data is from databases. Word can query and import data from a variety of databases, including spreadsheets and even plain text files. The imported data can be changed and updated whenever the data source changes.

This chapter first introduces the basics of copy and paste, including an explanation of how to retain or lose text formatting. It explains how to link data to live sources and query databases to creating tables and mail merge documents. Lastly, it explains how to export data. Many of the topics include macros to demonstrate automation.

Importing Information

By far the most common way of importing data is by using the copy and paste commands. Most users are familiar with the edit keys: **CTRL-C** (copy), **CRTL-V** (paste), **CTRL-X** (cut), and **CRTL-Z** (undo).

In short, you select the text or object from the source document, copy using **CTRL-C** and paste it into the target document using **CTRL-V**. You can copy and paste text, pictures, graphics, tables, and art work (including, smart art and text boxes). Any text formatting will be copied and pasted, but the way formatting pastes depends on the context, and will be discussed in the section titled "Text formatting and copy/paste" (p. 165).

The source of the copy matters. Selections originating from Microsoft Office applications copy and paste better than other sources. However, simple objects, such as text, do well regardless.

Copy and Paste Options

Of course nothing stays simple for long, and Word's copy and paste has become a complete system. Word, for instance, has 27 options controlling copy and paste behavior, most dealing with formatting. Procedure 8.1 describes how to view these options:

Procedure 8.1. View copy and paste options

1. Click **Office** icon and then click **Word Options**.

2. Click **Advanced** in the left pane.

3. Scroll to **Cut, copy and paste options**.

These controls can also change the defaults. Many users like to paste the text only, so for example, changing **Pasting between documents** to **Keep Text Only** makes that the default.

Then there is the **Paste Options** button ( ). This icon appears at the end of a pasted selection and presents additional formatting options (see Figure 8.1).

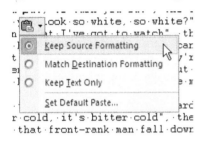

Figure 8.1. The Paste Options button with the options expanded.

You can make that button go away by pressing the **ESC** key. Many users prefer to turn this off (see Procedure 8.2).

Procedure 8.2. Suppress the Paste Options button display

1. Click **Office** icon and then click **Word Options**.

2. Click **Advanced** in the left pane.

3. Scroll to **Cut, copy, and paste** options.

4. Uncheck the **Show Paste Options buttons** check box.

Clipboard dialog

Copy and paste is generally considered a one-time action. That is, a user copies and pastes a text selection once and then may repeat the action with different text. The clipboard keeps the last item copied, and although you can paste that item several consecutive times, an intervening copy loses that item.

There are times when you may want to save some text to paste later. The Microsoft Office Clipboard stores up to 24 copied items from an Office application. The clipboard is available to any other

Office application (such as Excel or PowerPoint, though not other Microsoft applications like Internet Explorer). The clipboard retains all the items as long as at least one Office application remains open. After that, it retains only the last copied item.

Adding to the Office clipboard

Each time you copy or cut an item, it is automatically added to the clipboard.

Viewing the Office clipboard

From the **Home** tab in the **Clipboard** group, click the **Clipboard** Dialog Box Launcher. The **Clipboard** dialog displays. The available items display in that list.

Pasting from the Office clipboard

You can paste a selection by clicking on the clipboard item. To paste from the clipboard:

1. From the **Home** tab in the **Clipboard** group, click the **Clipboard** Dialog Box Launcher. The **Clipboard** dialog displays.

2. Click on the item to paste into the insertion point or the current selection.

Text formatting and copy/paste

Keeping the original format of the selected text has less to do with the copy process and more to do with the formatting of the source and target selections. The paste retains its formatting for text which has one of the following applied to it:

- **Direct formatting:** The text was directly modified, for example by using the Home tab Font selections such as bold, italic, or font colors.

- **Character formatting:** This is shown in the Styles dialog as a lower case a. This style can apply to individual characters.

- **Paragraph mark/section break.** The selection includes a paragraph mark – either an end of paragraph or end of document mark – or a section break. Each of these, especially the end of document paragraph mark, contains style information for the preceding paragraph, document, and section respectively. The selection before that mark will retain its current formatting. Any selection after one of those marks will follow the paste rules mentioned here.

All other style information is taken from the styles in effect at the insertion point or the start of the selected area.

If after pasting, the text blends in with the surrounding text, undo and try the paste again, this time selecting enough source text to capture the following paragraph mark. Styles introduced into a document this way will be retained in the target document.

This also introduces a common problem. Users frequently apply direct formatting to all the text. For example, they might select all the text and directly assign it Calibri 11. The selection would look like Normal style, but if you paste it into another document it will keep the Calibri font, seeming as if the formatting rules for paste didn't work.

If you want to use the target's style or formatting, use the **Paste options** button and select **Match Destination Formatting**. This option is useful when pasting selections that include paragraph marks whose style you don't want to keep, or if you want the new text to match the formatting of the target.

If all you want to do is paste the text without formatting, use the **Paste options** button and select **Keep Text Only**. This ensures hidden text and link information does not transfer.

Some users still paste the text into a Notepad document and then re-paste it into the target Word document; they feel this is an absolute way of cleaning text since Notepad does not support any formatting at all. **Keep Text Only** now does the same thing. You can also use **Paste Special Unformatted Text**; see below. Use can also use the keyboard equivalent by selecting the text and press **CTRL-[Space]**

You can copy and paste text selections into a target document and retain any revision marks and comments.

Procedure 8.3. Paste text, retaining revision marks

1. Make a selection from the source document.

2. Turn **Track Changes** off by toggling **Review|Tracking|Track Changes|Track Changes**.

3. Press **CRTL-C** to copy the text, or **CRTL-X** to cut the text to the Clipboard.

4. Choose a selection or an insertion point in the target document.

5. Turn Track Changes off (toggling **Review|Tracking|Track Changes|Track Changes**) in the target document.

6. Press **CRTL-V** to paste the text.

The Spike

This is an overlooked option. The name refers to the paper spindle of an earlier time used to impale pieces of paper, as kind of a mildly destructive inbox. This kept them in a specific place, and importantly, in a specific order: last in, first out.

Word's spike allows you to make a sequence of cuts and retain all the cut text in the order you collected them, until you do a paste operation. For example, at times you may have to go through a document gathering various text selections and pasting them elsewhere. The manual way would require you to cut some text, scroll to a new location, paste it, then scroll back to get the next text selection, and so on. The spike simplifies this by allowing you to collect several text selections together and then paste them in a single operation. Procedure 8.4 shows how to collect and paste text with the spike.

Procedure 8.4. Collect and paste text with the Spike

1. Select the text (also graphics) you want to collect and press **CTRL-F3**. This cuts the text from the document.

2. Repeat this for each item you want to collect.

3. Choose the destination, either as a selection or an insert point, and press **CTRL-SHIFT-F3**. This pastes the spike content at the destination. It also empties the spike so that you can't paste from the spike again without collecting new items.

The spike uses a separate clipboard, independent from the Office clipboard. Any cuts made with the spike do not display in the Clipboard dialog. Likewise, any conventional copy or cut command does not replace the spike clipboard, and a paste command does not paste from the spike clipboard.

To see the contents of the spike clipboard, use the **Building Blocks Organizer** dialog. Although this uses Building Blocks, you don't have to previously define the spike (as you would with other Building Blocks). Instead, the spike entry shows whatever is in the spike clipboard at that moment. To see the contents of the spike clipboard, use Procedure 8.5.

Procedure 8.5. View the contents of the Spike clipboard

1. Select the **Insert||Text|Quick Parts|Building Blocks Organizer**.

2. In the **Building Blocks** list, scroll down to to **Spike** . Note that the spike entry will display only if there is valid content to paste.

3. Select **Spike**. This displays the clipboard contents in the preview box on the right side.

The spike paste operation (**CTRL-SHIFT-F3**) empties its clipboard. To paste the spike clipboard without emptying it, use Procedure 8.6.

Procedure 8.6. Paste the contents without emptying the Spike

1. Select the **Insert|Text|Quick Parts|Building Blocks** Organizer.

2. In the **Building Blocks** list, scroll down to **Spike** . Note that the spike entry will only display if there is valid content to paste.

3. Select **Spike**. This displays the clipboard contents in the preview box on the right side.

4. Click **Insert**.

Example 8.1 is a macro that allows you to paste the spike clipboard without having to use the **Building Blocks**.

```
1 Sub SpikeWithoutDeletingText()
2   If Len(Selection.Range.Text) > 1 Then
3     Application.ScreenUpdating = False
4
5     Selection.Range.Copy
6     NormalTemplate.AutoTextEntries.AppendToSpike Range:=Selection.Range
7     ActiveDocument.Undo 1
8
9     Application.ScreenUpdating = True
10    Application.ScreenRefresh
11  End If
12 End Sub
```

Example 8.1. Using the Spike without deleting the clipboard

Actually, this macro does delete the text (it's required for the spike operation). However, the cut text is immediately pasted back into the same place (line 7, ActiveDocument.Undo 1). The ScreenUpdating statement determines whether the screen shows these changes. If set to False (line 3), you won't see the flicker of text being deleted and then re-added. If set to True (line 9), the display will change as usual. ScreenRefresh (line 10) forces a refresh, which in this case may not be needed, but it is there just to be sure.

Macros and VBA for Copy and Paste

The macro recorder is adequate when it comes to copy operations. The problem is that copy and paste operations tend to be manual. You have to find the text, select it, and after copying, then specify the paste location. Macros don't excel at that amount of interaction. You can write a macro that automatically finds certain text, but where and how to paste the text is another question.

The macro in Example 8.2 addresses part of this problem. In the past, you would have had to select and copy the text, activate the target document, find an insertion point, paste, and repeat. Example 8.2 allows you to select the text, and then copies and pastes it in a collection document. If you're making a series of copy and pastes, this procedure makes it faster and easier, with all the material pasted into one document. For this simple example, the source document has to be opened first, and then the target document (the one being pasted into) has to be opened. The macro should be assigned to a keyboard short cut or a convenient ribbon button to keep the number of actions down.

```
Public Sub MakeManyCopies()
    On Error GoTo MyErrorhandler

    Dim sourceDocument As Document
    Set sourceDocument = ActiveDocument

    If Len(Selection.Text) > 0 Then
        Selection.Copy
    End If

    'The targetDocument must be opened after the sourceDocument.
    Dim targetDocument As Document
    Set targetDocument = Application.Documents(1)

    Dim pasteRange As Range
    Set pasteRange = targetDocument.Range
    pasteRange.Collapse wdCollapseEnd
    pasteRange.Paste
    pasteRange.InsertParagraphAfter

    Exit Sub

MyErrorhandler:
    MsgBox "MakeManyCopies" & vbCrLf & _
        Err.Description & vbCrLf & Err.Number
End Sub
```

Example 8.2. Macro to make multiple copies

You can simplify pasting unformatted text even more with Example 8.3. For best results, assign it to a keyboard shortcut. Assigning it to **CTRL+V** effectively replaces the existing paste function as does naming it EditPaste. The code makes sure all the text pastes as unformatted text. Removing the macro from that key assignment or naming it differently restores the original **CTRL+V** paste or feature or EditPaste macro respectively.

```
Public Sub EditPaste()
    On Error Resume Next
    Selection.PasteSpecial DataType:=wdPasteText
End Sub
```

Example 8.3. Paste unformatted text

Example 8.4 is a variation that asks if you want to paste using formatted or unformatted text.

```
Sub EditPaste()
    On Error Resume Next
    If MsgBox("Paste Unformatted Text only?", _
            vbQuestion & vbYesNo, "Paste Options") = vbYes Then
        Selection.PasteSpecial DataType:=wdPasteText
    Else
        Selection.Paste
    End If
End Sub
```

Example 8.4. Prompting to paste as unformatted text

Paste Special

If the direct paste methods above don't do enough, there is the **Paste Special** menu. This menu provides additional options for pasting text. You can access **Paste Special** through the **Home|Clipboard|Paste|Paste Special** menu. The menu item selection changes with the type of object being pasted. Here are some common cases:

► **Unformatted Text and Unformatted Unicode:** Unformatted is just what is sounds like, the most plain text possible. Unformatted Unicode is still plain text, but in the Unicode code set.

► **Microsoft Word Document Object:** This pastes the selection as an embedded Word document and not as independent text. The text appears in the document, but is not directly editable. You can double click the selection, and it appears in a new, separate document, which you can edit. You can resize the inserted text region, but only to an area that displays all the text. If pasted with an icon, the icon appears in the target document instead of as text. Double clicking still displays the selection in a separate document.

► **Picture:** This inserts the text as a bitmap graphic in either Windows Metafile or Enhanced Metafile format. In general, the Metafile format supports printing and portability between documents and performs better for sharing than conventional graphics.

The Windows Metafile Format (WMF) is customized for Windows and is the native format for Office applications. As a result, this file format is generally the best fit for use in Office.

The Enhanced Metafile Format (EMF) includes additional capabilities, and many users consider it to be an improved file format. However, because it is extensible – that is, programmers can change or add to its capabilities – this format may not be as widely compatible as the Windows Metafile format.

Regardless of the original format of the picture, the selected file pastes in as a graphic that you cannot edit, convert back to text, or link back to the original source.

Dragging Text

You can drag a selection around in Word, which moves it to that new location. In the same way, if you drag a selection between documents, it moves to the target document and is cut from the source document. If you right click and drag, several options display (see Figure 8.2).

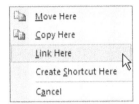

Figure 8.2. Copy, move, and link options

The **Move and Copy** option should be obvious. Here is brief summary of the other options:

Link Here (link field)

This creates a linked text connection between the selection in the source document and the copied selection in the target document. If the source changes, the linked target changes. If the target document is open when the text changes, the field updates automatically. Otherwise, it changes when the target document is next opened. The linked text in the target document can be changed, but it will revert to the source text the next time the field is updated, or is opened.

Linking is a powerful means of dynamically sharing data among documents. But, keep in mind that if the source files move to a new location, you will have to re-create the link, although you can convert the field into non-linked text (**CTRL-SHIFT-F9**). Alternatively, you can move the source file along with the target.

When links exist, the target location contains a bookmark noted as OLE (Object Linking and Embedding, Microsoft's technology specifically for embedding information in documents). The target selection is actually a field and may highlight according to the field highlight preferences in Word Options (see Figure 8.3).

```
· · · · · · They ·are ·hangin' ·Danny       [· · · · · · They ·are ·hangin' ·Danny ·Deever, ·they ·are ·marchin'
· · · · · · · They · 'ave · 'alted ·Danny          · · · · · · ·They · 'ave · 'alted ·Danny ·Deever ·by · 'is ·coffin ·on ·tl
· · · · · · An' · 'e'll ·swing ·in · 'ar:          · · · · · · An' · 'e'll ·swing ·in · 'arf ·a ·minute ·for ·a ·sneakin' ·:
· · · · · O ·they're ·hangin' ·Danny               · · · · · · O ·they're ·hangin' ·Danny ·Deever ·in ·the ·mornin'!¶
```

Figure 8.3. Side by side: linked text (left) and the bookmarked source (right)

Link Here is just a Link field. The advantage is that Link Here creates the field and bookmarks the source document automatically. You could manually insert a Link field and get the same results (you would have to include the entire file or create a bookmark). Although Link Here doesn't have a user interface for editing, the field code looks something like { LINK Word.Document.12 "C:\\folder1\\folder2\\sourcefile.docx" "OLE_LINK1" \a \r} .

IncludeText field

You could also pull material from another file, including non-Word files, with the **IncludeText** field (**Insert|Text|Quick Parts|Fields**), selecting **IncludeText**. The FileName path has to include double backslashes (see the Link notation above) instead of the usual single backslash. You can also specify a bookmark in the source document to get the text from, otherwise the entire file is included. The included text is not automatically updated as the Link field is (although opening the target file or manually updating the target field updates the material). An important switch is the Locked Field (\ !). This switch prevents Word from updating fields in the target text unless the source text has changed. While you can still explicitly update the field, automatic updates won't be applied. On the other hand, you can update the source file from the copy. That is, if you make changes within the target field, click **CTRL-Shift-F7** to update the source.

The difference between Link and IncludeText is subtle. IncludeText is recommended for text that is unlikely to change often or when you don't have a pressing need to have the most updated text. Use Link if you expect the information to change frequently. You can ensure the latest update by using \a (update automatically) with Link.

IncludePicture field

IncludePicture lets you place graphics into a document the same way **IncludeText** inserts text. The basic form is { INCLUDEPICTURE "C:\\folder1\\filename.ext"}. The file path name has to use double backslashes. If you use the ribbon (**Insert|Text|Quick Parts|Fields**, selecting **IncludeText**), single backslashes get converted for you. If you manually enter the field, you will have to type the double backslashes yourself. After placing the field, it gets replaced by the image immediately, and you can no longer use right click to edit and toggle the fields. To see the field code in this case, select the image and press **ALT-F9**; the same sequence displays the image again. Once placed, the image can be resized or modified using the **Picture Tools** tab of the ribbon.

Create shortcut here

A shortcut inserts an icon for the selection, but is otherwise similar to linked text. Clicking it opens the source document with the text selected.

Open File

Word can open text documents saved by other applications and in other formats, such as HTML. However, this is likely to be less effective than opening documents created by spreadsheets or presentation applications that Word knows about. When Word can't properly open a document, it may be better to copy and paste text into Word.

Insert Object

Inserting an object allows you to embed a document created by another application directly into a Word document. Usually the insertion comes from Microsoft Office applications, but not exclusively. For example, you can insert documents created by applications such as Adobe Acrobat, presentation and image applications, and even programming applications (such as Microsoft Visual Basic 6 or Microsoft Visual Studio). While technically this inserts the entire document, sometimes only a portion of the document displays. A wide spreadsheet, for example, may not display properly in a portrait-oriented Word document. Another example is that embedded spreadsheets are not scrollable.

Procedure 8.7 shows how to insert an object into a document:

Procedure 8.7. Insert an object into a document

1. From the **Insert|Text** , click **Object**. This displays the **Object** dialog.

2. Click either **Create New** tab, if you're going to type your own information into the object, or **Create from File**, if you want to use an existing file.

3. If you use **Create New**, select the type of application from the **Object** type list and browse for the existing file. If you use **Create from File**, navigate to the file.

4. Click **OK** to insert the object. The object displays. Different options will then appear depending on the inserted object.

Editing or opening an object

Right clicking presents a menu that includes the following two options (see Figure 8.4).

- ► **Edit:** Allows you to edit the entire object. This includes changing text, cropping the object, or changing the display area.

- ► **Open:** Opens the object within the application that created it. For example, if you open a spreadsheet object, you will see Excel's ribbon. Since the entire application is available, you can use more options for modifying the object than Edit alone allows.

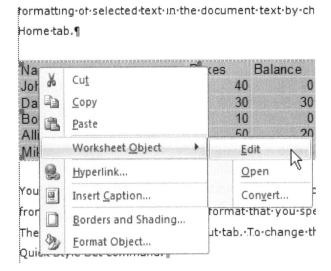

Figure 8.4. Worksheet object menu

You can modify the display of an object in one of two ways:

1. The first way is the default. After inserting the object, the display will either be the entire object, such as a slide from PowerPoint, or part of the object, as from Excel; more on that later. The area that gets shown in a Word document is a single selection and can't be edited directly. By selecting the object, you can change its shape with the resize handles. This behaves like a bit map when it comes to resizing. That is, the fonts may appear distorted or jagged when resized.

2. The second way is to change the display area. Double click the object, or select **Edit** from its right click pop-up menu. If it's a spreadsheet, the display area shows in an editable container, including the ribbon of the owning application. In this editable state, you can resize the visible region. When you're done, clicking outside the object (somewhere else in the Word document) returns the edit object back into a static display (see Figure 8.5).

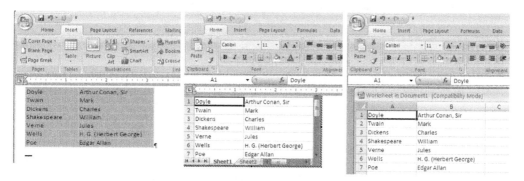

Figure 8.5. Changing the display area of an object

Other applications behave similarly, although there will be differences in selections and options.

CSV and tab-delimited files

Even though Word can't directly open an Excel spreadsheet, spreadsheet information can be saved in the CSV (comma separated value) format using the Excel **Save As** option: **CSV (Comma delimited)(.csv)**. This is a plain text format (one that Word is good at opening) with columns separated by a comma and rows by a paragraph mark. In the past, Word could only open a CSV file as plain text, and you would have to manually convert the contents into a table. Word 2007 and later versions change this depending how you open the file.

Going through the Open menu or the right click **Open with menu** option is the same before, and the material displays as plain text. Dragging the CSV file into an already open Word document creates an embedded table (see Figure 8.6).

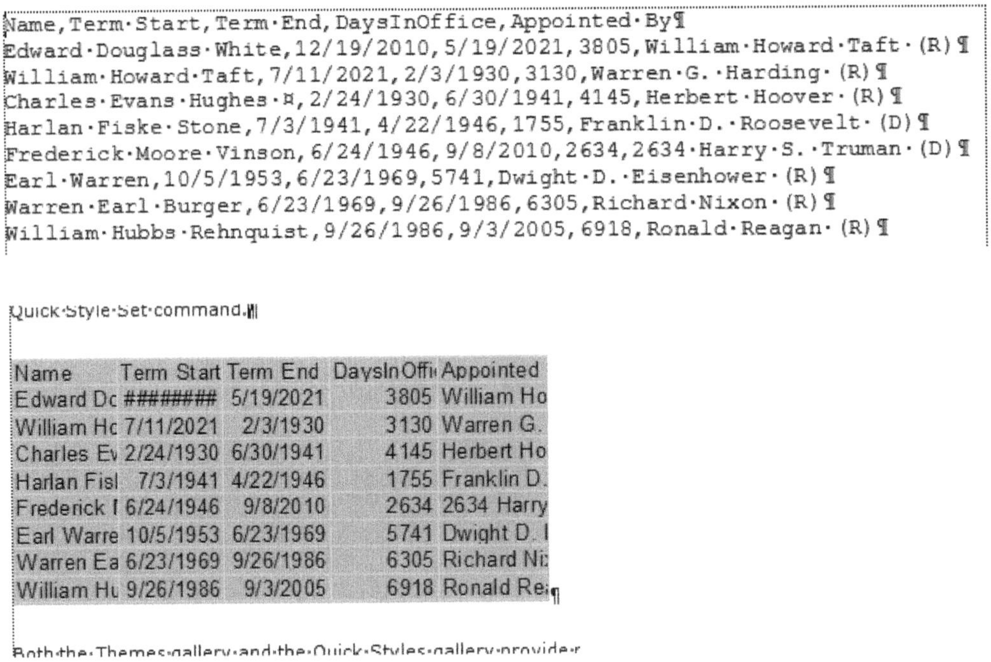

```
Name,Term·Start,Term·End,DaysInOffice,Appointed·By¶
Edward·Douglass·White,12/19/2010,5/19/2021,3805,William·Howard·Taft·(R)¶
William·Howard·Taft,7/11/2021,2/3/1930,3130,Warren·G.·Harding·(R)¶
Charles·Evans·Hughes·¤,2/24/1930,6/30/1941,4145,Herbert·Hoover·(R)¶
Harlan·Fiske·Stone,7/3/1941,4/22/1946,1755,Franklin·D.·Roosevelt·(D)¶
Frederick·Moore·Vinson,6/24/1946,9/8/2010,2634,2634·Harry·S.·Truman·(D)¶
Earl·Warren,10/5/1953,6/23/1969,5741,Dwight·D.·Eisenhower·(R)¶
Warren·Earl·Burger,6/23/1969,9/26/1986,6305,Richard·Nixon·(R)¶
William·Hubbs·Rehnquist,9/26/1986,9/3/2005,6918,Ronald·Reagan·(R)¶
```

Quick·Style·Set·command.¶

Name	Term Start	Term End	DaysInOffi	Appointed
Edward Dc	#######	5/19/2021	3805	William Ho
William Hc	7/11/2021	2/3/1930	3130	Warren G.
Charles Ev	2/24/1930	6/30/1941	4145	Herbert Ho
Harlan Fisl	7/3/1941	4/22/1946	1755	Franklin D.
Frederick I	6/24/1946	9/8/2010	2634	2634 Harry
Earl Warre	10/5/1953	6/23/1969	5741	Dwight D. I
Warren Ea	6/23/1969	9/26/1986	6305	Richard Ni:
William Hu	9/26/1986	9/3/2005	6918	Ronald Rei¶

Both·the·Themes·gallery·and·the·Quick·Styles·gallery·provide·r

Figure 8.6. Importing a CSV file

Another option is to save the spreadsheet as a tab-delimited file, using the Excel **Save As** option: **Text(Tab delimited)(.txt)**. This output format is also plain text, but it uses tabs between the fields rather than commas. The difference is that Word recognizes tabs differently. Opened from within Word, the file still displays as plain text, however, dragging the file onto a Word document creates an embedded file, not a table.

XML
Starting with Office 2007, Office is XML-based, a format partially introduced in Office 2003. The new file names end in "x," such as .docx or .xlsx, indicating the new format. This allows for easier data exchange among more types of applications and is not limited to Microsoft products.

Data Connection Wizard
In addition to cut and paste, linking, and object embedding, Word can also directly access database information. Accessing databases introduces a new dimension for automating documents. For example, you can query a company sales database to list the best selling products for that week, list changes in inventory, or produce a regional contact list.

Database sources can be Microsoft Access, Microsoft SQL Server, or Oracle. You can also use applications that support ODBC (Open Database Connectivity, a common protocol for accessing other databases) or OLE DB (Object Linking and Embedding, Database, a Microsoft technology used to access data sources other than traditional databases). Despite the similarity of names, OLE DB is not related to OLE. ODBC and OLE DB are commonly supported access methods. The popular, open-source database MySQL, for instance, supports ODBC access.

OLE DB is a more liberal access method, connecting to applications that might not otherwise be considered a database. For example, Excel is considered a database in this regard, as is a simple plain text file (if it is formatted properly).

Regardless of the source, using an OLE DB connection allows you to create your own database for a document and update it periodically without having to deal with a complex database or rely on support outside of your group.

Inserting a new table from a database

For the Microsoft databases, the connection is basically the same. This is true for spreadsheets, databases, or plain text files. You can query plain text files if they are comma- or tab-delimited. That is, each column or field is marked with a comma or tab, and paragraph marks separate rows. Many spreadsheets and databases can save reports in this format. The following example uses a spreadsheet as the source (CookieSales.xlsx, Excel), although a tab-delimited text file (CookieSales.txt), or Access Database file (CookieSales.accdb), would also work with almost the exact same procedures.

The example here is a list of customers who purchased cookies, along with their outstanding balance due, and a note if their payment is overdue. If the source is Excel, the cell could also be a formula or calculation; all that matters is the result. The data looks like this (see Figure 8.7):

CustomerName	BoxesOrdered	Balance	Overdue?
Jackie	50	$0	No
Tom	10	$20	No
Mark	5	$15	Yes
Ruth	25	$30	No
Randy	33	$0	No

Figure 8.7. Data for cookie sales example

The spreadsheet format presentation may be convenient, but you can also present the information as a Microsoft Word table. To insert the information as table use Procedure 8.8.

Procedure 8.8. Create a Word table from a database

1. Select **Insert|Text|Quick Parts**, then select **Fields**. This presents the **Field** dialog box.

2. From **Field names** select **Database**.

3. Click **Insert Database** from the **Field Properties** panel. The **Database** dialog displays. The buttons display in the order they should be clicked.

4. Click **Get Data**. The **Select Data Source** dialog displays.

5. Navigate to the source file containing the data (for this example, CookieSales.txt) and click **Open** to select the file. The **Select Table** dialog displays.

6. Plain text files may have an additional step for selecting the encoding. If a conversion dialog appears, most of the time the **Windows** format (the default selection) is adequate. Click **OK**.

7. Back in the **Select Table** dialog, click **OK**. The **Database** dialog displays again.

Procedure 8.9 shows how to set additional data options on the information.

Procedure 8.9. Set additional data options

1. In the **Database** dialog, click **Table Autoformat**, to set the format of the inserted table. Select one of the preset formats. Although this step is optional (a default style is already selected), the default isn't always the most pleasant looking.

2. Click **OK**.

To get the data, use Procedure 8.10

Procedure 8.10. Import Database Information

1. Still in the **Database** dialog, click **Insert Data**. This presents the **Insert Data** dialog.

2. Check **Insert data as field**. This makes the insert a Word table.

3. Click **OK**. The queried information inserts as a formatted table and a field (see Figure 8.8).

CustomerName¤	BoxesOrdered¤	Balance¤	Overdue?¤	¤
Jackie¤	50¤	$0·¤	No¤	¤
Tom¤	10¤	$20·¤	No¤	¤
Mark¤	5¤	$15·¤	Yes¤	¤
Ruth¤	25¤	$30·¤	No¤	¤
Randy¤	33¤	$0·¤	No¤	¤

Figure 8.8. Data inserted from a database

Setting query conditions

At this point you still have a table not much different than what you would get by pasting an Excel selection; it even updates the information as the source changes. The difference is that you can now query the data, sort it, or present entries conditionally. For example, you could list the people selling more than a certain number of boxes or those with overdue balances.

The next example queries the same database looking for overdue balances.

Editing a table from a database

1. Get back to the **Database** dialog using Procedure 8.8 and Procedure 8.9.

2. In **Database**, click **Query Options**.

The **Query Options** dialog presents three tabs: **Select Fields**, **Sort Records**, and **Filter Records**. The **Select Fields** tab allows you to include or exclude fields from the resulting table. Don't make any changes here for this example.

3. Click the **Sort Records** tab. **Sort Records** is similar to the **Sort** dialog in Word. You select the field or fields you want sorted, along with the order (ascending or descending).

4. In the first **Sort by** drop-down list, select **Balance** and click **Descending**. This is going to list who owes the most money first.

Click the **Filter Records** tab. This tab allows you to set the conditions to include or exclude items from the table. To set the criterion:

5. Select **Overdue** from the first **Field** box

6. Set the **Comparison** by selecting **Equal to**.

7. Set the **Compare To** value to **Yes**.

8. Click **OK**.

The **Filter Records** tab of the **Query Options** dialog displays a series of six possible conditions to filter the records. If you leave this entire tab blank or don't fill in any values, no filtering applies and it selects all the records.

However, you can also define conditions. These are known as "logical conditions." The value for the **Overdue** field was equal to Yes or No. By applying additional conditions, the filter becomes more restrictive. For example, we could make a second condition defining that the **Balance** has to be greater than $20.

Each condition is independent of the others. For example, one condition was based on the **Overdue** field, and the second was based on the **Balance**. Any item in the list meeting all the conditions gets included. In the example with two conditions, any person selected has be overdue (the **Overdue** field being Yes) and has to have a balance of more than $20). If the conditions are restrictive enough, it is possible to select no items.

Finally, get the data:

9. Click **Insert Data**.

10. Check **Insert data as field**.

11. Click **OK**.

The table inserts anew, but it only includes those items noted as overdue, starting with those owing the most. In this case only one person, Mark, has an overdue balance (see Figure 8.9).

CustomerName¤	BoxesOrdered¤	Balance¤	Overdue?¤	¤
Mark¤	5¤	15¤	Yes¤	¤

Figure 8.9. Data table filtered

Updating a table

Although presenting information from a new or edited query is laborious (you have to essentially define the table from scratch), updating it is the same as updating any other field. Select any part of the table, right click, and select **Update Field**. Alternatively, you could select part of the table and press **F9**. The update checks the data source using the same query it was set up with and returns a corresponding list. In this example, Tom has yet to pay his balance and his account has become overdue. If this was changed in the spreadsheet, the updated table would look like Figure 8.10.

CustomerName¤	BoxesOrdered¤	Balance¤	Overdue?¤	¤
Tom¤	10¤	20¤	Yes¤	¤
Mark¤	5¤	15¤	Yes¤	¤

Figure 8.10. Data table updated

Using field codes

A table can be inserted as a field (which allows it to be updated). In fact, the examples above use **Insert|Quick Parts|Fields** to create the table. As a field, you have full access to the field codes, and you can directly change the parameters. Due to the complexity of the code, it might be better to stick to Word's dialogs. For example, the field code for the last query of Figure 8.10 would look like Figure 8.11.

```
{·DATABASE··\d·"C:\\folder1\\CookieSales.xlsx"·\c·"Provider=Microsoft.ACE.OLEDB.12.0;User·
ID=Admin;Data·Source=·C:\\folder1\\CookieSales.xlsx;Mode=Read;Extended·
Properties=\"HDR=YES;IMEX=1;\";Jet·OLEDB:System·database=\"\";Jet·OLEDB:Registry·Path=\"\";Jet·
OLEDB:Engine·Type=37;Jet·OLEDB:Database·Locking·Mode=0;Jet·OLEDB:Global·Partial·Bulk·Ops=2;Jet·
OLEDB:Global·Bulk·Transactions=1;Jet·OLEDB:New·Database·Password=\"\";Jet·OLEDB:Create·System·
Database=False;Jet·OLEDB:Encrypt·Database=False;Jet·OLEDB:Don't·Copy·Locale·on·Compact=False;Jet·
OLEDB:Compact·Without·Replica·Repair=False;Jet·OLEDB:SFP=False;Jet·OLEDB:Support·Complex·
Data=False"·\s·"SELECT·*·FROM·`Sheet1$`"·\|"4"·\b·"191\h·}¶
```

Figure 8.11. Field code for Figure 8.10

Using macros and VBA to handle field codes *WITH XL*

Macros can be used to handle field codes efficiently, and the generated code is relatively clean. A recorded macro would speed up creating a table if the same query is used each time. Example 8.5 shows the recorded query, although the file path, here `C:\cookies.xlsx`, may be different on your computer.

```
Sub InsertOrUpdateDatabaseField()
    Selection.Range.InsertDatabase Format:=1, Style:=191, _
        LinkToSource:=True, _
        Connection:= _
        "Provider=Microsoft.ACE.OLEDB.12.0;User ID=Admin;" & _
        "Data Source=c:\Cookies.xlsx;Mode=Read;Extended " & _
            "Properties=" & _
            """HDR=YES;IMEX=1;"";" & _
        "Jet OLEDB:System database="""";Jet OLEDB:Registry " & _
            "Path="""";" & _
        "Jet OLEDB:Engine Type=37;Jet O", _
        SQLStatement:= _
        "SELECT `CustomerName`, `BoxesOrdered`, `Balance`, " & _
            "`Overdue?` FROM" & _
        "`Sheet1$` WHERE ((`Overdue?` = 'Yes')) ORDER BY " & _
            "`Balance` DESC" _
        & "", PasswordDocument:="", PasswordTemplate:="", _
            WritePasswordDocument _
        :="", WritePasswordTemplate:="", DataSource:= _
        "c:\Cookies.xlsx ", From:=-1, _
        To:=-1, IncludeFields:=True
End Sub
```

Example 8.5. Insert database query table *WITH XL*

Example 8.6 is a variation that allows you to select accounts that are either overdue or not.

```
Sub ShowOverDueBalancesOrNot()
    Dim msgboxReturn As Long
    msgboxReturn = MsgBox(prompt:="Click 'Yes' for showing " & _
        "overdue balances. " & _
    vbCrLf & "'No' for not overdue or " & vbCrLf & _
    "Cancel to end the macro.", buttons:=vbYesNoCancel, _
        Title:="Query Type")

    Dim compareValue As String
    Select Case msgboxReturn                    ❶
        Case vbYes
            compareValue = "Yes"
        Case vbNo
            compareValue = "No"
        Case vbCancel
            Exit Sub
        Case Else
    End Select

    Selection.Range.InsertDatabase Format:=1, Style:=191, _
        LinkToSource:=True, _
```

```
            Connection:="", SQLStatement:= _
            "SELECT CustomerName, BoxesOrdered, Balance, Overdue " & _
                "FROM C:\Cookies.xlsx WHERE " & _
            "((Overdue = '" & compareValue & "'))" _
            & "", PasswordDocument:="", PasswordTemplate:="", _
            WritePasswordDocument:="", WritePasswordTemplate:="", _
            DataSource:=" C:\Cookies.xlsx ", From:=-1, To:=-1, _
                IncludeFields:=True
End Sub
```

Example 8.6. Select overdue or not overdue accounts   *WITH XL*

❶   The variable `compareValue` is set to `Yes` or `No` in the `Select Case` statement depending on whether the user clicks `Yes`, `No`, or `Cancel`.

    It is not a good practice to use the Message box dialog controls of `Yes`, `No`, and `Cancel` for purposes other than Yes, No, or Cancel. Here, they're used solely for convenience, but in widespread use you will likely just confuse your users.

Expanding the previous example to include all accounts regardless of their overdue status requires the changes shown in Example 8.7.

```
Sub ShowOverDueBalancesOrNotOrAll()
  Dim msgboxReturn As Long
  msgboxReturn = MsgBox(prompt:="Click 'Yes' for showing " & _
  "overdue balances. " & _
    vbCrLf & "'No' for not overdue or " & vbCrLf & _
    "Cancel to end the macro.", buttons:=vbYesNoCancel, _
    Title:="Query Type")

  Dim compareStatement As String
  Select Case msgboxReturn
    Case vbYes
      compareStatement = "SELECT CustomerName, " & _              ❶
        "BoxesOrdered, Balance, " & _
        "Overdue FROM Cookies.xlsx " & _
        "WHERE ((Overdue = 'Yes'))" & ""
    Case vbNo
      compareStatement = "SELECT CustomerName, " & _
        "BoxesOrdered, Balance, " & _
        "Overdue FROM Cookies.xlsx " & _
        "WHERE ((Overdue = 'No'))" & ""
    Case vbCancel
      compareStatement = "SELECT CustomerName, " & _
        "BoxesOrdered, Balance, " & _
        "Overdue " & _
        "FROM H:\MyStuff\Development\CookieSales.txt" & ""
    Case Else
  End Select

  Selection.Range.InsertDatabase Format:=1, Style:=191, _
    LinkToSource:=True, _
```

```
        Connection:="", SQLStatement:=compareStatement, _
        PasswordDocument:="", PasswordTemplate:="", _
        WritePasswordDocument:="", WritePasswordTemplate:="", _
        DataSource:=" Cookies.xlsx ", From:=-1, To:=-1, _
        IncludeFields:=True
End Sub
```

Example 8.7. Select all accounts *WITH XL*

❶ Since the query changes to show all the accounts, the macro's basic structure had to change too. The variable `compareStatement` now has to contain the entire query, not just a `Yes` or `No` part of it.

Other Data Sources

Word can query a wide variety of databases and data sources. The examples above use built-in connections, namely those for the Microsoft Office applications. However, you can use almost any database that supports an OBDC or OLE DB connection. Creating those connections may require the assistance of an IT expert. However, once you make the database connection, you can use these techniques to access the information.

Mail Merge

You can also use this type of data import to implement a mail merge capability. Mail merges lets you supply fields from a database to fields in a Word document automatically and selectively. The database can be almost any kind of file, including a formal database such as Microsoft Access or Oracle, a Microsoft Excel spreadsheet, a Word document, or even a plain text file. Regardless of the source, the information in the source file has be consistently formatted and labeled. In these examples, we use the Excel file `Cookies.xlsx`.

The term "mail merge" is also used in a general sense. The classical use is to create mailing labels or form letters. Many users store recipient mailing information in a source such as Excel and then print all the labels at one time. You can still do this, but you are not limited to labels. Word offers five kinds of mail merge (documents (also called letters), e-mail messages, envelopes, labels, and directories, or a listing by category). Regardless, the procedures are similar.

This example continues the previous one (from Data Connection Wizard) which accesses a cookie selling database in an Excel file `Cookie-Sales.xlsx`. This example prints a form letter for each overdue account. The procedure is almost the same as creating a table (Procedure 8.8 (p. 175)). There is a new first step, which creates a document in Word that you will use as the mail template. The word "template" is misleading, as this file doesn't have to be saved in any particular format or even saved at all. Template just means a document with mail merge notations in it. The resulting generated files will not modify the template, but will create new files. You can either put all of the generated instances in one file or put them in separate files.

For this example, the completed file will look like this:

> Dear Ruth,
>
> We hope you enjoyed your 25 boxes of cookies. Please promptly pay the outstanding $30 balance.

The underlined text won't be underlined in the letter, it indicates where the inserted fields are.

Creating a Mail Merge Letter

Here is how you create the mail merge letter:

1. Select **Mailings|Start Mail Merge|Select Recipients**, and choose **Use Existing List**. This presents the **Select Data Source** dialog.

2. Navigate to the file `Cookie-Sales.xlsx` and click **Open**. You may be presented with a **Select Table** dialog. If so, select a worksheet, in this case **Sheet1$**. Click **OK**.

Now, define each data field:

3. Write the letter information in the document. As a starting point, you can use the exact text from letter above, including the name and numbers. The actual information will be inserted in the next step.

4. For the **name** field, select *Ruth* (if you used the letter above), or position the cursor where you want the name to appear. Select **Mailings|Write & Insert Fields|Insert Merge Field**. The drop-down list or the **Insert Merge Field** dialog lists the recognized fields from the source file. Select *CustomerName*. The selection or insertion point will insert *CustomerName* into the document. This will be a field (which will be highlighted if you have field highlighting on), enclosed in double brackets («»). The double brackets indicate this is a mail merge field.

5. Repeat for each of the following in the template document: **BoxesOrdered** and **Balance** (include the dollar sign for **Balance**, since the data source includes that symbol as part of the field). If you double click existing text to select it, be sure to exclude any trailing white space, such as a space character.

The document should look like this:

> Dear «CustomerName»,
>
> We hope you enjoyed your «BoxesOrdered» boxes of cookies. Please promptly pay the outstanding «Balance» balance.

Since this is being sent only to those with an outstanding balance, you need to set the selection condition as follows:

6. Click **Mailings|Start Mail Merge|Edit Recipient List**. This displays the **Mail Merge Recipients** dialog. This dialog combines several individual dialogs, but more helpful is that it displays the receipt list along with all the associated fields and their values on the screen. As you set include or exclude conditions, this dialog shows the currently selected items.

7. Click **Filter**. The **Filter and Sort** dialog displays. This dialog will set conditions that can include or exclude receipts. In the **Filter Records** tab (the default), perform the following actions:
   - **Field:** Select **Overdue?** from the drop-down list.
   - **Comparison:** Select **Equal to** from the drop-down list.
   - **Compare to:** Enter **Yes**. This entry corresponds to the literal value (it's also case sensitive) from the database. Since the resulting **Mail Merge Recipients** displays the currently selected names, you can double-check the query results before continuing.
   - Click **OK**.
   - Click **OK** again to close the **Mail Merge Recipients** dialog.

The last step is to implement the merge:

8. Select **Mailings|Finish|Finish & Merge**, choosing **Edit Individual Documents**. The **Merge to New Document** dialog displays.

9. Select **All**; this is the default.

10. Click **OK**.

This creates a new Word document with sections for each recipient who has an overdue account. Each field completes with the correct information.

Mail merge is actually a type of a field. if you have field shading on (**Office|Word Options|Advanced**, Show document content, Field Shading), you can see which ones are fields and you can even toggle the field to see the field codes. You can see the fields that relate directly to the Mail Merge options from the **Field** dialog by selecting **Mail Merge** from the **Categories** drop-down list. That also means, you can insert many of the merge fields through the Field dialog (**Insert|Quick Parts|Text**, Fields). In that regard, the **Mailings|Write & Insert Fields|Insert Merge Field** button is a convenience button, since it presents the merge field name (such as CustomerName or Boxes Ordered from the previous example) automatically. If you manually inserted the merge field name you might misspell it, displaying an **Invalid Merge Field** error dialog when you try to run the merge.

Because mail merge is a field, you can use other fields in the mail merge template. The other fields are independent of the mail merge field and can be use normally. For example, you could insert the current date, shown here expanded.

{ DATE \@ "MMMM d, yyyy" }

Dear «CustomerName»,

We hope you enjoyed your «BoxesOrdered» boxes of cookies. Please promptly pay the outstanding «Overdue» balance.

You can also make the form more interactive. For example, you can add an FILLIN field so you can specify a due-by date.

{ DATE \@ "MMMM d, yyyy" }

Dear «CustomerName»,

We hope you enjoyed your «BoxesOrdered» boxes of cookies. Please promptly pay the outstanding «Overdue» balance by { FILLIN "Have the customer pay the amount by:" \d "the first Monday of the month" \o }.

The **FILLIN** field prompts you to include a payment due date and displays the result in the text. The \o switch at the end means the field will be invoked once for the mail merge run. If omitted, it will prompt for each record, which could be annoying for even shorter mail merge runs. If you need to use that response in more than one location in the document, use the ASK field. ASK stores the response as a bookmark that can be referenced multiple times.

Be aware that you can encounter problems when using fields in a mail merge. Some of the fields survive the mail merge process intact, that is, as still functioning fields. For example, the **DATE** field is not changed, which means the display date will change dynamically after customers get the document.

Converting a date to a static field

To force **DATE** fields to be static dates after the merge, use { QUOTE { DATE } }. You can include any formatting options and switches you need. This example shows the date down to the seconds:

```
{ QUOTE { DATE \@ "M/d/yyyy h:mm:ss am/pm" } }
```

Formatting numbers and currency

You can control the number and currency formatting by using a numeric picture switch. To format number and currency text:

Procedure 8.11. Format numbers and currency

1. Select the field and reveal the field coding (use **Shift-F9** or right click and select **Toggle Field Codes**). The field will look like {MERGEFIELD MyNumber}.

2. Edit the field with the switch information at the end. For example:

```
{MERGEFIELD MyData \# $,0.00}
```

3. Update the field (using **F9** while positioned in the field or right click and select **Update Field**). Updating the field doesn't show an actual value (other than the mail merge field name) until the mail merge is run.

The numeric picture switch has several options:

\# 0	Displays rounded whole numbers.
\# ,0	Displays rounded whole numbers with a thousands separator.
\# ,0.00	Displays numbers with two decimal places, with a thousands separator.
\# $,0	Displays rounded whole dollars with a thousands separator.
\# $,0.00;($,0.00);'-'	For currency, with brackets around negative numbers and a hyphen for 0 values. If you use a final ";" in the formatting switch with nothing following, (\# $,0.00;($,0.00);) zero values will be suppressed. Note that this suppresses zeros resulting from empty fields and from fields containing the value zero.

The precision (the displayed number of decimal points) is controlled by the string "0.00". You can use anything from 0 to 0.000000000000000 (15 places).

Procedure 8.12. Replace a missing or empty value

If a record has a missing or empty value, the mail merge output will be blank. You can replace a missing or empty value with a placeholder of zero.

1. In your mail merge template, select a numeric merge field. In the cookie sale example, select «Balance».

2. Press **CTRL-F9**, which encloses the selection in a new field. The result looks like:

    ```
    {«Balance»}
    ```

3. Enter Set Value at the start of the field. The result looks like:

    ```
    { Set Value «Balance»}
    ```

4. After the existing field, insert a new field. Move the insertion point after the field and press **CTRL-F9**. The result looks like:

    ```
    { Set Value «Balance»}{}
    ```

5. Enter =Val \# "$,0.00" into the new field. The result looks like:

    ```
    {Set Val «Value»}{=Val \# "$,0.00"}
    ```

6. Run your mail merge. Any missing or empty {«Balance»} fields will display *$0.00*.

Using math with mail merge

Mail merge fields can use math functions in the same as other fields. In this example, the fields calculate the late fee of 10% on the outstanding balances.

Procedure 8.13. Basic mail merge math

1. In your mail merge template, select the numeric merge field. In the previous examples, add a new line ("New balance including late fee: ").

2. Add a mail merge field based on the balance (**Mailings|Write & Insert Fields|Insert Merge Field**, selecting **Balance**.

3. Select the new field «Balance». Press **CTRL-F9**, which encloses the selection in a new field. The result looks like:

   { «Balance» }

4. Before the «Balance» field, insert an equal sign (=), and after the «Balance» field insert * 1.1 \# "$,0.00". The resulting field should look like:

   { = {«Balance»} * 1.1 \# "$,0.00" }, or fully expanded:

   { = {MERGEFIELD Balance} * 1.1 \# "$,0.00" }

5. Run your mail merge.

Using dates with mail merge

Date formats vary widely among different databases, computer regional settings, internal application formats, and even connection types. For example, when Word connects to an OLE DB data source, Word treats dates as if they are in the American mm/dd/yy format, regardless of the format in the data source. Formatting switches in fields address that, making consistency possible, regardless of the format is used in the data source or otherwise.

To explicitly set a date format, you can use a combination of d (day), M (upper case for month), y (year), h (hour), m (lower case for minutes), and s (second). A good set of examples is presented in the **Field** dialog (**Insert|Text|Quick Parts**, selecting **Fields**) in the **Date formats** list of the **Date** field. The corresponding field code displays as you click different listed formats. For months, a single M represents the numeric value of the month (*3* for March, for example), MM as a two digit month number (*03* for March), MMM as the three letter abbreviation (*Mar* for March), and MMMM with the full name (*March* for March). In a similar way, d (for day) represents the date a single number, dd, a two digit number, ddd for the abbreviated day of the week (*Fri* for Friday), and dddd as the full name of the day (*Friday* for Friday).

Table 8.1 contains some date format examples.

Table 8.1. Sample date expressions

Expression	Result
{ «MyDate» \@ "dddd, d MMMM yyyy"; }	Friday, 4 March 2011
{ «MyDate» \@ "ddd, d MMMM yyyy"; }	Fri, 4 March 2011
{ «MyDate» \@ "d MMM yyyy"; }	4, Mar 2011
{ «MyDate» \@ "dd/MMM/yyyy"; }	04/Mar/2011
{ «MyDate» \@ "d-MM-yy"; }	4-Mar-11

Masking a US Social Security Number

If you store US Social Security Numbers in the standard format of 123-45-6789, you can use fields to display only the last four digits of the number. The field below, SSN is the merge field name containing the number.

```
{QUOTE{SET ID {MERGEFIELD SSN}}{SET Part3{=({ID}*(-1)-ID)/2}}"XXX-XX-
"{Part3 \# 0000}}
```

Including a picture

IncludePicture can be used in mail merges to place pictures. For example, you might want to customize a signature by using a graphic file of the person's signature or include a picture of the product a customer ordered.

To use **IncludePicture**, the name of the graphic file needs to be included in the source database. That file name can either be the complete path name of the file, a partial path name, or just the name of the graphic file. In the last two cases, the **IncludePicture** field code must include the rest of the path name to completely identify the target file. Procedure 8.14 shows how to create a mail merge **IncludePicture** field.

Procedure 8.14. Create a mail merge IncludePicture field

1. Create a mail merge template file.

2. Insert the **IncludePicture** field where you want it. You can either use the ribbon (**Insert|Text|Quick Parts|Fields** , selecting **IncludeText**) or insert the field manually using **CTRL-F9** in create the field brackets.

3. Construct the field to look like this:

   ```
   { INCLUDEPICTURE "{ IF TRUE "{MERGEFIELD SignatureFile}"}" \d}
   ```

   The IF TRUE statement is a trick needed to unlink the picture from its source. You can leave it out but will have to update the picture, either manually or with an automatic update event.

SignatureFile is the database label for the path to the graphic. Normally, an **IncludePicture** file path name requires the path to have double backslashes (such as c:\\folder1\\folder2\\filename.jpg). However, in a mail merge either double slashes or single backslashes (such as c:\folder1\folder2\filename.jpg) may be used. A partial path name may be used in the database. For example, if only the file name (such as signature1.jpg) were used, the field should look like:

```
{ INCLUDEPICTURE
  "{ IF TRUE "C:\\folder1\\folder2\\{MERGEFIELD SignatureFile}"}" \d}
```

With a partial path name (such as \\folder2\\signature1.jpg) it should look like:

```
{ INCLUDEPICTURE
  "{ IF TRUE "C:\\folder1\\{MERGEFIELD SignatureFile}"}" \d}
```

The inserted graphic file cannot be resized automatically. If you need this done, there are only two options: Resize the image at the source by modifying the source file, or resize the images after the mail merge. If you see the rendered graphic in the mail merge template file, do not directly modify the picture. Modifying the picture will freeze the field (it deletes the field and replaces it with the graphic) to the last rendered image, an action that you can't undo. To reset the dynamic mail merge picture, you have to insert the field anew.

Export

You can use the techniques above to import information into a Word document. You can still paste into a Word document and create a link back to the spreadsheet in the same way you can paste and link between documents. Word can export information to other applications or save it in different formats.

Using Copy/Paste to Export Information

One of the easiest ways to transfer information from Word to another application is through the copy and paste operation. Select and copy the data from the Word document and paste it into the target document or application. Other applications may not allow data to be pasted in as easily as Word will. In those cases, see the documentation for that application. Data is usually transferable among Microsoft Office applications.

Using Macros and VBA to Export Information

Macros and VBA can be used to copy and paste information among Microsoft Office applications. In our previous examples, the macro operations were wholly contained within Word, but you can involve other applications, such as Excel. However, you can't record a macro to do this because Word will not record the Excel portions of the sequence. The same is true if you try recording the macro with Excel.

Instead, you have to modify the code. For example, the macro in Example 8.8 copies the selection from Word and pastes it into the active Excel spreadsheet in its active cell. Since Word is issuing commands to another application, Word has to load the target's object model before running this. To add Excel's object model to the VBA IDE, use Procedure 8.15.

Procedure 8.15. Add Excel document object model

1. Click **Developer|Code|Visual Basic** to launch the IDE. Select the **Tools** menu, choosing **References**. This displays the **References** dialog.

2. Check the **Microsoft Excel 12.0 Object Library**. This is a reference to Office 2007's Excel, which is numbered as version 12; each Office release will be different.

3. Click **OK**. The Excel object model and functions are now available for Word to use.

Example 8.8 runs from Word; a spreadsheet has to be open before running the macro.

```
Sub CopyFromWordToExcel()
  Selection.Copy

  Dim excelApplication As Excel.Application
  Set excelApplication = GetObject(, "Excel.Application")

  Dim targetSpreadsheet As Excel.Worksheet
  Set targetSpreadsheet = _
    excelApplication.ActiveWorkbook.Sheets(1)

  targetSpreadsheet.Paste
End Sub
```

Example 8.8. Copy a selection from Word to Excel

Using Save As to Export Information

You can save the contents of a document to a different format. To change the format, use **Save As** and select the new format in the **Save As Type** drop-down list. The formats aren't as specialized as Excel's, but that's due more to the nature of the Word document. For example, Excel can save as a CSV and tab-delimited file, but only because of the tabular nature of the spreadsheet format. Word can save as plain text, but loses the table and formatting. When formatting is important, you may want to copy the tables to Excel, then save the file in another format.

Copying a table into a spreadsheet

Although Word doesn't have the tabular nature of Excel, you can still save or copy information directly into a spreadsheet and preserve the columns. Copying and pasting a table from Word into Excel is straightforward. You can manually copy a table, but the paste into Excel may include unwanted borders. To get around that, you have to change the **Match Destination Formatting** option. A macro can help, but a recorded macro won't record the Excel procedures.

The macro in Example 8.9 copies a table by selecting the entire table, or a part of it, and pasting it as text, without the border formatting, into the active cell of an open spreadsheet. Before running, you need to add a reference to the Microsoft Excel 12.0 Object Library (see Procedure 8.15).

```
Sub CopyTableToSpreadsheet()
  On Error GoTo MyErrorhandler

  'Selects the entire table
  Selection.Tables(1).Range.Copy

  'Excel Information
  Dim excelApplication As Excel.Application
  Set excelApplication = GetObject(, "Excel.Application")
  excelApplication.ActiveWorkbook.Sheets(1).PasteSpecial _
    Format:="HTML", Link:=False, DisplayAsIcon:=False, _
    NoHTMLFormatting:=True

  Exit Sub
```

```
MyErrorhandler:
  If Err.Number = 429 Then
    MsgBox "No spreadsheet is opened. Please open one."
  Else
    MsgBox "CopyTableToSpreadsheet" & vbCrLf & _
        Err.Description & vbCrLf & Err.Number
  End If
End Sub
```

Example 8.9. Copy a Word table to an Excel spreadsheet

This macro also has error handling in case a spreadsheet has not been opened. It traps error number 429, which says there is no open spreadsheet and displays a more useful message.

Saving Word Form Information to Excel

Word allows you to create a form, which is a document that has fields a user can enter information into. Of course you can save the document as a whole, but you can also save just the information in the fields to a text file. For example, if you have a valid form open in Word, to save only the user entered information, use Procedure 8.16.

Procedure 8.16. Save form information

1. Click the **Office** icon and then click **Word Options**

2. Click **Advanced** on the left.

3. In **Preserve fidelity when sharing this document**, check **Save form data as delimited text file**.

4. Click **OK**.

5. Save the file. The default file type is a text file (`.txt`), instead of `.docx`.

The saved file will have each field within quotes and separated by commas. Excel or Word recognizes this format as a legitimate data source: a comma separated values (CSV) file. The point is to be able to collect information from users and export the information into some kind of database, including Excel. But Microsoft only goes half way toward that end.

First, the **Save form data as delimited text file** option is not persistent. That is, it applies to one document and just for one save operation. Assuming you have collected many of these files it becomes annoying to reset that option each time. Furthermore, the users of the form are unlikely to remember or care to set this option. And even if they did, you would still end up with many individual files that still have to get into a database.

The macro in Example 8.10 addresses these issues. The macro goes through a predetermined folder, searches for all `.docx` files, and extracts the information into a single Excel spreadsheet. You need to be sure that the folder only contains the completed forms saved as `.docx` files and not as plain text files (`.txt`).

Before running this macro, you need to add references for Microsoft Excel 12.0 Object Library and Microsoft Scripting Runtime Library (see Procedure 8.15 (p. 188)).

```
 1 Public Sub GetFileInformation()
 2   On Error GoTo MyErrorhandler
 3
 4   Dim myFolderPath As String
 5   'Excel Information
 6   myFolderPath = "c:\enter your\path to the\forms folder"
 7   Dim excelApplication As Excel.Application
 8   Set excelApplication = GetObject(, "Excel.Application")
 9
10   Dim targetSpreadsheet As Excel.Worksheet
11   Set targetSpreadsheet = _
12     excelApplication.ActiveWorkbook.Sheets(1)
13
14   'File System object
15   Dim FSO As New FileSystemObject
16
17   Dim oFolder As Folder
18
19   Set oFolder = FSO.GetFolder(myFolderPath)
20
21   Dim oFiles As Files
22   Set oFiles = oFolder.Files
23
24   Dim TmpDoc As Document
25   Dim oFile As File
26   For Each oFile In oFiles
27     Debug.Print oFile.Name
28
29     If LCase$(Right$(oFile.Name, 5)) = LCase$(".docx") Then
30       Set TmpDoc = Documents.Open(FileName:=oFile.Path, _
31         Visible:=True)
32
33       TmpDoc.SaveAs FileName:=oFolder & "\tempFile.txt", _
34         FileFormat:=wdFormatText, AddToRecentFiles:=False, _
35           SaveFormsData:=True
36
37       TmpDoc.Close wdDoNotSaveChanges
38       Set TmpDoc = Nothing
39
40       Set TmpDoc = Documents.Open(FileName:=oFolder & _
41         "\tempFile.txt", Visible:=True)
42
43       Dim copyRange As Range
44       Set copyRange = TmpDoc.Range
45       copyRange.Find.Execute findtext:="""","""", _
46         replacewith:="""""" & vbTab & _
47         """""", Replace:=wdReplaceAll
48       copyRange.Find.Execute findtext:=Chr(34), _
49         replacewith:=vbNullString, _
50         Replace:=wdReplaceAll
51
52       TmpDoc.Range.Copy
53       TmpDoc.Close wdDoNotSaveChanges
54       Kill oFolder & "\tempFile.txt"
55
```

```
56        Dim availableRow As Long
57        availableRow = _
58          targetSpreadsheet.Cells( _
59          targetSpreadsheet.Rows.Count, 1). _
60              End(xlUp).Offset(1, 0).Row
61        targetSpreadsheet.Cells(availableRow, 1).Select
62        targetSpreadsheet.Paste
63      End If
64
65      DoEvents
66    Next
67
68    Exit Sub
69
70 MyErrorhandler:
71    MsgBox "GetFileInformation" & vbCrLf & _
72        Err.Description & vbCrLf & Err.Number
73 End Sub
```

Example 8.10. Extract information from multiple forms into a single Excel spreadsheet

To use Example 8.10 you need to enter the path name to your folder with the form files, into the variable myFolderPath (line 6). Open the target, an Excel spreadsheet, before running the macro. The macro automatically selects the active cell. The mechanics of going through the folder for files are handled by FileSystemObject (see line 15), which is a library that handles file operations that VBA or Office don't normally handle.

The macro opens each file (line 30) and saves it with the **Save form data as delimited text file** option (line 33), thus keeping only the field information. It then opens the resulting text file (line 40), changes the commas outside of any quotation marks (since commas could be part of the data itself), removes the quotation marks, and then copies and pastes the text into a spreadsheet (lines 43-62). The text pastes into columns because Excel uses tabs for that purpose; using only commas would enter everything in a single cell. The two Find statements (lines 45 & 48) make those changes. Finally, the macro deletes the temporary text file (line 53) and searches for the next .docx file.

Summary

Word has many capabilities for importing and exporting data. This makes it a versatile tool, not just for moving data from one format to another, but also for creating new reports, documents, and dynamic, updatable charts. This starts with the venerable copy and paste. For the same amount of effort, you can link data to another document. You can insert a document or show part of a spreadsheet. Finally, you can query databases – anything from a plain text file to a corporate database – and import, update, and format that data into your own documents. Although all of these options are available through the ribbon, automation and macros allow you to speed this up. In some cases, you can easily perform tasks that would be prohibitively time consuming if done without automation.

Code Samples

This appendix takes a different approach to introducing programming concepts. The topics and code here are examples and partial programs, called snippets. I encourage you to use the samples as a starting point for your macros, or add them to your existing macros as needed. Of course, the samples are not complete and do not exhaustively represent each topic. As with other parts of this book, they do not attempt to solve any one problem – given the range of requirements for all users this would be prohibitively complex – rather, they present a range of possible solutions. This allows you to create a framework and hopefully a starting point to meet your challenges.

This is not a programmer's guide to VBA. I do not attempt to provide every detail about each VBA call or to cover the VBA language. For example, the SaveAs function has 16 parameters, but only two are discussed here. Instead, I try to highlight the most common or most useful parameters. You can see the full range of options for any function using the IDE or IntelliSense. I encourage you to further explore these options. These examples may be used by themselves or used to modify examples elsewhere in this book to meet your needs.

This appendix introduces the examples by topic. Along with each example are notes describing the purpose of the code and its usage. Most of the examples are not complete functions, but are meant to be included in macros. At the end of the appendix are several complete examples.

Macro Structure

Macros follow a well defined structure. Although the code inside each macro can vary considerably, the macro itself has three basic structure members: declaration type, scope, and parameters.

Declaration Type

A macro must be declared as one of two types: Function or Sub (subroutine). A Function returns a value, a Sub does not. Each may also be referred to as a *routine* or *macro*. Macros declared as subroutines are more common. The macro recorder in Word generates only subroutines; functions have to be hand-written or hand-modified.

Subroutine declarations

Here is the basic declaration for a subroutine:

```
Sub SubName()
End Sub
```

Example A.1 simulates rolling a six-sided die and displays the result (such as *You rolled a: 5*).

```
Sub RollSixSidedDie()
    MsgBox "You rolled a: " & Int(6 * Rnd) + 1
End Sub
```

Example A.1. Dice simulation subroutine

Function declarations

A function returns a value. That means that a calculation or string value can be passed back to the calling routine and used there. In addition, functions cannot be called from the **Macros** Dialog. Here is the basic declaration for a function:

```
Function SubName() As returnType
    Dim x As returnType
    SubName = x
End Sub
```

In this case, the return value is a variable defined in the last line. That line (SubName = x) looks like an assignment, but it assigns the value to the function name, rather than to a normal variable. Only one value can be returned.

Example A.2 returns the result of rolling a six-sided die.

```
Function RollDieFunction () As Long
        RollDieFunction = Int(6 * Rnd) + 1
End Function
```

Example A.2. Dice simulation function

Example A.3 shows how to call a function from a subroutine.

```
Sub ShowDieRollResult()
    MsgBox "You rolled a: " & RollDieFunction()
End Sub

Function RollDieFunction() As Long
        RollSixSidedDieFunction = Int(6 * Rnd) + 1
End Function
```

Example A.3. Calling a function from a subroutine

The macro ShowDieRollResult calls RollDieFunction and displays the result. By separating the actual die rolling into another routine (either as a Sub or Function) it can be used in more than one place without having to copy the critical part of the code more than once. The critical code here is simple (`Int(6 * Rnd) + 1`) but in other cases it could be more complex. Example A.4 simulates rolling two six-sided dice by calling `RollDieFunction` twice:

```
Sub ShowDieRollResult()
    MsgBox "You rolled a: " & RollDieFunction() + RollDieFunction()
End Sub
```

Example A.4. `RollDieFunction` **called twice**

Another advantage to using a function is that you can change what the function does – for example, the number of sides the die can have – by adding a parameter, without changing the calling macro. Parameters are described in the section titled "Parameters".

Scope

The scope determines which code modules can see a subroutine or function. Two scope definitions are available: `Public` and `Private`. `Public` allows a routine to be called from different modules. Only `Public` routines can be called from the **Macros** dialog. `Private` limits a routine to only the immediate code module. If omitted, the routine is considered `Public`. Word's macro recorder does not explicitly generate the Public definition. Example A.5 shows declarations for `Public` and `Private` functions and subroutines.

```
Public Sub SubName()
End Sub

Private Sub SubName()
End Sub

Public Function FunctionName() as returntype
End Sub

Private Function FunctionName() as returntype
End Sub
```

Example A.5. `Public` **and** `Private` **declarations**

Parameters

Parameters (also called arguments) represent variables that can be passed to a routine. Example A.6 shows function and subroutine calls with parameters.

```
Sub SubName(parametername as type)
End Sub

Function FunctionName(parametername as type) as returntype
End Sub
```

Example A.6. Calls with parameters

A macro can be defined with any number of parameters (however, Word's macro generator does not record macros with parameters). To pass in multiple parameters, separate them by commas.

Example A.7 takes two parameters:

```
Sub SubName(parametername1 as type,
            parametername2 as type)
End Sub
```

Example A.7. Macro with two parameters

Example A.8 takes three:

```
Function FunctionName(parametername1 as type,
                      parametername2 as type,
                      parametername3 as type) as returntype
End Sub
```

Example A.8. Macro with three parameters

Example A.9 shows how Example A.2 (p. 194) can be modified to add a parameter that indicates how many sides a die has.

```
Function RollDieFunction(dieSides As Long) As Long
    RollDieFunction = Int(dieSides * Rnd) + 1
End Function
```

Example A.9. `RollDieFunction` with parameter

The calling routine can specify any number. Example A.10, " `RollDieFunction` called with a value of two" passes in two; essentially flipping a coin. Calling with a value of six would give you a conventional die roll, but you can choose any value.

```
Sub ShowDieRollResult()
    MsgBox "You rolled a: " & RollDieFunction(2)
End Sub
```

Example A.10. `RollDieFunction` called with a value of two

Code Examples

With the three basic parts of a macro defined, the rest of the macro contains the code specific to the task. This section contains examples of code snippets that you can use to form macros.

Assigning a Document

Although referring to the currently-used document with the `ActiveDocument` object is common, it's generally better to use an explicit variable in case the user switches among several open documents while the macro is running. Example A.11 shows how to do this.

```
Public Sub GetActiveDocument()
    Dim currentDocument As Document
    Set currentDocument = ActiveDocument()
End Sub
```

Example A.11. Assigning the active document to a variable

Selection

These operations select text or an item. In Word programming, the act of highlighting a range of a text or items is called a Select, and the collection of highlighted text or items is the Selection. Using the Selection is a common and perhaps overused convenience. Even though each opened document can have text or objects selected, Word considers the Selection to be only in the active document. You might get unexpected results if you refer to the Selection and the user changes the active document while the macro is running (this might happen if the macro runs for a long time or at least longer than the user's attention span). I prefer to use the Range object.

Here are some Selection examples:

```
ActiveDocument.Select
```
Selects the entire document using `ActiveDocument`.

```
currentDocument.Select
```
Selects the entire document using `currentDocument`.

```
currentDocument.Paragraphs(1).Range.Select
```
Selects the first paragraph.

```
currentDocument.Words(1).Select
currentDocument.Words(10).Select
```
Selects the first word; selects the tenth word.

```
currentDocument.Characters(1).Select
currentDocument.Characters(100).Select
```
Selects the first character; selects the 100th character.

```
currentDocument.Sections(1).Range.Select
currentDocument.Sections(3).Range.Select
```
Selects the entire first section; selects the third section.

```
currentDocument.Sections(2).Range.Words(10).Select
```
Selects the tenth word of the second section.

```
currentDocument.Range(10, 20).Select
```
Selects the tenth through 20th characters of the document. This method uses a `Range` object to define the selection but the Selection object is also considered a `Range`.

```
Selection.Text = "Newly added text."
```
Replaces the selected text with "Newly added text."

```
Selection.Font.Name = "Verdana"
Selection.Font.Size = 8.5
```
Changes the selected text to 8.5 pt Verdana.

```
Selection.Font.Bold = True
Selection.Font.Underline = wdUnderlineSingle
```
Changes the selected text to bold. The underline is a single line but there are 18 options available.

```
ActiveDocument.Paragraphs(1).Range.Font.ColorIndex = wdDarkYellow
```
Changes the color of a Range object, here set to the first paragraph, font to dark yellow.

Microsoft defines the ColorIndex values to include: wdBlack, wdRed, wdGray25, wdTurquoise, wdYellow.

The ColorIndex is a value from a set number of colors. wdBlack, for example, is defined as 1 and is the first value in that set.

```
Selection.Font.Color = vbRed
```
Changes the color of the selected font to red. Visual Basic defines several colors that are commonly used: vbBlack, vbRed, vbGreen, vbYellow, vbBlue, vbMagenta, vbCyan, vbWhite.

The Color property, unlike ColorIndex, is not from a set of colors but defines the color in the three components of red, green, and blue (the RGB model).

```
Dim myRange As Range
Set myRange = ActiveDocument.Paragraphs(1).Range
myRange.Font.Color = wdColorDarkRed
```
Changes the color of a Range object – here set to the first paragraph – font to green.

Microsoft Office has its own set of defined colors, over 70, which include: wdColorBlack, wdColorBrown, wdColorGray10, wdColorLightTurquoise, wdColorDarkYellow.

```
ActiveDocument.Paragraphs(1).Range.Font.Color = RGB(255, 0, 0)
```
Set the font color of the first paragraph to red.   →RED

The color is defined using the RGB model. The first value is the red component, followed by the green, and finally blue. Each value can be zero through 255.

```
Selection.Move
```
Moves the selection one character to the left. After the move the selection is collapsed to become a single character insertion point.

```
Selection.Move unit:=wdWord, Count:=3
```
Moves the selection and new insertion point three words to the left. If the Count value was negative, it would move three words to the right.

Possible values for unit are: wdCharacter, wdWord, wdSentence, wdParagraph, wdSection, wdStory, wdCell, wdColumn, wdRow, wdTable.

```
Selection.Expand unit:=wdSentence
```
Expands the selection to include entire current sentence.

Possible values for unit are: wdCharacter, wdWord, wdSentence, wdParagraph, wdSection, wdStory, wdCell, wdColumn, wdRow, wdTable.

```
Selection.Extend Character:="T"
```
Extends the selection from the start of the selection to the next occurring "T".

```
Selection.Move unit:=wdWord, Count:=3
ActiveDocument.Bookmarks("\word").Range.Select
```

Move the selection ahead three words and then selects the next word. The bookmark "\word" is part of a class of predefined bookmarks that are always available, remain current after each operation, and cannot be deleted.

Possible values for predefined bookmarks are: \Line, \Char, \Para, \Section, \Dock, \Page, \StartOfDoc, \EndOfDoc, \Cell, \Table.

You can specify more complex ranges by setting the Start and End points, You can start with a range, say the main story, and then trim the beginning and/or ending positions by assigning a new value. Example A.12 uses a Range object. Ranges, which have to be declared and set ahead of time, are internal representations of areas within the document and are more versatile than Selection. Example A.12 initially sets the range to be the main story of currentDocument (line 6) and then defines the range to include the second and third paragraphs (lines 8 & 9).

```
 1 Public Sub SelectRangeFromDocument()
 2     Dim currentDocument As Document
 3     Set currentDocument = ActiveDocument
 4
 5     Dim myRange As Range
 6     Set myRange = currentDocument.Range
 7
 8     myRange.Start = currentDocument.Paragraphs(2).Range.Start
 9     myRange.End = currentDocument.Paragraphs(3).Range.End
10     myRange.Select
11 End Sub
```

Example A.12. Using a `Range` object

Example A.13 combines the range definition into a single command:

```
Public Sub SelectRangeFromDocument()
    Dim currentDocument As Document
    Set currentDocument = ActiveDocument

    Dim myRange As Range
    Set myRange = currentDocument.Range
    Set myRange = _
        currentDocument.Range( _
            Start:=currentDocument.Paragraphs(2).Range.Start, _
            End:=currentDocument.Paragraphs(3).Range.End)
    myRange.Select
End Sub
```

Example A.13. Using a `Range` object – alternate

A range can be calculated. Example A.14 creates a range that begins with the first word and extends for N more words, where N is a random number between one and six.

```
Public Sub SelectRangeFromDocument()
    Dim currentDocument As Document
    Set currentDocument = ActiveDocument

    Dim myRange As Range
    Set myRange = currentDocument.Range

    myRange.Start = currentDocument.Words(1).Start
    myRange.End = currentDocument.Words(Int(6 * Rnd) + 1).End
    myRange.Select
End Sub
```

Example A.14. `Range` **object with calculated range**

Copy

This function makes a copy of the selected text or object in the Office Clipboard. The Copy function is usually accompanied by the Paste function.

```
Selection.Copy
```
Copies the currently selected text or object.

```
ActiveDocument.Range.Copy
```
Copies the entire document using ActiveDocument

```
currentDocument.range.copy
```
Copies the entire document using currentDocument.

```
Dim myRange As Range
Set myRange = currentDocument.Range
Set myRange = _
currentDocument.Range(_
Start:=currentDocument.Paragraphs(2).Range.Start, _
End:=currentDocument.Paragraphs(3).Range.End)
myRange.Copy
```
Copies the second and third paragraph of a document

Example A.15 copies the body content of the active document to a new document.

```
Public Sub GetActiveDocument()
    Dim currentDocument As Document
    Set currentDocument = ActiveDocument()

    Dim targetDocument As Document
    Set targetDocument = Documents.Add()

    currentDocument.Range.Copy
    targetDocument.Range.Paste
End Sub
```

Example A.15. Copy active document contents to a new document

Expanding that example, Example A.16 is a simple "Save Copy As" routine. It makes a copy of the open document and saves it but keeps the current copy open, which is useful for making periodic backups. In contrast, the Windows Save As feature closes the current document and makes the new version the active one.

```
Public Sub SaveCopyAs()
    On Error GoTo MyErrorHandler

    Dim sourceDocument As Document
    Set sourceDocument = ActiveDocument

    Dim docFullName As String
    docFullName = sourceDocument.FullName

    Dim newDocument As Document
    Set newDocument = sourceDocument.Application.Documents.Add
    sourceDocument.Range.Copy
    newDocument.Range.Paste
    With Dialogs(wdDialogFileSaveAs)
        .Name = "Copy of " & sourceDocument.Name
        .Show
    End With

    newDocument.Close wdDoNotSaveChanges
    Exit Sub

MyErrorHandler:
    MsgBox "SaveCopyAs" & vbCrLf & vbCrLf & _
           "Err = " & Err.Number & vbCrLf & _
           "Description: " & Err.Description
End Sub
```

Example A.16. Save Copy As routine

Paste

The Paste function pastes the contents of the Office Clipboard into the specified range. The range can also be the Selection.

`Selection.Paste`
> Pastes the clipboard items into the currently selected text or object.

`ActiveDocument.Range.Paste`
> Pastes the clipboard items into the `ActiveDocument`, wholly replacing the existing contents with the pasted material.

`currentDocument.Range.Paste`
> Pastes the clipboard items into the `currentDocument`, wholly replacing the existing contents with the pasted material.

`myRange.paste`
> Pastes the clipboard items into the defined `Range`, wholly replacing the existing contents with the pasted material.

Example A.17 copies the first paragraph of the active document and pastes it at the end of that document.

```
Public Sub GetActiveDocument()
    Dim currentDocument As Document
    Set currentDocument = ActiveDocument()

    Dim copyRange As Range
    Set copyRange = currentDocument.Paragraphs(1).Range
    copyRange.Copy

    Dim pasteRange As Range
    Set pasteRange = currentDocument.Range
    pasteRange.Collapse wdCollapseEnd
    pasteRange.Paste
End Sub
```

Example A.17. Copy first paragraph to end of document

Delete

The Delete function deletes the text or object in the specified range, which can be the Selection.

`Selection.Delete`
> Deletes the currently selected text or object.

`ActiveDocument.Range.Delete`
> Deletes all content in the `ActiveDocument`.

`currentDocument.Range.Delete`
> Deletes all content in the `currentDocument`.

```
Dim myRange As Range
Set myRange = Selection.Range
myRange.Delete
```
Deletes the contents in the defined Range. myRange is the current selection.

Looping

Looping repeats a sequence of actions. A loop can have a fixed number of iterations or a variable number that depends on some characteristic like the number of lines in the file or the number of items to be processed. Loops are commonly used to repeat an action throughout an object structure, for example finding all the misspellings or all the characters in a document.

There are three types of loops: For...Next, For Each, and Do While.

For...Next loops

The For...Next loop sets a variable to a starting value, executes a block of code, increments the variable, and repeats until the value of the variable reaches a defined ending point.

Example A.18 counts from 1 to 10, printing the result in the Immediate window of the IDE. The DoEvents call lets the system handle other events. If your program gets into an infinite loop, DoEvents lets you interrupt the routine without exiting Word. I recommend using DoEvents at least while debugging.

```
Dim i As Long
For i = 1 To 10
    Debug.Print i
    DoEvents
Next
```

Example A.18. Simple For...Next loop

Example A.19 sets i to 3 and then increments it by 2 until it is greater than 100. The value of i/3 is displays in the Immediate window of the IDE.

```
Dim i As Long
For i = 3 To 100 Step 2
    Debug.Print i / 3
    DoEvents
Next
```

Example A.19. For...Next loop with step increment

Example A.20 selects each of the first 100 words in the document.

```
Dim i As Long
For i = 1 To 100
    ActiveDocument.Words(i).Select
    DoEvents
Next
```

Example A.20. For...Next loop to select words

Example A.21 selects each word in the document. The starting and ending values for i can also be variables. This example uses the number of words in the document (ActiveDocument.Words.Count) as the ending value.

```
Dim i As Long
For i = 1 To ActiveDocument.Words.Count
    ActiveDocument.Words(i).Select
    DoEvents
Next
```

Example A.21. For...Next loop to select each word in document

Example A.22 starts at 100 and counts down to 1.

```
Dim i As Long
For i = 100 To 1 Step -1
    Debug.Print i / 3
    DoEvents
Next
```

Example A.22. For...Next loop with countdown

Example A.23 deletes each misspelling in the document. Deleting a misspelled word recalculates the SpellErrors collection. Therefore, you have to count backwards, deleting words from the end of the document first.

```
Dim i As Long
For i = ActiveDocument.SpellingErrors.Count To 1 Step -1
    ActiveDocument.SpellingErrors(i).Delete
    DoEvents
Next
```

Example A.23. For...Next loop to delete misspelled words

For Each loops

The For Each loop repeats a loop based on the number of items in an object. The advantage is that you don't have to know how many items there are (if there are no objects, the loop will not be entered). For Each loops are generally faster than For...Next loops.

Example A.24 selects each word in the document. The variable myWord is assigned the value of the current word on each iteration.

```
Dim myWord As Range
For Each myWord In ActiveDocument.Words
    myWord.Select
    DoEvents
Next
```

Example A.24. For Each loop to select each word in a document

Example A.25 selects each bookmark in the document.

```
Dim myBookmark As Bookmark
For Each myBookmark In ActiveDocument.Bookmarks
    myBookmark.Select
    DoEvents
Next
```

Example A.25. `For Each` **loop to select each bookmark in the active document**

Example A.26 selects each hyperlink in the document.

```
Dim myHyperlink As Hyperlink
For Each myHyperlink In ActiveDocument.Hyperlinks
    myHyperlink.Range.Select
    DoEvents
Next
```

Example A.26. `For Each` **loop to select each hyperlink in the active document**

Example A.27 selects each misspelling in the document. In the previous examples the object and the collection are obviously related (`Hyperlink` object in the **Hyperlinks** collection, and `Bookmark` in the **Bookmarks** collection). This case is not as obvious (`Range` object in the **SpellingErrors** collection). Check the document from time to time to make sure the object/collection matches.

```
Dim myMisspelling As Range
For Each myMisspelling In ActiveDocument.SpellingErrors
    myMisspelling.Select
    DoEvents
Next
```

Example A.27. `For Each` **loop to select spelling errors in the active document**

`Do While` **loops**

Unlike the other two types of loops, which have a definite starting and ending point, the `Do While` loop has a starting point, but it runs until an end condition is met. You must carefully state the end condition and make sure that condition can be met. Otherwise, the loop will never terminate, a condition called an "endless loop" or "infinite loop".

Example A.28 repeats the loop ten times. The condition is checked at the start of loop. When i becomes 10, the loop stops.

```
Public Sub ShowDoLoop()
    Dim i As Long
    i = 0
    Do While i < 10
        Debug.Print i
        i = i + 1
        DoEvents
    Loop
End Sub
```

Example A.28. `Do While` **loop that repeats ten times**

Example A.29 also repeats the loop ten times, but the condition is checked at the bottom of loop. This guarantees that the loop will run at least once.

```
Public Sub ShowDoLoop()
    Dim i As Long
    i = 0
    Do
        Debug.Print i
        i = i + 1
        DoEvents
    Loop While i < 10
End Sub
```

Example A.29. `Do While` **loop with test at bottom of the loop**

Example A.30 attempts to repeat the loop ten times. There is check (i = 7) to leave the loop early using the Exit Do statement. This is the preferred way to exit a loop early.

```
Public Sub ShowDoLoop3()
    Dim i As Long
    i = 0
    Do While i < 10
        Debug.Print i
        i = i + 1
        If i = 7 Then Exit Do
        DoEvents
    Loop
End Sub
```

Example A.30. `Do While` **loop with early exit**

The While...Wend statement (see Example A.31) is an alternative to Do While. The two are functionally equivalent and may be used interchangeably.

```
Public Sub ShowDoLoop4()
    Dim i As Long
    i = 0
    While i < 10
        Debug.Print i
        i = i + 1
        DoEvents
    Wend
End Sub
```

Example A.31. While...Wend loop

Example A.32 deletes misspellings in a document. The loop always deletes the first remaining misspelling until there are none left. Checking the condition at the bottom of the loop will not work since the document may not contain any spelling errors, in which case attempting to delete the first one results in an error.

The Select statement isn't required, but is included for debugging purposes. It highlights the misspelled word so you can see the word before it gets deleted. This is helpful if you're stepping through the code one line at a time.

```
Public Sub ShowDoLoop()
    Dim currentDocument As Document
    Set currentDocument = ActiveDocument

    Do While currentDocument.SpellingErrors.Count > 0
        currentDocument.SpellingErrors(1).Select
        currentDocument.SpellingErrors(1).Delete
        DoEvents
    Loop
End Sub
```

Example A.32. Do While loop to delete misspellings

Example A.33 also deletes misspellings in a document. The loop uses a variation, the Do Until statement. Each loop deletes the first misspelling until the misspelling count becomes zero.

```
Public Sub ShowDoLoop()
    Dim currentDocument As Document
    Set currentDocument = ActiveDocument

    Do Until currentDocument.SpellingErrors.Count = 0
        currentDocument.SpellingErrors(1).Select
        currentDocument.SpellingErrors(1).Delete
        DoEvents
    Loop
End Sub
```

Example A.33. Do Until loop to delete misspellings – alternate

Tables

Tables are a popular feature that allows information to presented in a tabular or matrix format.

Example A.34 selects each table in a document.

```
Dim myTable As Table
For Each myTable In currentDocument
    myTable.Range.Select
    DoEvents
Next
```

Example A.34. Select tables

Example A.35 deletes each table in a document.

```
Dim i As Long
For i = currentDocument.Tables.Count To 1 Step -1
    currentDocument.Tables(i).Select
    currentDocument.Tables(i).Delete
    DoEvents
Next
```

Example A.35. Delete tables

Example A.36 adds a table at the current selection point. The table is identified as a specific object (the Set myTable statement) so that you can reference that specific table by name (myTable.Borders.Enable = True).

```
Dim myTable As Table
Set myTable = currentDocument.Tables.Add(Range:=Selection.Range,
            numRows:=5, NumColumns:=5)
myTable.Borders.Enable = True
```

Example A.36. Add a table

Example A.37 adds a table at the current selection point. The table is identified by its position within the document. In this case, it is the last table in the document (currentDocument.Tables.Count).

```
currentDocument.Tables.Add Range:=Selection.Range,_
    numRows:=5, NumColumns:=5
currentDocument.Tables(currentDocument.Tables.Count).Borders.Enable = True
```

Example A.37. Add a table – alternate

Example A.38 retrieves the text from the cell at row 1, column 2. Text retrieved from table cells always have two character appended at the end of the string. The Left statement removes those two characters so the text appears by itself.

```
Dim cellString As String
cellString = _
  currentDocument.Tables(currentDocument.Tables.Count).Cell(1, 2).Range.Text
Debug.Print Left(cellString, Len(cellString) - 2)
```

Example A.38. Retrieve text from a table

Example A.39 inserts text into the cell at row 1, column 2.

```
currentDocument.Tables(currentDocument.Tables.Count). _
    Cell(1, 2).Range.Text = "Hello, cell"
```

Example A.39. Insert text into a table

Example A.40 selects each row of a table. The table used is the first table (if there more than one) that is contained in the current selection. This includes the cursor if it is in a table. An error occurs if the selection or cursor does not include a table. This code results in an error if any cells have been merged.

```
Public Sub SelectTableRows()
    Dim myTable As Table
    Set myTable = Selection.Tables(1)

    Dim myRow As Row
    For Each myRow In myTable.Rows
        myRow.Select
        DoEvents
    Next
End Sub
```

Example A.40. Select rows in a table

Example A.41 checks if there is a table within the selection (line 2). If there is, it selects each column within the table. This code results in an error if any cells have been merged.

```
 1 Public Sub SelectTableCols()
 2     If Selection.Tables.Count > 0 Then
 3         Dim myTable As Table
 4         Set myTable = Selection.Tables(1)
 5
 6         Dim myColumn As Column
 7         For Each myColumn In myTable.Columns
 8             myColumn.Select
 9             DoEvents
10         Next
11     End If
12 End Sub
```

Example A.41. Look for a table in a selection

Example A.42 selects each cell. This is the classic matrix or table approach.

```
Public Sub SelectTableCells()
    If Selection.Tables.Count > 0 Then
        Dim myTable As Table
        Set myTable = Selection.Tables(1)

        Dim currentRow As Long
        Dim currentColumn As Long
        For currentRow = 1 To myTable.Rows.Count
            For currentColumn = 1 To myTable.Columns.Count
                myTable.Cell(currentRow, currentColumn).Range.Select
                DoEvents
            Next
        Next
    End If
End Sub
```

Example A.42. Select each cell in a table

Example A.43 selects each cell. This approach is more efficient for VBA.

```
Public Sub SelectTableCells2()
    'The document selection must be in table.
    If Selection.Tables.Count > 0 Then
        Dim myTable As Table
        Set myTable = Selection.Tables(1)

        Dim currentCell As Cell
        For Each currentCell In myTable.Range.Cells
            currentCell.Select
            DoEvents
        Next
    End If
End Sub
```

Example A.43. Select each cell in a table – alternate

Example A.44 converts the selected table to text.

```
Public Sub ConvertTableToText()
    'The document selection must be in table.
    Dim myTable As Table
    Set myTable = Selection.Tables(1)
    myTable.ConvertToText
End Sub
```

Example A.44. Convert table to text

Example A.45 converts the selected table to text and then changes the newly created text to bold.

```
Public Sub ConvertTableToText2()
    'The document selection must be in table.
    Dim myTable As Table
    Set myTable = Selection.Tables(1)

    Dim convertedTextRange As Range
    Set convertedTextRange = myTable.ConvertToText()
    convertedTextRange.Font.Bold = True
End Sub
```

Example A.45. Convert table to text and make text bold

Example A.46 converts the selected text to a table.

```
Public Sub ConvertTextToTable()
    'Text must be selected, with each paragraph
    'becoming a table row.
    Selection.ConvertToTable
End Sub
```

Example A.46. Convert text to a table

If the selection is not a single insertion point, Example A.47 converts the selection to a table with a border.

```
Public Sub ConvertTextToTable2()
    'The selection must be at least two characters.
    If Selection.Start <> Selection.End Then
        Dim newTable As Table
        Set newTable = Selection.ConvertToTable()

        'Adds a border
        newTable.Borders.Enable = True
    End If
End Sub
```

Example A.47. Convert text to a table with a border

Documents

These functions operate on the document itself and include features such as opening, closing, saving, making active/inactive, hiding, or naming.

Example A.48 opens a document named test.txt located at the root directory of the C drive.

```
Public Sub OpenADocument()
    'Change 'c:\test.txt' to any valid path and file name
    Application.Documents.Open "c:\test.txt"
End Sub
```

Example A.48. Open a document

Example A.49 opens a document named test.txt located at the root directory of the C drive. The newly opened file is assigned to the testDocument object. This allows that file to be specified along with any other open file.

```
Public Sub OpenADocument2()
    'Change 'c:\test.txt' to any valid path and file name
    Dim testDocument As Document
    Set testDocument = Application.Documents.Open("c:\test.txt")
End Sub
```

Example A.49. Open a document and assign to an object

Example A.50 sets a document object to the first opened document. This does not change the ActiveDocument. This is useful when you want to access another document (for example, to read from or write to) but do not want to change the ActiveDocument.

```
Public Sub OpenADocument3()
    'Gets the document that was last opened.
    Dim myDocument As Document
    Set myDocument = Documents(1)
End Sub
```

Example A.50. Set document object to first opened document

Example A.51 sets a document object to the opened document named Status_Report.docx. This does not change the ActiveDocument.

```
Public Sub OpenADocument4()
    'Change 'Status_Report.docx' to real document name.
    Dim myDocument As Document
    Set myDocument = Documents("Status_Report.docx")
End Sub
```

Example A.51. Set document object to named document

Example A.52 displays the number of currently opened documents.

```
Public Sub ShowNumberOfOpenDocuments()
    MsgBox "Number of opened documents: " & Documents.Count
End Sub
```

Example A.52. Display the number of currently opened documents

Example A.53 displays a message box with all the currently opened documents. The constant vb-CrLf (lines 5 & 8) is the character code for inserting a new line (carriage return and line feed).

```
Public Sub ShowNumberOfOpenDocuments()
    Dim displayString As String
    Dim myDocument As Document
    For Each myDocument In Documents
        displayString = displayString & myDocument.Name & vbCrLf
        DoEvents
    Next
    MsgBox "The list of opened documents:" & vbCrLf & displayString
End Sub
```

Example A.53. Display a message box with all currently opened documents

Example A.54 closes the active document and saves any changes. If the document has not been saved previously, the **Save As** dialog displays.

```
Public Sub CloseActiveDocument()
    'If the file has not be previously saved
    'a Save As dialog displays.
    ActiveDocument.Close wdSaveChanges
End Sub
```

Example A.54. Save and close the active document

Example A.55 saves the active document but doesn't close it. If the document has not been saved previously, the **Save As** dialog displays.

```
Public Sub SaveActiveDocument()
    'If the file has not be previously saved
    'a Save As dialog displays.
    ActiveDocument.Save
End Sub
```

Example A.55. Save the active document

Example A.56 saves the document currentDocument as c:\test.htm and in HTML format.

```
Public Sub SaveActiveDocument2()
    'You can change 'c:\test.htm' to another path and file.
    currentDocument.SaveAs FileName:="c:\test.htm", fileFormat:=wdFormatHTML
End Sub
```

Example A.56. Save a document in a file

Example A.57 creates a new document and assigns it to the newDocument object name.

```
Public Sub CreateNewDocument()
    Dim newDocument As Document
    Set newDocument = Application.Documents.Add
End Sub
```

Example A.57. Create a new document

Example A.58 sets the named object currentDocument window to visible. False sets it to not visible

```
Public Sub MakeActiveDocumentVisible()
    Dim currentDocument As Document
    Set currentDocument = ActiveDocument

    currentDocument.Windows(1).Visible = True
End Sub
```

Example A.58. Set currentDocument to visible

Example A.59 moves the named object currentDocument window's top left corner to 100, 150

```
Public Sub MoveActiveWindow()
    Dim currentDocument As Document
    Set currentDocument = ActiveDocument

    currentDocument.Windows(1).Top = 100
    currentDocument.Windows(1).Left = 150
End Sub
```

Example A.59. Move top left corner of currentDocument

Example A.60 inserts text at the end of the active document. The second statement inserts a paragraph after. The two statements are often used together.

```
Public Sub WriteToDocument()
    'Inserts text at the end of the document
    ActiveDocument.Range.InsertAfter "Hello, there."
    ActiveDocument.Range.InsertParagraphAfter
End Sub
```

Example A.60. Insert text at end of currentDocument

Example A.61 inserts text after the second paragraph.

```
Public Sub WriteToDocument2()
    'Inserts text after the second paragraph.
    'The document has to be begin with at least two paragraphs
    ActiveDocument.Paragraphs(2).Range.InsertAfter "Another sample."
End Sub
```

Example A.61. Insert text after the second paragraph

Example A.62 also inserts text after the second paragraph. This example is similar to Example A.61, except that a range object is used. Using ranges gives you more control over placement of text or other items.

Note that using a range to insert text or objects does not change the location of the cursor or previously selected text.

```
Public Sub WriteToDocument3()
    'Inserts text after the second paragraph.
    'The document has to be begin with at least two paragraphs
    Dim insertRange As Range
    Set insertRange = ActiveDocument.Paragraphs(2).Range
    insertRange.InsertAfter "New text."
    insertRange.InsertParagraphAfter
End Sub
```

Example A.62. Insert text after the second paragraph using `Range` object

Revisions

Revisions are the collection of all the revision marks made in the document. While revisions are turned on, each addition and deletion is recorded in this object. You can selectively review this collection, looking for revisions of interest.

Example A.63 displays the number of revisions in the Immediate window of the IDE

```
Public Sub ShowNumberOfRevisions()
    Debug.Print ActiveDocument.Revisions.Count
End Sub
```

Example A.63. Display number of revisions

Example A.64 accepts all the revisions in the `ActiveDocument`

```
Public Sub AcceptAllRevisions2()
    ActiveDocument.Revisions.AcceptAll
End Sub
```

Example A.64. Accept all revisions

Example A.65 rejects all the revisions in the `ActiveDocument`.

```
Public Sub RejectAllRevisions1()
    ActiveDocument.Revisions.RejectAll
End Sub
```

Example A.65. Reject all revisions

Example A.66 selects each revision in the `ActiveDocument`.

```
Public Sub SelectEachRevision()
    'There should be revisions in the active document.
    Dim myRevision As Revision
    For Each myRevision In ActiveDocument.Revisions
        myRevision.Range.Select
        DoEvents

    Next
End Sub
```

Example A.66. Select revisions

Example A.67 selects the revision if the revision is an insert. The property myRevision.Type is an enumerated property. That means each type of revision is noted with a code. The code wdRevisionInsert in this example is for an insert. Another common value is wdRevisionDelete, which is for deletes. There are 19 codes in all.

```
Public Sub SelectEachRevision2()
    Dim myRevision As Revision
    For Each myRevision In ActiveDocument.Revisions
        If myRevision.Type = wdRevisionInsert Then
            myRevision.Range.Select
        End If
        DoEvents
    Next
End Sub
```

Example A.67. Select insert revisions

Example A.68 displays the author (myRevision.Author) of the revision if the revision is a delete type of change. The Author is the User Name from the Word Option dialog.

```
Public Sub SelectRevisiontType()
    Dim myRevision As Revision
    For Each myRevision In ActiveDocument.Revisions
        If myRevision.Type = wdRevisionDelete Then
            Debug.Print myRevision.Author
        End If
        DoEvents
    Next
End Sub
```

Example A.68. Display author of a revision

Fields

Fields allow you to insert automatically formatted and updated information into your document. You can use fields to display the author's name, the current page number, or a link to other documents.

Example A.69 displays the document name and the number of fields in that document in a message box dialog.

```
Public Sub ShowNumberOfFields()
    MsgBox "Number of fields in " & _
        ActiveDocument.Name & ": " & _
        ActiveDocument.Fields.Count
End Sub
```

Example A.69. Display document name in a field

Example A.70 selects each field in the `ActiveDocument`.

```
Public Sub ShowNumberOfFields2()
    Dim myField As Field
    For Each myField In ActiveDocument.Fields
        myField.Select
        DoEvents
    Next
End Sub
```

Example A.70. Select each field in the `ActiveDocument`

Example A.71 deletes each field in the `ActiveDocument`.

The `Select` statement isn't required but is included for debugging purposes.

```
Public Sub DeleteFields()
    Dim i As Long
    For i = ActiveDocument.Fields.Count To 1 Step -1
        ActiveDocument.Fields(i).Select
        ActiveDocument.Fields(i).Delete
        DoEvents
    Next
End Sub
```

Example A.71. Delete each field in the `ActiveDocument`

Example A.72 inserts the author's field in the Selection. The `wdFieldAuthor` parameter is the field type. There are 94 defined field types; consult the Object Browser in the IDE to see all the enumerated type names.

```
Public Sub InsertField()
    ActiveDocument.Fields.Add Selection.Range, wdFieldAuthor
End Sub
```

Example A.72. Insert Author field in the Selection

Example A.73 creates a field at the insertion point or insertion range.

```
Public Sub InsertField2()
  Selection.Fields.Add Range:=Selection.Range, Type:=wdFieldEmpty, _
    Text:="ASK FavBookType ""What kind of books do you like?"" " & _
        "\d ""True Crime"" ", _
    PreserveFormatting:=True
End Sub
```

Example A.73. Create field at the insertion point

Example A.74 updates all the fields in the document.

```
Sub UpdateFields()
    ActiveDocument.Fields.Update
End Sub
```

Example A.74. Update all fields

Example A.75 updates the specified field, in this case the seventh one. An error would result if there was no seventh field in the document.

```
Sub UpdateFields()
    'There has to be at least seven fields in the document
    ActiveDocument.Fields(7).Update
End Sub
```

Example A.75. Update a specific field

Example A.76 updates only the ASK fields (type wdFieldAsk).

```
Sub UpdateAFieldType()
    Dim myField As Field
    For Each myField In ActiveDocument.Fields
        If myField.Type = wdFieldAsk Then
            myField.Update
        End If
        DoEvents
    Next
End Sub
```

Example A.76. Update ASK fields

Shapes

A shape is an object that represents a drawing. These include the typical drawn shapes such as rectangles, lines, and smart art shapes, but they also include comments, diagrams, pictures, and charts. There are two basic types of shapes: **Shape** and **InlineShape**. An important difference between the two is that a **Shape** can be positioned anywhere on the page. In that regard, it is considered to be "floating" over the text. An **InlineShape** is positioned alongside the text and can positioned at the insertion point along with other text. Altogether, there are 26 different kinds of shapes.

Shapes include text boxes, pictures, charts, lines, or other shapes selected from the **Insert|Illustrations|Shapes** menu. You can treat any shape object similar to other shape objects.

Example A.77 selects each **Shape** object in the document:

```
Sub SelectShape()
    Dim currentDocument As Document
    Set currentDocument = ActiveDocument

    Dim myShape As Shape
    For Each myShape In currentDocument.Shapes
        myShape.Select
        DoEvents
    Next
End Sub
```

Example A.77. Select every `Shape`

Example A.78 selects each **InlinerShape** object in the document:

```
Sub SelectInlineShape()
    Dim currentDocument As Document
    Set currentDocument = ActiveDocument

    Dim myShape As InlineShape
    For Each myShape In currentDocument.InlineShapes
        myShape.Select
        DoEvents
    Next
End Sub
```

Example A.78. Select every `InlineShape`

Example A.79 creates a text box shape at 50, 100 within the document that is 200 points wide and 75 points high. Then, it adds text to that text box.

Other possible values for creating a shape include: `AddCallout`, `AddCanvas`, `AddChart`, `AddCurve`, `AddLabel`, `AddShape`, `AddPolyline`, `AddPicture`, `AddLine`, `AddTextbox`, `AddTextEffect`. Each shape has its own set of parameters.

```
Sub CreateShape()
    Dim currentDocument As Document
    Set currentDocument = ActiveDocument

    Dim myShape As Shape
    Set myShape = _
        currentDocument.Shapes.AddTextbox( _
            Orientation:=msoTextOrientationHorizontal, _
            Left:=50, Top:=100, Height:=75, Width:=200)
    myShape.TextFrame.TextRange.Text = "Text for the textbox."
End Sub
```

Example A.79. Create a text box

Example A.80 deletes each shape in the `currentDocument` object.

The `Select` statement isn't required, but is included for debugging purposes.

```
Sub CreateShape()
    Dim currentDocument As Document
    Set currentDocument = ActiveDocument

    Dim shapeCount As Long
    For shapeCount = currentDocument.Shapes.Count To 1 Step -1
        currentDocument.Shapes(shapeCount).Select
        currentDocument.Shapes(shapeCount).Delete
        DoEvents
    Next
End Sub
```

Example A.80. Delete every shape in the document

Example A.81 deletes all the charts in the document.

Values for `Shape.Type` include: `msoCallout`, `msoChart`, `msoComment`, `msoDiagram`, `msoLine`, `msoPicture`.

```
Sub CreateShape()
    'There needs to be a Smart Art diagram in the document.
    Dim currentDocument As Document
    Set currentDocument = ActiveDocument

    Dim shapeCount As Long
    'SmartArt shapes are 'InlineShape' objects rather than 'Shape' object
    For shapeCount = currentDocument.InlineShapes.Count To 1 Step -1
        currentDocument.InlineShapes(shapeCount).Select
        If currentDocument.InlineShapes(shapeCount).Type = _
         wdInlineShapeSmartArt Then
            currentDocument.InlineShapes(shapeCount).Delete
        End If
        DoEvents
    Next
End Sub
```

Example A.81. Delete every chart in the document

Example A.82 aligns each Shape object in the document to the right margin.

Since the placement is relative to the left margin, the calculation is based on the page width less the left and right margins. The chart's left coordinate (myShape.Left) is then set to the effective page width less the width of the chart (line 13).

```
 1 Sub MoveShapes()
 2     Dim currentDocument As Document
 3     Set currentDocument = ActiveDocument
 4
 5     Dim myShape As Shape
 6     For Each myShape In currentDocument.Shapes
 7         myShape.Select
 8
 9         Dim myRightMargin As Long
10         myRightMargin = currentDocument.PageSetup.PageWidth - _
11             currentDocument.PageSetup.RightMargin - _
12             currentDocument.PageSetup.LeftMargin
13         myShape.Left = myRightMargin - myShape.Width
14         DoEvents
15     Next
16 End Sub
```

Example A.82. Align charts to the margin

Error Handling

Errors are inevitable. During development, you encounter errors as you try new ideas or discover new cases. Some objects will be empty or nonexistent, users may close documents without you knowing, or they may change the active document during a macro's execution. And, sometimes there are bugs in Word. Occasionally you may have to actually generate or depend on errors to continue processing.

In VBA, it's generally best to try to handle errors in each routine. Anticipate as many errors as you can by doing things like checking values before using them or making sure an object has been properly set. For example, before executing the math equation $1/x$, test to be sure x is not equal to zero.

Because you can't avoid all errors in advance, you should also provide code to catch errors. This allows you to either fix or handle the error before it causes the the macro to stop unexpectedly, or worse, make Word itself quit. Error handling statements should be placed as close to the potentially offending lines as possible. In most cases, knowing the exact line ahead of time is not realistic, so consider placing error handling statements to cover the entire routine. In most of the examples listed, the On Error statements are the first lines in the routine.

Trapping errors is easy. Effective error handling is more difficult. Figuring out how to fix an error depends on the situation and your code. Experience is the most useful guide, so the more you write and experiment, the better you will get at error handling. During development, don't be afraid of errors. In fact you need to get them to make the code better. After all, development is the time to find errors, rather than after the code is deployed.

Here are some examples of common ways to handle errors.

Example A.83 displays the standard error dialog when an error is encountered. This is the default handler, so even if you don't explicitly add this statement, an error will by default cause the standard error dialog to be displayed.

```
On Error Goto 0
```

Example A.83. Go to standard dialog on error

Example A.84 ignores the error and continues the program. The next statement is executed. This does not fix the error, it simply ignores it and continues. Depending on the error, the macro may or may not stop. Ignoring errors can be useful, but you need to be careful that an error you skip doesn't crash or stop the macro.

```
On Error Resume Next
```

Example A.84. Ignore errors

Example A.85 transfers execution of the program to the line after the MyErrorHandler label.

```
On Error Goto MyErrorHandler
```

Example A.85. Go to named location on error

The Resume statement transfers control back to the line causing the error, and the Resume Next statement transfers control back to the line after the one causing the error. These statements can only be called while handling an error.

Example A.86 sets a collection to all unique misspellings in a document. Because the collection can only hold unique items, trying to add an existing item will result in an error. However, this error is not really an error; after all, duplicate misspellings are not unlikely in a document. The error statement (On Error Resume Next, line 6) forces the routine to continue to the next line. This is a case where you're relying on an error to good effect.

```
 1 Sub CollectMisspellings()
 2     Dim currentDocument As Document
 3     Set currentDocument = ActiveDocument
 4
 5     Dim myCollection As New Collection
 6     On Error Resume Next
 7     Dim myGrammarError As Range
 8     For Each myGrammarError In currentDocument.SpellingErrors
 9         myCollection.Add myGrammarError.Text, myGrammarError.Text
10         DoEvents
11     Next
12 End Sub
```

Example A.86. Collect misspelled words

Example A.87 sets a collection to all unique misspellings in a document. The code is similar to Example A.86, except a conditional test is made based on the error. Here, error number 457 ("This key is already associated with an element of this collection") is detected (line 11) and a warning is displayed to the user (lines 12 & 13).

```
 1 Sub CollectMisspellings2()
 2     On Error Resume Next
 3     Dim currentDocument As Document
 4     Set currentDocument = ActiveDocument
 5
 6     Dim myCollection As New Collection
 7     Dim myGrammarError As Range
 8     For Each myGrammarError In currentDocument.SpellingErrors
 9         myCollection.Add myGrammarError.Text, myGrammarError.Text
10
11         If Err.Number = 457 Then
12             MsgBox "The word '" & myGrammarError.Text & _
13                     "' has already been added."
14         End If
15
16         DoEvents
17     Next
18 End Sub
```

Example A.87. Detect duplicate misspelled words and display warning

Example A.88 sets a collection to all unique misspellings in a document. The code is similar to Example A.87, except that the error handling is processed at the end of the routine (line 14).

The Exit Sub statement (line 12) is needed to end the routine, otherwise the code will execute into the MyErrorHandler code.

```
 1 Public Sub ErrorHandling2()
 2     Dim myCollection As New Collection
 3
 4     On Error GoTo MyErrorHandler
 5     Dim myGrammarError As Range
 6     For Each myGrammarError In ActiveDocument.SpellingErrors
 7         myCollection.Add myGrammarError.Text, myGrammarError.Text
 8
 9         DoEvents
10     Next
11
12     Exit Sub
13
14 MyErrorHandler:
15     If Err.Number = 457 Then
16         MsgBox "The word '" & myGrammarError.Text & _
17                 "' as already been added."
18         Resume Next
19     End If
20 End Sub
```

Example A.88. Detect duplicate misspelled words and display warning – alternate

Comprehensive Example

Example A.89 collects the misspellings in a document and lists them in a separate document. Rather than just listing the misspelled words, the routine lists the sentence each word appears in (see line 30, myGrammarError.Expand wdSentence) to provide context. The error handling routine (MyErrorHandler) is at line 46 and the On Error statement is at line 2.

Finally, each document object is closed (see line 42, Set outputDocument = Nothing statement). This closes the VBA reference to the document but not the document itself.

 Making the output document invisible is not required (see line 23, outputDocument.Windows(1).Visible = False). However, for longer documents doing this can speed up processing. It may also reduce confusion for the user by hiding the document update and only showing the results when the routine is finished.

```vba
1 Public Sub FindAndListGrammarErrors()
2     On Error GoTo MyErrorHandler
3
4     Dim currentDocument As Document
5     Set currentDocument = ActiveDocument
6
7     'If there are no misspelled words, leave the routine.
8
9     If currentDocument.SpellingErrors.Count = 0 Then
10        MsgBox "There are no misspellings in document: " & _
11                currentDocument.Name
12        Exit Sub
13    End If
14
15    'There are misspelled words, so add a document for the output.
16
17    Dim outputDocument As Document
18    Set outputDocument = Documents.Add()
19
20    'Hide the output document. This is optional, but generally makes
21    'the routine run faster.
22
23    outputDocument.Windows(1).Visible = False
24
25    'Loop through each misspelling and write to the output.
26
27    Dim myGrammarError As Range
28    For Each myGrammarError In currentDocument.SpellingErrors
29        myGrammarError.Select 'Optional; for debugging
30        myGrammarError.Expand wdSentence 'List just the misspelling.
31        myGrammarError.Select 'Optional; for debugging
32
33        outputDocument.Range.InsertAfter myGrammarError.Text
34        outputDocument.Range.InsertParagraphAfter
35
36        DoEvents
37    Next
```

```
38
39        'Finally, show the output document
40
41        outputDocument.Windows(1).Visible = True
42        Set outputDocument = Nothing
43        Set currentDocument = Nothing
44        Exit Sub
45
46 MyErrorHandler:
47        MsgBox "Error: " & Err.Number & vbCrLf & _
48               "Error description: " & Err.Description
49 End Sub
```

Example A.89. Comprehensive example

The Autos

"The Autos," as they are referred to informally, are calls that execute automatically. There are five Autos: AutoOpen, AutoClose, AutoNew, AutoExec and AutoExit, By default none of them are defined, and you have to create them explicitly in order to use them. By creating them, you can perform special actions. For example, you might want to make sure all opened documents have the company template attached. In that case, you might define AutoOpen to run that code.

Two of the Autos, AutoOpen and AutoClose, are document level macros that run whenever the document they are attached to either opens or closes, respectively. The three other Autos – AutoNew, AutoExec, and AutoExit – are template level. They must be defined in a template.

Table A.1 summarizes when and where each auto macro can be used.

Table A.1. The Autos

Macro	Location		
	In document	In attached template (document template)	In global template (Normal.dotx, or dotx in Word startup folder)
AutoOpen: Runs when the document is opened.	Yes	No	No
AutoClose: Runs before the document is closed.	Yes	Yes	Yes
AutoExec: Runs after a globally loaded template is loaded.	No	No	Yes
AutoExit: Runs before a globally loaded template is unloaded.	No	No	Yes
AutoNew: Runs when a document is created.	No	Yes	Yes

Examples of the Autos

Example A.90 displays the document name when the document is opened.

```
Sub AutoOpen()
   MsgBox " This document is named: " & ActiveDocument.Name
End Sub
```

Example A.90. Display document name on open

Example A.91 displays a message when the document is closed.

```
Sub AutoClose()
   MsgBox "Closing document: " & ActiveDocument.Name
End Sub
```

Example A.91. Display message on close

Example A.92 displays a message when a document is created. Place this macro in a template, and it will be executed when a document is created from that template. `AutoOpen` and `AutoNew` are mutually exclusive.

```
Sub AutoNew()
   MsgBox "Creating a new document."
End Sub
```

Example A.92. Display message a document is created

Example A.93 displays a message when a document is launched. `AutoExec` must be placed in a global template, that is, either in Word's startup location or in `Normat.dot` or `Normal.dotm`.

```
Public Sub AutoExec()
   MsgBox "Running AutoExec"
End Sub
```

Example A.93. Display message when a document is launched

Example A.94 displays a message when Word Quits. `AutoExit` must be placed in a global template, that is, either in Word's startup location or in `Normat.dot` or `Normal.dotm`.

```
Public Sub AutoExit()
   MsgBox "Running AutoExit"
End Sub
```

Example A.94. Display message when Word quits

Example A.95 disables all Auto macros after the statement runs.

```
WordBasic.DisableAutoMacros True
```

Example A.95. Disable macros

Example A.96 enables the macros for the remainder of the document's session.

```
WordBasic.DisableAutoMacros False
```

Example A.96. Enable macros

 The state of the Autos (enabled or disabled) is not retained between sessions. They will be enabled the next time the document or template is started. To disable all Autos, hold down the **SHIFT** key while opening a document.

Special Characters

Special characters are best defined by what they are not. They are not letters, numbers, symbols, or punctuation. They include control characters and formatting characters. Table A.2 describes the special characters Visual Basic defines for use in VBA macros.

Table A.2. Special characters

Common Name	VBA Name	ASCII	Description
Carriage return/ Line feed	vbCrLf	13, 10	These two characters together represent a paragraph mark, also called a hard carriage return. They mark the end of a paragraph and add formatting and spacing.
Manual line feed	vbVerticalTab	11	Manual line break, also called a soft carriage return. Paragraph formatting is not applied. Instead, a line break is inserted and the following text is considered part of the same paragraph.
Tab	vbTab	09	Tab
Null String	vbNullString	(null)	Empty string. This is the preferred way to set a string to be empty (myString = vbNullString).
Non-breaking space	chr(160)	160	Similar to a conventional space, but it prevents the line from being broken at its location.
Non-breaking hyphen	chr(30)	30	Characters or words on both sides of a non-breaking hyphen must be kept on the same line.
Soft hyphen	chr(173)	173	Indicates where a hyphen may be inserted inside a word. Only displayed if the word is split.

Examples Using Special Characters

The following examples demonstrate how to use special characters

Example A.97 inserts two lines separated by a paragraph mark.

```
ActiveDocument.Range.InsertAfter "This is one line," & vbCrLf & _
    " and this is another."
```

Example A.97. Insert paragraph mark

Example A.98 inserts three lines separated by line feeds.

```
Public Sub InsertTextInDocument()
    Dim myString As String
    myString = vbNull
    myString = "Item 1" & Chr(11)
    myString = myString & "Item 2" & Chr(11)
    myString = myString & "Item 3"

    ActiveDocument.Range.InsertAfter "1" & vbTab & "2"
End Sub
```

LINE FEED (handwritten annotation)

Example A.98. Insert line feeds

Example A.99 inserts the text "Microsoft Windows" with a non-breaking space between the words. This means the two words will not be separated.

```
Public Sub InsertTextInDocument2()
    ActiveDocument.Range.InsertAfter "Microsoft" & Chr(160) & "Windows"
End Sub
```

SPACE (handwritten annotation)

Example A.99. Insert words separated by non-breaking space

Example A.100 inserts soft hyphens in the text. A soft hyphen indicates where a word or phrase can be broken.

```
Public Sub InsertTextInDocument3()
    ActiveDocument.Range.InsertAfter _
        "stre" & Chr(173) & "ngth" & Chr(173) & "ed"
End Sub
```

SPACE (handwritten annotation)

Example A.100. Insert soft hyphens

Summary

This appendix contains examples of code to handle common situations such as opening and closing documents, copying and pasting text, and moving around inside a document. You can use these code snippets freely in your own macros.

B

Automation Related Topics

The Developer Tab

In Office 2007, the Developer tab is where you can access all the development tools. This includes running macros and getting to the IDE (integrated development environment), XML tools, and the controls for forms and content controls. During installation, the Developer tab is not displayed by default. To see the tab use Procedure B.1.

Procedure B.1. Display Developer tab

1. Click the **Microsoft Office** button in the top left of the Word window.

2. Click **Word Options**.

3. Click **Popular** on the left side.

4. In **Top options for working with Word** section, check **Show Developer tab** in the Ribbon.

5. Click **OK**.

How Do You Find Automation Projects?

Technical communicators face a dizzying array of tasks, which can vary daily for each writer. These tasks can be broadly categorized in three ways:

► Simple but time consuming tasks that are purely procedural. These include formatting tables, removing comments, accepting revision marks, checking footers, and just about anything you can imagine doing from the user interface.

► Tasks that require decision making. These are also highly procedural, but require using conditional text, collecting a subset of information using selective criteria, or prompting the user to make a decision.

► Creating new information. This kind of task may be accomplished by compiling information from the document itself (for example, collecting all the comments in a separate document or assembling a parts number list) or from an outside source, such as a collection of error numbers from the development team, last month's revenue figures from the sales department, or lists from the company database.

The best ideas for projects will come from you. Every writer's challenges are different, and they change from day to day. Here are some suggestions on selecting projects for automation:

- **Think small:** Automation doesn't have to be anything more than just using the **F4** key to repeat the last action. Don't fall into the trap of making the problem bigger than it really is. Programmers are likely to want to create an independent application, complete with menus and buttons. Although they may create an excellent solution, the real goal here is to empower individuals so they can create their own solutions.

- **Think local:** There's nothing fancy or elaborate about what automation should be. Quite the opposite. Be aware of the most mundane tasks. That's where the low hanging fruit with the highest payback can be found. The most likely candidates are repetitious actions. Notice when you're doing the same action or set of actions over and over: formatting text, creating and formatting tables, extracting part numbers, adding section headers, and so on.

One team I worked with had to make sure all part numbers were displayed in a bold typeface. Since part numbers varied in format (six to eight characters, some had alphanumerics, others had hyphens, and so forth.), the process was essentially manual. Within 15 minutes I created a macro to find all the part numbers and make them bold. A process that previously had taken a half-day per document was reduced to less than five seconds.

- **Think Easy:** In the same way that candidates for automation don't have to elaborate, neither does the automation itself. For Office, use the built-in macro recorder. Record the sequence as a macro and save it.

- **Think about doing an automation audit:** Even though the payoff for creating the part number macro was huge, the writers themselves did not identify that process as a candidate for automation. It was discovered while tracking down an unrelated problem. To find the less obvious candidates, consider an automation audit, where an automation programmer meets with writers and walks through their procedures looking for automation opportunities. This doesn't need to be a formal audit, nor does it need to take a long one.

After seeing what a quick automation audit can find, it is likely that your writers will generate the next round of ideas, usually in the form of "Can you do this?" questions. The general response should be that you'd be disappointed if you couldn't.

What Makes a Good Automation Project

Having identified a potential project, understand that not all projects make for good automation. Before starting any project, consider the time investment needed to automate the process versus the benefits it may provide. Automation is about making things better, faster, or more reliable, so it needs to improve at least one of those three. Selecting projects carefully and understanding the limitations of automation is important to creating a successful project. The following considerations should be made before starting a project:

- **Consistency:** By far the most important consideration in deciding whether to automate is the consistency of the data. If the original data is not consistent, or if it is difficult to flag, then automation will be more difficult. For example, if you're parsing a file that is supposed to be tab-delimited – that is, tabs separate the fields – and some tabs are missing, superfluous ones are present, or commas are used instead, then the data will not parse properly.

Inconsistency doesn't make automation impossible, it just adds one more hindrance. For example, with a tab-delimited file, if you know that commas should be treated like tabs, then you can anticipate this by replacing commas with tabs, then parsing the file. Of course, even in that example there is consistency since you know all commas are supposed to be tabs. If some commas should be tabs, but others should remain commas, you have to make assumptions for the user and risk being wrong, or your code has to prompt the user to confirm. Clearly, this makes the task more complex.

► **True one-time use:** The mantra for automation projects is that if it's used once, it's likely to be used again. However, there are occasions when a procedure will be used only once. In those cases, automation is probably not worth the time or money. Extremely easy tasks may not be worth it. For example, having a macro to replace two spaces at the end of a sentence with one might be just as easily done with the **Find** dialog. That dialog is widely understood, and being built-in, doesn't require any development.

► **Don't rewrite an existing feature:** Don't write functions that already exist. Office has a rich set of features, many of which users may not know about. For example, in addition to the many built in commands on the ribbon, Word comes with over 100 macros (see **Developer tab,** **Macros** button of the **Code** panel, **Macros In: Word Commands**). Check out these existing capabilities first.

► **Concentrate on what Word does best:** Word is a word processor, and although it has some math capabilities, Excel is better at math and has a more extensive set of math features. In the same way, using Excel to format a textual document is usually counterproductive.

► **You are the customer:** Creating automation projects for yourself is very different than creating them for others. You tend to be much more clear with requirements and expectations when it's for yourself. You know the data, the data source, the end requirements, and the limitations. You will know when the scope expands too far.

In contrast, working with others can add communication problems. Others may not understand your vision or agree with the user interface, and they may have assumptions and expectations that are different from yours. Start by solving your immediate issues, and then with experience and success, consider sharing the results with others or creating custom projects for others.

► **Too large a scope:** The surest way to fail is to over-estimate what you can do and over-promise results. Start with projects that accomplish one task. Then, consider expanding the scope after the first few successes.

► **Unclear requirements:** If the project is your own design, that is, you are creating the tool to solve a specific problem for yourself, the requirements will likely be clear and precise. If you're working with others, the requirements may be less clear, causing frustration for both you and the user. Regardless, stay focused on the task. The ultimate vision may be noble, but limit the scope at first. If all the tool has to do is convert a database query to a table, don't make it do more.

► **Understand the difference between magic and programming:** It may seem unlikely, but it is common to get requirements that could not be implemented without "magic." The promise of automation is easily misunderstood, leading to requirements that assume code "just knows" which data to select. A person may be a subject expert and know which sentences should or shouldn't be included, but unless there's a clear test for selecting the text you need to act on, automation can't be used.

Planning for Automation

Once you decide a project is a good candidate for automation, consider the following to keep the project on track:

- **Solve one problem at a time:** The scope of the solution is to address one and only one problem. Whether it's getting information from a database, checking the styles within a Word document, or generating pages in HTML, limit the scope. Don't combine solutions until you're more comfortable with automation concepts and implementation.

- **Don't write overly robust tools:** You're writing scripts for a one-time, specific purpose and scope. Therefore, you don't need extensive error checking or online help. A common time sink is trying to make the tool bulletproof. If your audience is one specific writer or editor, you can specify exactly how to run the code or what parameters to enforce. Again, the point is to get a specific task done.

- **Tools have a limited lifespan:** Because the tool is designed to do one specific task, it may have a short lifespan. That's alright. Besides, good and useful tools will evolve over time.

- **Reuse the code, not the tools:** For each new solution create a new tool. Don't keep adding on to the same tool. This will only make it unusable for any purpose. Certainly, you can base the new tool on an existing one that does a similar task, but always start from a copy and modify it. Over time you will end up with a large collection of tools, applications, and scripts. Think of this collection not as a tool library, but as an example library. Reuse portions of the code for other projects. For example, code that opens different files in a single directory or writes to an external file will likely be needed at other times. You will gain speed and proficiency over time from familiarity with the code.

- **Understand what is possible with your writing tools:** Visual Basic and VBA capabilities access virtually any aspect of a document, Word or otherwise. You may not use all the capabilities at first, but knowing what is possible will encourage you to push your solutions.

- **Feature creep:** Possibly worse than unclear requirements are requirements that change during the development process. This phenomenon is known as feature creep. Users introduce new requirements or request changes to existing ones while the project is being worked on. This can be frustrating for all parties and can cause delays, as you rewrite and re-test code and macros.

  But, not all feature creep is bad. As others get used to the tools or start to understand what automation can do for them, it's natural for them to ask for more features or capabilities. My favorite part of project management is when a customer has an epiphany and starts requesting new features. It takes negotiations to balance all the requirements, but some really good ideas can emerge. No doubt in your own automation projects you'll be tempted to keep improving or adding features. The distinction between this being good or bad is up to you and how the changes affect you.

- **Keep focused:** When you want to hang a picture, a hammer is not the solution, a picture hanging on the wall is. The same thing applies to automation. You will not be judged by the look or the elegance of the tool; chances are, nobody will even know about those things. Rather, you will be judged on the tool's results and ultimately its ability to meet the goal. In other words, automation is a means to an end, not the end itself.

Problems with Automation

Automation isn't solely a programmer's world, but you are entering a programming realm, and the more you know about the process, the more valuable and proficient you can be. There are plenty of good books about macro writing, Office programming, and automation in general. All these books discuss what happens when things go right. In a sense, they idealize the development process. The problem is that few books mention what happens when things go wrong – and they will go wrong. Obvious cases include errors in macro logic. Less obvious are actions that the author has little or no control over. These cases include a user's inattention to detail, inconsistent document formatting, and Word's behavior. Regardless of the reason, all of these things can detract from the development process, frustrating everyone

Some detracting factors can't be avoided. Others can be. In either case, recognizing them early and coming up with workarounds can save the project. The following is a list of common detractions, and how to work with them.

Programming Issues

The following issues relate to the programming side of macros.

Handling errors

Office's macro recorders make it easy to create macros. However, a significant failing is that macros created this way don't include error handling. For example, the following macro expects a specifically named style to be present:

```
Public Sub Macro1()
    Selection.Style = "ChapterHeaderBold"
End Sub
```

If a style with that name is not present when the code is run, an error is returned. Unfortunately, native Office errors are anything but helpful, as you can see in Figure B.1.

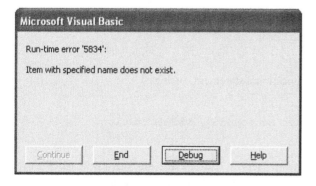

Figure B.1. Unknown name error

The solution is to add error handling code. In Example B.1, line 2 (On Error GoTo) traps any error and sends the code to line 5 (MyErrorHandler). Since you know the code number (from the system error display above), you can use that to test the error condition.

```
 1 Public Sub Macro1()
 2 On Error GoTo MyErrorHandler
 3     Selection.Style = "ChapterHeaderBold"
 4     Exit Sub
 5 MyErrorHandler:
 6     If Err.Number = 5834 Then
 7         MsgBox Prompt:="The named style is not in the document."
 8     Else
 9         MsgBox "Err = " & Err.Number
10 End If
11 End Sub
```

Example B.1. Error handling example

Figure B.2 shows the plain language error message the user will see.

Figure B.2. Plain language error message

One statement has turned into nine but the macro is more helpful. Your users will appreciate this, as will you when use the macro four months from now, after you have forgotten the particulars.

Macros can't do everything

Macros alone can't provide all the resources for a robust automation tool. Like error handling, features such as warning dialogs, input boxes, and to some extent, open dialogs, can't be recorded. These have to be added afterwards. Here is a simple example: to display a message at the end of a procedure, use the following line of code before the Exit Sub statement:

```
MsgBox "Done processing.", vbExclamation
Exit Sub
```

This can be used in combination with a conditional statement, such as:

```
If searchString <> targetString Then
    MsgBox "Requested text cannot be found.", vbInformation
End If
```

Input boxes are dialogs that request input from users. In Example B.2, an InputBox asks the user for a number. This code also checks the findCount variable, which will be null (or empty) if the user did enter a value.

```
Dim findCount As String
findCount = InputBox("Enter the number of items to find:")
If findCount = vbNullString Then
    MsgBox "No value was entered.", vbCritical
End If
```

Example B.2. Input dialog to prompt user for a number

Figure B.3 shows the input box for Example B.2.

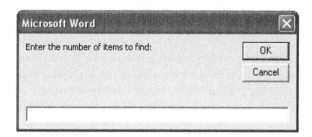

Figure B.3. Input box

Figure B.4 shows the resulting warning dialog. A better warning would be to suggest a course of action to fix the error, for example, "Please enter a number greater than zero."

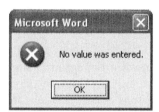

Figure B.4. Warning dialog

Limited testing

Like a written document, macros are rarely perfect after being written. They require testing and debugging, a process that helps ensure that the macro runs as it should. Lack of testing allows bugs or problems to get to users, and that causes a lot of frustration for everyone. It is important to make sure that you anticipate the possible ways the macro could be used and the conditions under which it will be invoked. Cases may include testing to see if a word begins highlighted or not, if another file has to be opened, or if the search phrase is not in the document or is in the document more than once? Test the macro on different documents. One common problem is that the macro is developed using only one document. This kind of tunnel vision may result in other mistakes or cases never being tested. By using several documents, you make your macro more robust.

Others as users

If a macro is useful to you, chances are it will be useful to others. That leverage is important, but it requires additional effort. While the macro author knows how to use it, others won't know and will have to be told. Some of this can be done by documentation. A better way is to remember that you are writing this macro for other people and not yourself. For example, instead of assuming a specific file is already available, include an open dialog. Similarly, anticipate errors (such as the named style not being found) or provide graceful error messages. The macro doesn't have to stop when it gets an error as long as the error is handled well.

A good test for clarity is to not use the macro for a month or two and then go back to it. What is unclear to you at that time will likely be unclear to others.

Microsoft Office-Related Issues

In addition to programmatic considerations, Word itself may introduce issues.

Office has bugs

Like any other software, Office applications have bugs. To guard against data loss, Word comes with an automatic recovery capability that tries to save documents when it crashes. Other bugs show up in the user interface, such as mismatching page numbers, headers that move around on their own, and revision tracking that enters endless loops. These bugs show themselves as problems that you think shouldn't be there, for example when a macro keeps getting errors in odd places, or a wrong value displays.

Although Word has bugs, don't assume that every error is a result of an Office bug. More often, the problem will be in your code. Check your code carefully, making sure that required documents are opened and that values are properly set. If you feel your code and logic is correct, check the Internet to try and confirm the error or speak with one of your company's developers for more information.

Word can be slow

A macro may seem quick enough when run on a small example, but when run against a large document it may slow to a virtual stop. It's natural to assume that everything takes longer in a large document, but while that's true to some extent, there may be other reasons. Some operations are just slow. For example, opening or creating a document or extracting information from a table can take some time. Doing an operation many times is going to take a disproportionate amount of time.

Review the code and logic. Remove any unnecessary steps. It's surprising how much time can be lost in even the smallest and most innocuous looking loops. Minimize opening and closing documents, hide the document or even hide Word itself when doing long operations (updating the information on the screen takes significant time), don't move the insertion point around to insert or delete text, and don't use selection or highlighting.

Unexpected things

It's been said that Word never misses a chance to frustrate. No matter how well planned a macro is, there is always a chance of unexpected problems. For example, if the document has another language introduced into it (quite easy to do if multiple users edit the same document), a user may get a message about proofing tools or a specific spelling library not being available. Other instances may include a security message about running macros, or a **Find** dialog that is opened in another Word document. Any of these things can interrupt the macro, which can be frustrating since there may or may not be a warning for the user. The macro could just appear to be frozen. In addition, each Office suite program is its own server and can send or receive information at any time. For example, Outlook usually responds to new e-mail when a message is received. It is possible for this to interfere with a running macro, especially if Word is the e-mail editor.

Short of anticipating every possible option, which is unrealistic, just be aware things like this can happen.

User-Related Issues

The following items are related to other user's actions.

Unreliable formatting

Inconsistent or improper document formatting is likely to be the single largest problem area. Macros often rely on specific text formats, text combinations, or formatting. If those things are not there, at best the results will be incomplete, at worst the macro will get an error. This problem may be largely out of your control if you're helping another team. If others use the macro, you won't necessarily be around help.

You can try to proactively enforce document standards and fix problems at the source. However, realistically, the best you can do is to make the macro more forgiving by attempting to recognize reasonable variations (such as the text being correct, but not styled consistently). Beyond that, consider using warning dialogs to notify users of non-conforming cases.

Users don't read messages

As much as technical communicators may complain about users not reading their notes, the truth is that when communicators themselves are the audience, they don't fare much better. This is made worse because macro authors have to go out of their way to show text. That means most of the feedback users receive while running macros is likely be error messages. Even if you display proper error messages, there's a good chance the user isn't going to read them. Instead, you may get a call or e-mail even though the message is there.

This issue is hard to work around. Some users will assume that since it's an in-house tool, it's more likely to break than a commercial one and that any message won't be meaningful. It would be too easy to blame users for not reading messages, but the risk is that they'll stop using the tool out of frustration. One solution is to make notes clearer. The earlier message, "The named style is not in the document," could be re-written as "The style (**ChapterHeaderBold**) is not in the document. Please add the style to the original document and rerun this tool."

How Do You Get Started?

With a project in mind that you think is a good candidate for automation, how do you get started? A general rule is to start simply and then get more complex as you go. If the solution is procedural, then record the sequence as a macro. This might take several attempts to get correct; performing a sequence for recording is sometimes harder than it looks. Keep in mind, for example, that mouse clicks are not recorded, so selecting text or ranges must be done with the keyboard. Since the macro isn't time-based, you can go slowly and think about each step and its options. After recording your macro, test it. If you like the results, keep going; if not, go back and correct it.

If you're only using the recording feature, and not taking a coding approach, you will have to re-record the macro each time you want to make changes or add new features. For relatively simple sequences, this is easy enough, but it gets more difficult with longer or more complex sequences. This leads some users eventually into coding.

Taking a coding approach requires additional patience since more can go wrong. Like before, think about each step carefully. If you're new to coding, consider adding one line of code at a time, then testing with each addition. It sounds laborious but it's surprising how many errors you can discover with this method.

What is a Document Object Model?

A Word document has many systems and subsystems working together. There are individual characters, which group to form words, words to sentences, paragraphs, and stories. In addition, there are revision marks, hyperlinks, footers, end notes, spell checks, lists, and more. From your perspective everything works together seamlessly (or at least should).

To make all of this work, each system is tracked individually and internally in the document. Each system is called an "object." Collectively, the set of objects form the "document" and since this is a well-defined grouping, in a general sense it's a "model." Therefore, this is called the "document object model," or DOM. The concept is not unique to Microsoft Office or even Microsoft itself. Each Office suite tool has its own DOM. These can be viewed online at MSDN (Microsoft Developer's Network, http://msdn.microsoft.com).

Each system in Word has a corresponding object in the DOM, and that object defines the structure needed to store that system's particular information. This information – the names and values – are required to be used if you modify an object. At the highest level – the document itself – there are about 200 objects. There's an object for handling each character, should you need to examine individual characters. Another object handles sentences, and so on. Any object itself can contain other objects.

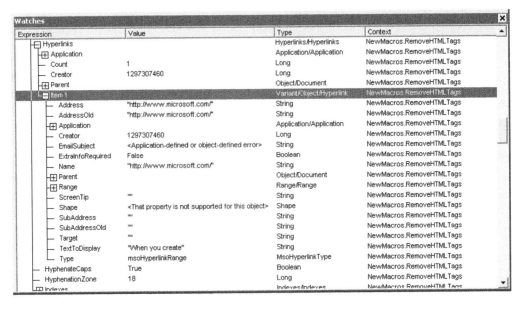

Figure B.5. Partial display of Word's DOM as seen through the IDE

There are several ways to see or visualize the model. The first is through Word's IDE debugger, which shows the structure in a tree format..Figure B.5 displays the hyperlinks for the document, along with other objects (indicated by the **expand** +/- buttons). Other useful information includes the **Count**, which shows how many hyperlinks there are in the document or the selection. The debugger displays information about each link individually.

Another way these features show up is through code with the help of **IntelliSense**. **IntelliSense** is a form of autocompletion in which available options display in a list as you type. The IDE provides a drop-down list of known objects, properties, and methods. Figure B.6 is an example.

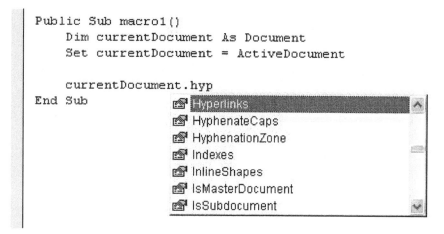

```
Public Sub macro1()
    Dim currentDocument As Document
    Set currentDocument = ActiveDocument

    currentDocument.hyp
End Sub
```

- Hyperlinks
- HyphenateCaps
- HyphenationZone
- Indexes
- InlineShapes
- IsMasterDocument
- IsSubdocument

Figure B.6. Intellisense showing possible options.

A third option is through the IDE's object browser, a list of all known objects. In the IDE, click **View|Object Browser**, or **F2**. A screen displays with a search and list.

Why Not Use Selection?

The habit of highlighting text is ingrained from the Word experience. While writing, we have to select or highlight text. This is used for many functions, including changing fonts, setting styles, and modifying or deleting text, to name only a few examples.

When programming or debugging, it is often convenient to use the Selection to see which text or part of the document is being worked on. However, the Selection becomes a liability if not handled correctly. A number of problems occur by using the Selection in macros. The most immediate one is that the Selection refers to the active document only. Regardless how many documents are open or how many of those have highlighted text, Word considers the Selection to be in the active document only. If the user switches documents while the macro is running, the moment the macro encounters the code line affecting the Selection, the active document is used, which may not be the document you wanted the macro to use. A lot of users who record macros or write VBA code forget that other documents could get activated after the macro starts.

There are other technical and less interesting reasons. Using the Selection is slow and using many Selection statements can slow down a macro excessively. Lastly, it may simply be disorienting to the user to have the cursor or selected text move around, or at least not be in the same place when the macro ends.

The macro recorder uses the Selection liberally, arguably overusing it. If you're trying to learn VBA by recording macros, you may get an unsafe dependence on the Selection. Using Word programmatically requires a different approach. There are two workarounds for avoiding the Selection:

- First, use the Range object. Technically a Selection is a range object, but in the code samples in this book, each Range is explicitly defined. You can have multiple ranges defined, each pointing to its own region, and there will never be any conflicts.

- Second, use ActiveDocument only once per routine or sequence. Like Selection, ActiveDocument uses the active document at the moment the line of code is run. As just pointed out, this may be different from the active document at the start of the macro. Example B.3 shows both of these workarounds.

```
 1 Sub Macro1()
 2     Dim currentDocument As Document
 3     Set currentDocument = ActiveDocument
 4
 5     'Range example 1
 6     currentDocument.Range(10, 20).Font.Bold = True
 7
 8     'Range example 2
 9     Dim myRange As Range
10     Set myRange = currentDocument.Range(10, 20)
11     myRange.Font.Bold = True
12 End Sub
```

Example B.3. Using Range and ActiveDocument

Assigning the active document to its own variable (currentDocument, line 3) means that all actions will take place within currentDocument, whether it's active or not. Many of the examples use two documents, which are called sourceDocument and targetDocument in this discussion. Referring to these documents explicitly avoids any conflicts, and each uses the ActiveDocument call only once.

Tips for Using For Loops

The document object model (DOM) provides an invaluable service by grouping objects together. For example, all the bookmarks in the DOM are in a single location, and there are hundreds of similar objects that group links, fields, characters, pictures, and so on.

Of course, the properties and characteristics will be different for each type of object but important similarities exist. Typically, each has a Count property showing the total number of objects of that type. The Count may be zero, indicating none of those objects exist, or it may be a very large number, such as the number of characters in a long document. The other important similarity is that each item within an object group is available individually. Occurrences are listed as an "Item", starting from Item1. These two characteristics provide a useful, convenient, and (most of the time) quick way to go through the entire list of objects. For programming, this is usually done by looping.

VBA supports two kinds of For loops: For...Next and For Each. While both do similar things, there are differences. A For...Next loop uses a counter and a range (a limiting value, not a

Range object). Example B.4 is an example of a simple For . . . Next loop that counts from one to ten and displays the result in the **Immediate** window of the IDE.

```
Public Sub ForLoopDemo()
    Dim i as long
    For i = 1 to 10
        Debug.Print i
    Next i
End Sub
```

Example B.4. For . . . Next loop

Example B.5 applies a For . . . Next loop to the DOM.

```
Public Sub ForTest()
    Dim currentDocument As Document
    Set currentDocument = ActiveDocument

    Dim i As Long
    For i = 1 To currentDocument.Words.Count
        Debug.Print currentDocument.Words(i)
        DoEvents
    Next i
End Sub
```

Example B.5. For . . . Next loop applied to the DOM

The loop in Example B.5 goes through all the words in the document and displays them in the **Immediate** window. You don't have to know how many words there are, the value of current-Document.Words.Count provides that for you.

In contrast, the For Each loop doesn't use Count at all. Instead it just goes through a structure until it runs out of items. If there no items, the code inside the loop doesn't ever run. That seems like a minor distinction, but there are important implications. Not the least is that you don't need a special case for zero items. Example B.6 cycles through the words in the current document using a For Each loop.

```
Public Sub ForEachTest()
    Dim currentDocument As Document
    Set currentDocument = ActiveDocument

    Dim myWord As Range
    For Each myWord In currentDocument.Words
        Debug.Print myWord.Text
        DoEvents
    Next
End Sub
```

Example B.6. For Each loop

A control item is still needed to terminate the loop. Instead of a numeric variable (i in Example B.4 and Example B.5), Example B.6 uses myWord (which is a Range object). The loop looks for all items defined the same as `myWord` in the structure `currentDocument.Words`. It may be confusing since you might expect `myWord` to be text. It's a Range because any word in a document not only has text associated with it, but also fonts, color, styles, possible hyperlinks, the position in the document, and many other items. In the same way individual characters are ultimately defined as a Range as well.

When would you use one instead of the other? For the most part, it's a personal choice. The `For Each` loop tends to be quicker, although that's not always the case. And, it's generally considered more sophisticated, if you're trying to impress people.

There is one exception. If you want to delete some or all of the items in a list, use the `For...Next` loop, but count down instead of up. Deleting an item changes the list and can throw the `For Each` loop off, miss some items altogether, hang the macro in an endless loop, or worse yet, crash Word. Example B.7 shows how to delete items.

```
Public Sub DeleteTest()
    Dim currentDocument As Document
    Set currentDocument = ActiveDocument

    Dim i As Long
    For i = currentDocument.Words.Count To 1 Step -1
        currentDocument.Words(i).Delete
        DoEvents
    Next i
End Sub
```

Example B.7. `For...Next` loop to delete items from a list

Example B.7 counts backwards, starting at the end of the item list – here the words in the document – to the beginning. This makes sure that the counter will never encounter a deleted item, since the item is deleted only after the counter has passed it.

These loops are mentioned because the macro recorder, for all its good attributes, is not smart enough to generate loops. For example, if you record a session doing repeated deletes, the recorder will create the code for deleting each item individually.

Don't Learn VBA With the Recorder

Inside every Office suite application is a built-in set of tools for automation. Although referred to collectively as VBA (Visual Basic for Applications), this is actually a comprehensive set of up to three tools: A language component (VBA), a code editor (the IDE, also called the integrated development environment), and a macro recorder.

The VBA language itself is an interpreted language loosely based on earlier versions of the BASIC language. It is akin to VBScript and the VB language series. Keeping the term "BASIC" in the name was a good idea since at the time nearly everyone liked the BASIC language, and those who didn't had enough information to stay clear of it; a win-win situation for all. VBA's evolution was from a previous language, WordBasic, which was designed specifically, as the name may imply, to work with Word. Realizing the language's scope needed to expand to include all the Office suite applications, Microsoft created VBA in Word 95. Curiously, WordBasic still survives and there are some useful WordBasic calls that have not been converted to VBA.

Some complexity was introduced due to the document object model (DOM) of the Office suite applications.

Many users see the macro recorder as a good way to learn VBA. Perhaps it is, up to a point. It's useful when you want to create simple macros. In this case you don't have to know anything about the language, which is what it was designed for initially. Second, it's convenient if you don't know how to programming a topic. You can record a macro and use that as the starting point.

As for learning the language, it's not that useful, for three reasons:

► First, it doesn't handle looping. One of VBA's most powerful features is that it can go through an extensive amount of material in a few lines of code. It can loop through the longest of documents a character at a time in three lines of code. You can loop through all the links, misspellings, comments, paragraphs, bookmarks, and fields the same way. But the VBA recorder can't record that kind of looping, and there's no way you can force it to. If you want to do an action twice in a recorded macro, you have to perform that action twice.

► Second, it can't create decision making code, like `if` or `switch` statements. There is no way to force it to record decision statements. Together, loops and decisions are key to program control in VBA. Looping through all the words in a document may be powerful but what if you wanted to stop on each occurrence of a specific word? An `if` statement can handle that easily, but the recorder can't capture an `if` statement.

► Lastly, the code the macro recorder produces is largely inefficient. While the recorded code may do what it's supposed to do, it's not exemplary code, does not follow good practices (for example, see the section titled "Why Not Use Selection?" (p. 239)), and often produces superfluous code – lots of it.

Example B.8 shows this last point clearly. It contains code generated by the macro recorder for setting the paragraph style.

```
Sub Macro1()
    With Selection.ParagraphFormat
        .LeftIndent = InchesToPoints(0)
        .RightIndent = InchesToPoints(0)
        .SpaceBefore = 0
        .SpaceBeforeAuto = False
        .SpaceAfter = 10
        .SpaceAfterAuto = False
        .LineSpacingRule = wdLineSpace1pt5
        .Alignment = wdAlignParagraphLeft
        .WidowControl = True
        .KeepWithNext = False
        .KeepTogether = False
        .PageBreakBefore = False
        .NoLineNumber = False
        .Hyphenation = True
        .FirstLineIndent = InchesToPoints(0)
        .OutlineLevel = wdOutlineLevelBodyText
        .CharacterUnitLeftIndent = 0
        .CharacterUnitRightIndent = 0
        .CharacterUnitFirstLineIndent = 0
        .LineUnitBefore = 0
```

```
        .LineUnitAfter = 0
        .MirrorIndents = False
        .TextboxTightWrap = wdTightNone
    End With
End Sub
```

Example B.8. Macro recorder code for setting the paragraph style

Example B.8 was recorded by simply opening the **Paragraph** dialog, changing the line spacing to 1 1/2, and then closing the dialog. VBA is already a slow language. Using so much code is going to further slow down the process. There's also a code maintenance concern. If you have to go back and look at the code after three months or a year (when you will have forgotten the subtleties of the code), trying to change it will be much more difficult. Example B.9 does the same thing as Example B.8 in many fewer lines.

```
Sub Macro1()
    Selection.ParagraphFormat.LineSpacingRule = wdLineSpace1pt5
End Sub
```

Example B.9. Hand written code for setting the paragraph style

Differences Between Word's Paragraph Marks and Carriage Returns

The paragraph mark is often taken for granted. Many don't give it a second thought when they conclude a paragraph. But it controls more than that one function. You need to understand it in order to get the most out of, and sometimes into, a document.

The paragraph mark ("¶") is called a "pilcrow," and is created by the **enter** key. It serves several purposes. Its intent is to indicate a carriage return. In the early days of computers, displays were usually teletypes, and an electronic marker had to be used return the typing head back to the beginning of its track. This marker was typically used in combination with a line feed, so that the paper advanced and no overtyping occurred. The terms survived and you may occasionally hear it called a carriage return/line feed.

One obvious use is to end a line and start a new one. This is the simplest cases, hailing directly from pre-monitor days. Using the paragraph mark this way forces a line break. For a typewriter, that would be appropriate, but in electronic publishing, this can prevent the proper flow of text. Now that several generations of users have been brought up on computers and keyboards, this use is becoming less common.

The next obvious use is similar: It ends one paragraph and starts a new one. This is generally considered the proper use of the paragraph mark. This also illustrates the difference between line spacing and paragraph spacing. Line spacing is the space between lines as they wrap automatically. In the past, this was typically described as single spacing or double spacing, although in Word this distance can be finely tweaked. Paragraph spacing is the space between the last line of one paragraph and the first line of the next one. The paragraph mark controls this distance, which is independent of line spacing and can also be finely tweaked.

The paragraph mark itself is just like any other character. It can be inserted, deleted, found, replaced, and styled. But it is also different from the other characters. A paragraph is an object and is defined as all the characters and material from after the preceding paragraph mark up to and including the next paragraph mark. This means that the style information for a paragraph is contained in the ending paragraph mark. Therefore, deleting the pilcrow also deletes the formatting information for that paragraph, and the material will assume the formatting of the next paragraph.

You can delete the paragraph mark, but the result is not the same as deleting other characters. If the paragraph mark is part of selected text, you can cut or delete that text and the paragraph mark will remain with the selection and be included when the selection is pasted. However, the paragraph mark remains in the source document, too. It doesn't get removed along with the other text. To delete it, it has to be selected by itself or the Selection has to include the paragraph mark as the last character.

Collecting Acronyms

Many companies, as well as the military, require an acronym list at the end of their documents. Certainly with the proliferation of acronyms and the often absurd forms they take, this is understandable. Yet many underestimate the task of finding them.

Consider first the instance of the classic upper case-only acronym. Examples include: NATO (North Atlantic Treaty Organization), SAT (was Scholastic Aptitude Test), and FAQ (frequently asked questions)

Word's **Find** feature with wildcards can locate this kind of acronym, and you can also use a macro (see Example 4.15, "The FindAcronyms macro")

However, consider the additional forms acronyms can take. Here are just a few variations:

► **Plurals:** This simple variation introduces ATMs (automatic teller machines), CDs (compact discs), or JPEGs (joint photographic experts group).

► **Mixed case:** Scuba, Radar, and Modem.

► **Collisions:** Not all acronyms are technically misspellings. Some "collide" with commonly used words. For example: USA PATRIOT Act (Uniting and Strengthening America by Providing Appropriate Tools Required to Intercept and Obstruct Terrorism), BATMAN (Biochemistry and Temporal Mechanisms Arising in Nature), and ROBIN (Robustness of Biologically-Inspired Networks); the government goes out of its way to contrive terms.

► **Multiple words:** Some acronyms are multiple words: US Lab (U.S. Laboratory, a space station module), Ku-Band (part of the electromagnetic spectrum). Although not strictly acronyms, this class of terms uses multiple words as if they were one term.

► **Abbreviations:** For example, A.M. and P.M. (ante meridiem / post meridiem) use periods after each letter. While that practice may be dated, it is still used enough to be a consideration for finding acronyms.

Therefore, being able to automatically find all acronyms is difficult. The most basic task is to define what an acronym is in the first place. Your team will have to decide that.

ASCII Table

ASCII (American Standard Code for Information Interchange) is a character coding schematic. Each character is defined as a numeric value, and by using that value, you can insert a specific character or search for one. Many languages defined the values differently. The table here, Windows-1252 (also called CP-1252), is a Latin alphabet widely adopted for English and some other Western languages because of the pervasiveness of the Microsoft Windows operating system.

The ASCII table is split into two basic parts. Values 0 – 127 are the fundamental character set. Values 128 – 255 is called the extended ASCII table and extends the character set another 128 values. This last range is not standard and may vary by computer manufacturer. The extended ASCII information presented is Microsoft Windows Latin-1 version. This is considered the most common set and is available to Microsoft Word.

Control Characters: 0 – 31

The first 32 characters in the ASCII table are historically non-printing control codes and are used to control peripherals such as printers. The values presented here are Word's use of them. Although their use is common, each program may have different applications of the values.

Table C.1. Table of ASCII control values

Value	Character	Explanation
0	(nul)	Null char. Used in Word as a null character. In VBA, use vbNullChar.
1	(soh)	Start of Heading. Not typically used with Word.
2	(stx)	Start of Text. Not typically used with Word.
3	(etx)	End of Text. Not typically used with Word.
4	(eot)	End of Transmission. Not typically used with Word.
5	(enq)	Enquiry. Not typically used with Word.
6	(ack)	Acknowledgment. Not typically used with Word.
7	(bel)	Bell. Not typically used with Word.
8	(bs)	Back Space. Not typically used with Word.
9	(ht)	Horizontal Tab. Used in Word as a tab. In VBA, use vbTAB.
10	(nl)	Line Feed. Not typically used with Word.
11	(vt)	Vertical Tab. Used in Word as a manual line break; also SHIFT ENTER. In VBA, used vbVerticalTab.
12	(np)	Form Feed. Used in Word as a manual page break. In VBA, used vbFormFeed.
13	(cr)	Carriage Return. Used in Word as a paragraph marker; also RETURN. In VBA, use vbCRLF.
14	(so)	Shift Out / X-On. Used in Word as a column break.
15	(si)	Shift In / X-Off. Not typically used with Word.
16	(dle)	Data Line Escape. Not typically used with Word.
17	(dc1)	Device Control 1. Not typically used with Word.
18	(dc2)	Device Control 2. Not typically used with Word.
19	(dc3)	Device Control 3. Not typically used with Word.
20	(dc4)	Device Control 4. Not typically used with Word.
21	(nak)	Negative Acknowledgement. Not typically used with Word.
22	(syn)	Synchronous Idle. Not typically used with Word.
23	(etb)	End of Transmit Block. Not typically used with Word.
24	(can)	Cancel. Not typically used with Word.
25	(em)	End of Medium. Not typically used with Word.
26	(sub)	Substitute. Not typically used with Word.
27	(esc)	Escape. Not typically used with Word.
28	(fs)	File Separator. Not typically used with Word.
29	(gs)	Group Separator. Not typically used with Word.
30	(rs)	Record Separator. Used in Word as a non-breaking hyphen.
31	(us)	Unit Separator. Used in Word as a optional hyphen.

Basic ASCII codes: 32 – 127

The basic character set, which contains printable characters, letters, digits, punctuation marks, and common symbols. Except for the value 127, each value is accessible through the keyboard.

Table C.2. Table of basic ASCII values

Value	Character	Value	Character	Value	Character	Value	Character
32	(sp)	56	8	80	P	104	h
33	!	57	9	81	Q	105	i
34	"	58	:	82	R	106	j
35	#	59	;	83	S	107	k
36	$	60	<	84	T	108	l
37	%	61	=	85	U	109	m
38	&	62	>	86	V	110	n
39	'	63	?	87	W	111	o
40	(	64	@	88	X	112	p
41	)	65	A	89	Y	113	q
42	*	66	B	90	Z	114	r
43	+	67	C	91	[	115	s
44	,	68	D	92	\	116	t
45	-	69	E	93	]	117	u
46	.	70	F	94	^	118	v
47	/	71	G	95	_	119	w
48	0	72	H	96	`	120	x
49	1	73	I	97	a	121	y
50	2	74	J	98	b	122	z
51	3	75	K	99	c	123	{
52	4	76	L	100	d	124		
53	5	77	M	101	e	125	}
54	6	78	N	102	f	126	~
55	7	79	O	103	g	127	(del)

Extended ASCII codes: 128 – 255

The extended character set. Values 128 – 159 use the Microsoft Windows Latin-1 extended character values.

Table C.3. Table of extended ASCII values

Value	Character	Value	Character	Value	Character	Value	Character
128	€	160		192	À	224	à
129	unused	161	¡	193	Á	225	á
130	‚	162	¢	194	Â	226	â
131	ƒ	163	£	195	Ã	227	ã
132	„	164	¤	196	Ä	228	ä
133	…	165	¥	197	Å	229	å
134	†	166	¦	198	Æ	230	æ
135	‡	167	§	199	Ç	231	ç
136	ˆ	168	¨	200	È	232	è
137	‰	169	©	201	É	233	é
138	Š	170	ª	202	Ê	234	ê
139	‹	171	«	203	Ë	235	ë
140	Œ	172	¬	204	Ì	236	ì
141	unused	173		205	Í	237	í
142	Ž	174	®	206	Î	238	î
143	unused	175	¯	207	Ï	239	ï
144	unused	176	°	208	Ð	240	ð
145	'	177	±	209	Ñ	241	ñ
146	'	178	²	210	Ò	242	ò
147	"	179	³	211	Ó	243	ó
148	"	180	´	212	Ô	244	ô
149	•	181	µ	213	Õ	245	õ
150	–	182	¶	214	Ö	246	ö
151	—	183	·	215	×	247	÷
152	˜	184	¸	216	Ø	248	ø
153	™	185	¹	217	Ù	249	ù
154	š	186	º	218	Ú	250	ú
155	›	187	»	219	Û	251	û
156	œ	188	¼	220	Ü	252	ü
157	unused	189	½	221	Ý	253	ý
158	ž	190	¾	222	Þ	254	þ
159	Ÿ	191	¿	223	ß	255	ÿ

Code Examples

The following code examples use character coding to insert text into a document or dialogs. Example C.1 inserts an ASCII character using the VBA `Chr()` command:

```
ActiveDocument.Range.InsertAfter "Display a character: " & Chr(65)
```

Example C.1. Insert an ASCII character using `Chr()`

Example C.2 inserts the capital letter "A" into the active document:

```
 1 Public Sub AddCharacters()
 2   On Error GoTo MyErrorHandler
 3
 4   Dim currentDocument As Document
 5   Set currentDocument = ActiveDocument
 6
 7   currentDocument.Range.InsertAfter "Display a character: " & Chr(65)
 8
 9   'Insert a line break
10   currentDocument.Range.InsertAfter Chr(13)
11
12   currentDocument.Range.InsertAfter "Display a tab: " & Chr(9)
13   Exit Sub
14
15 MyErrorHandler:
16   MsgBox "AddCharacters" & vbCrLf & vbCrLf & _
17         "Err = " & Err.Number & vbCrLf & _
18         "Description: " & Err.Description
19   End Sub
```

(handwritten annotations: "↳ CHAR "A"", "CARRIAGE RETURN", "HORIZONTAL TAB")

Example C.2. Insert character into active document

Example C.3 inserts two lines, one ending with capital letter "A" (line 7) and the next one, a tab marker (line 13). You may need to **Show Paragraph marks (Home|Paragraph|Show/Hide)** or press **CTRL-*** (**CTRL-SHIFT-8**). When a VBA-defined constant is available, use that instead. In Example C.3, I use the `vbCrLf` constant, which represents a line break.

```
 1 Public Sub AddCharacters2()
 2     On Error GoTo MyErrorHandler
 3
 4     Dim currentDocument As Document
 5     Set currentDocument = ActiveDocument
 6
 7     currentDocument.Range.InsertAfter "Display a character: " & Chr(65)
 8
 9     'Insert a line break through a VBA constant
10     currentDocument.Range.InsertAfter vbCrLf
11
12     'Insert a line break as part of a string
13     Dim tempString As String
14
15     tempString = "This is line 1" & vbCrLf & "This is line 2"
16     currentDocument.Range.InsertAfter tempString
```

```
17
18      Exit Sub
19
20 MyErrorHandler:
21      MsgBox "AddCharacters2" & vbCrLf & vbCrLf & _
22              "Err = " & Err.Number & vbCrLf & _
23              "Description: " & Err.Description
24 End Sub
```

Example C.3. Insert characters on two lines

Example C.4 inserts line feeds using the VBA vbCrLf constant, directly inserting it in the active document (line 7) and as part of a string (line 11). The same string can be used in a dialog.

```
 1 Public Sub AddCharacters3()
 2      On Error GoTo MyErrorHandler
 3
 4      Dim currentDocument As Document
 5      Set currentDocument = ActiveDocument
 6
 7      currentDocument.Range.InsertAfter vbCrLf
 8
 9      'Insert a line break as part of a string
10      Dim tempString As String
11      tempString = "This is line 1" & vbCrLf & "This is line 2"
12      currentDocument.Range.InsertAfter tempString
13
14      'Display a line break in a dialog box
15      MsgBox tempString
16
17      Exit Sub
18
19 MyErrorHandler:
20      MsgBox "AddCharacters3" & vbCrLf & vbCrLf & _
21          "Err = " & Err.Number & vbCrLf & _
22          "Description: " & Err.Description
23 End Sub
```

Example C.4. Insert line feeds using the VBA vbCrLf function

The resulting message box displays two lines. The opposite of inserting a character with Chr() is getting the ASCII value of a character. The Asc() function retrieves the ASCII value of a character. For example, Asc("A"), returns the value 65.

Example C.5 displays the value of each character in a selection of the active document in **Immediate** window of the IDE:

```
Public Sub SeeCharacterCodes()
    On Error GoTo MyErrorHandler

    Dim theString As String
    theString = Selection.Text
    Dim i As Long

    For i = 1 To Len(theString)
        Debug.Print "'" & Mid(theString, i, 1) & "' '" & _
            Asc(Mid(theString, i, 1)) & "'"
    Next i

    Exit Sub

MyErrorHandler:
    MsgBox "SeeCharacterCodes" & vbCrLf & vbCrLf & _
    "Err = " & Err.Number & vbCrLf & _
    "Description: " & Err.Description
End Sub
```

Example C.5. Display character values

Glossary

argument

An "argument", also called a parameter, is a value passed into a procedure that helps calculate or produce a result. Arguments are declared in the first line of a procedure and are used as variables throughout that procedure. Functions and subroutines may have arguments. A procedure with arguments must be called from another procedure because that is the only way you can supply the arguments it needs. Procedures with arguments are not displayed in the Macros dialog, cannot be called from it, and cannot be part of the ribbon.

This example is a subroutine calling a function that calculates the area of a triangle. Two parameters are passed, the base and height measurements of the triangle.

```
Public Sub SubroutineCallingAFunction()
    MsgBox "The area = " & AreaOfATriangle(3, 4)
End Sub

Public Function AreaOfATriangle(base As Double, _
        height As Double) As Double
    AreaOfATriangle = (base * height) / 2
End Function
```

See also: function, macro

digital certificate

A "digital certificate" (also known as a digital ID) is a form of electronic credentials that verify the identity of the certificate holder. It can be compared to an ID card, such as a passport or driver's license. In either instance, you provide proof of identify to a third party – in the case of a driver's license it would be the state – and the third party issues a certificate that identifies you. The certificate, (the driver's license), is trusted since the issuer, the state, is trusted. In the same way, if file recipients trust the issuer of the certificate, then they can be assured that the macro came from the source the issuer says it came from. There is a strict certification process and usually a cost for a third party issuer, which is called a certificate authority or certification authority (CA). You can create a certificate yourself, called "self-certification," but the certificate is valid only on the computer that created it.

A digital certificate may contain the holder's name, address, serial number, expiration date, digital signature, and encryption information, along with other data. When an application, for example a Web browser, attempts to make a secure connection, it reviews the digital certificate from the site. The browser verifies the information, and if no problems are found, completes the secure connection.

digital signature

A "digital signature" is an electronic signature used to authenticate the identity and possible timestamp of a document or macro author. It verifies that the content of the document or macro has not changed since it was signed. If you trust the signer, then a valid digital signature indicates that the document or macro is exactly as the signer intended and that it has not been since modified. The signed document can be any a kind of document, such as Word document or an e-mail message, and does not have to be encrypted. The digital signature simply means the document has not changed since it was signed.

function

A "function" is a procedure that returns a value. VBA has many built-in functions, such as Time (returns the current time), CurDir (returns the current directory), and Abs (returns the absolute value of a number). Functions have to be called from another function or subroutine.

The first example uses built-in function Date, which returns the current date.

```
Public Sub ShowCurrentDate()
    MsgBox Date
End Sub
```

The second example is a user-defined function. It takes no arguments and returns the value of pi to two decimal places.

```
Public Function GetPi() As Double
    GetPi = 3.14
End Function
```

See also: subroutine, macro

IDE

An "IDE" (integrated development environment) is an application that provides a comprehensive environment for programming. It allows you to enter and write code, run the code, and debug it. You can observe the execution of your code line by line and look at variables and outputs as you go. An IDE also provides a set of tools to help program and manage projects.

See also: function, Intellisense, subroutine

IntelliSense

"IntelliSense" is Microsoft's implementation of auto-completion. In the IDE (integrated development environment, or the Office's VBA coding application), IntelliSense appears as you type code. If a partial word is recognized as an object from the coding model, the IDE displays all the possible completions for that word in a list. You can then select an item in the list, which then completes the word. In addition to the actual code word being typed, IntelliSense displays options, including the list members, parameter information, and in some cases, values for the parameter or statement.

macro

A "macro" is set of commands that can be played back to re-create a task. You can create a macro by recording it from the user interface or writing one directly in the IDE (integrated development environment). Word uses a scripting language, VBA (Visual Basic for Automation) for macros. A macro can be a single set of commands or it can call other macros.

This is an example of a macro recorded from from Word. It inserts text into a document at the current selection or insertion point.

```
Sub Macro1()
'
' Macro1 Macro
'
'

    Selection.TypeText Text:="This macro is recorded."
End Sub
```

See also: function, subroutine

module

A "module" contains programming code organized into procedures. There are three types of modules: code, form, and class. A code module is for general code use. All of the examples in this book use code modules. Form modules are used to define user interface forms such as dialogs and all the items on that dialog. A class module is for creating your own class or object.

object

An "object" is a self-contained entity in VBA. It can contain procedures you can call to perform operations such as selecting, highlighting, or deleting itself. It can also contain properties that describe itself, such as its position on the screen or the values currently assigned to it. Objects are an important aspect of Word VBA programming. Objects such Document, Range, and Shape provide access to the many features of Word. Objects are defined prior to use with the `Set` operator.

This example displays the name of a document by accessing the `Name` property of the object called `currentDocument`, which is an object of type `Word.Document`. `Word.Document` is an object type that contains properties, methods, and other objects related to a document.

```
Public Sub ShowDocumentName()
    Dim currentDocument As Word.Document
    Set currentDocument = ActiveDocument
    MsgBox currentDocument.Name
End Sub
```

procedure

A "procedure", also called a routine, is a collection of VBA statements that perform an operation or task. A procedure contains lines of code, along with comments that explain the code or provide programmer's notes for the reader. There are two types of procedures: functions and subroutines.

See also: subroutine, function, macro

QAT

A "QAT" (Quick Access Toolbar) is a small, customizable toolbar in Word that allows you to add buttons and commands that are not available in other parts of the ribbon or to make existing commands more convenient to access. By default, it is located in the upper left corner of Word next to the Office icon, although you move it to under the ribbon. It allows up to 20 commands and buttons.

ribbon

The "ribbon" is the set of controls and buttons in Microsoft Office, including Word, used to manipulate a document. Since Office 2007, it replaces the sets of tool bars and is one part of the new graphical user interface. The ribbon is a series of tabs, each with its own set of controls. The ribbon is not highly configurable or customizable in Office 2007, but has been further developed in Office 2010.

selection

A "selection" in Word is the highlighted area in a document. If no area is highlighted then the selection is the insertion point. Regardless of the number of documents open or how many documents contain highlighted areas, only the active document is considered to contain the current selection.

subroutine

A "subroutine" also called a Sub, is a procedure that doesn't return a value. Subroutines are perhaps the most common procedures. VBA user interface items often require their own subroutine to respond to events such as mouse clicks, keystrokes, or closing a document.

This is an example of a subroutine:

```
Public Sub SimpleSubroutine()
    MsgBox "This is a simple subroutine"
End Sub
```

This subroutine calls the GetPi function shown in the glossary entry for function:

```
Public Sub SubroutineCallingAFunction()
    MsgBox GetPi()
End Sub
```

See also: function, subroutine, macro

trusted publisher

A "trusted publisher" is a Microsoft Office digital signature and digital certificate management system that lets you choose which digital certificate issuers you trust and add them to a library. Office can be set up to run all macros (and ActiveX controls, add-ins, and applications extensions) from developers defined as being trusted publishers. This designation simplifies accepting new macros and changes without re-validating the developer's credentials every time.

Resources

Books

[1] Driza, Scott. 2009. *Word 2007 Document Automation with VBA and VSTO*. Jones & Bartlett. ISBN: 978-1598220476.

[2] Gonzalez, Juan Pablo, Cindy Meister, Suat Ozgur, Bill Dillworth, and Anne Troy. 2006. *Office VBA Macros You Can Use Today: Over 100 Amazing Ways to Automate Word, Excel, PowerPoint, Outlook, and Access*. Holy Macro! Books. ISBN: 978-1932802061.

[3] Powers, Hilary J. 2007. *Making Word Word for You: An Editor's Intro to the Tool for the Trade*. Editorial Freelancers Association. ISBN: 978-1880407226.

[4] Ruby, Jennie. 2009. *Editing with Microsoft Word 2007, "Skills and Drills" Learning*. IconLogic. ISBN: 978-1932733310.

[5] Savikas, Andrew. 2004. *Word Hacks: Tips & Tools for Taming Your Text*. O'Reilly Media. ISBN: 978-0596004934.

[6] Twain, Mark. 1889. *A Connecticut Yankee in King Arthur's Court*. Project Gutenberg, http://www.gutenberg.org/ebooks/86. Originally published in 1889.

[7] Wempen, Faithe. 2007. *Special Edition Using Microsoft Office Word 2007*. Que. ISBN: 978-0789736086.

Web Sites

[8] Companion website for this book. http://xmlpress.net/wordsecrets.html This site contains errata, up-to-date versions of the code examples, and other relevant information related to the book.

[9] Field Codes in Word. http://office.microsoft.com/en-us/word-help/field-codes-in-word-HA010100426.aspx Microsoft article describing Field Codes.

[10] Microsoft Smart Tag Software Development Kit. http://www.microsoft.com/downloads/en/details.aspx?familyid=c6189658-d915-4140-908a-9a0114953721&displaylang=en&pf=true You can find this link at the companion website for this book.[8] You can also find the Smart Tag SDK by searching for "Smart Tag SDK" on http://www.microsoft.com

Index

Q

QAT (see Quick Access Toolbar)
query conditions
    setting, 176
Quick Access Toolbar, 8
    accessing a macro using, 20
    definition, **258**
Quick Parts
    listing entries, 133
    selection, 127

R

recording a macro, 10, 15
regular expressions, 63-66
    Smart Tag examples, 153
    Smart Tags and, 152
    used in a macro, 65
replace, 37-66
replace a missing/empty value, 185
return values, 29
reuse, 232
revision marks
    retain in paste, 166
revisions, 215-216
ribbon
    creating fields, 67
    definition, **258**
runtime errors, 32

S

samples (see examples)
scope, 195
security, 24-27
    (see also digital certificate)
    (see also digital signature)
    (see also trusted provider)
security level, 25
selection, 197-200
    definition, **258**
    problems with, 239
setting breakpoints, 35-36
shapes, 218-221
sharing macros, 23-24
shortcuts
    fields, summary, 95
showing bookmarks, 84
smart defaults, 70
Smart Tags, 137-162
    collecting text, 154
    deploying, 146
    MOSTL, 144-152
    regular expressions and, 152

removing, 143
    SDK, 149
    VBA and, 153
    XML, 147
    XML reference, 157
special characters, 227-228
    find and replace, 39
    table, 227
spell checking, 49
spike, 166-168
    view clipboard, 167
stepping through code, 33
subroutine
    calling, 53
    declaration, 194
    definition, **258**

T

tab-delimited files
    inserting, 173
tables, 208-211
    fields in, 88
    inserting from a database, 175
    updating, 178
template
    adding, 125
    document, 125
    document Building Blocks, 126
    global, 126
    Normal.dotm, 16
term list
    adding, 151
    compiling, 150
    decompiling, 151
    file, 147-152
    using, 149
terms
    adding, 118
text
    collecting with spike, 166
    dragging, 170
    inserting, 126
    pasting with spike, 166
three-step find and replace, 38
trojan horse, 24
trusted locations, 26-27
trusted publisher, 25
    definition, **258**

U

Unicode, 40
    paste special, 169
    saving term list as, 149

Colophon

About the Book

The Secret Life of Word was written in Microsoft Word, then converted to HTML using some of the techniques described in the book. It was converted to DocBook XML and formatted using a customization of the DocBook stylesheets (http://docbook.sourceforge.net), the Saxon XSLT processor (http://saxon.sourceforge.net), and the RenderX XEP FO Engine. (http://renderx.com).

About the Author

Robert Delwood is a senior systems analyst in the NASA Johnson Space Center community. He writes Microsoft Office solutions using VB/VBA and .NET's VSTO, helping departments automate their tasks, simple and complex. A writer turned programmer, he bridges the worlds of writing and technology.

About XML Press

XML Press (http://xmlpress.net) specializes in concise, practical publications about social media, management, technical writing, XML, and supporting technologies for technical communicators, managers, engineers, and marketers.

The cover design was inspired by Wordle (http://wordle.net), a web site that creates word clouds. The XML Press logo was designed by Vicki Fogel Mykles, Write Image, Fort Collins, CO.

Lightning Source UK Ltd.
Milton Keynes UK
UKOW05f0341181215

264918UK00001B/34/P